PRAISE *for* TOBY THOMPSON

Positively Main Street

"A first-rate novelistic account of Thompson's own psyche as he uncovers the Dylan few people know. A new look at young Dylan, done with kindness, enthusiasm, and superb language."

William Kennedy
Look magazine

"Essential reading. Thompson, unprecedentedly, managed to interview not only Echo Helstrom, almost certainly the 'Girl of the North Country,' but Dylan's mother and brother, his uncle, his friends."

Michael Gray
Bob Dylan Encyclopedia

"Toby Thompson was there first."

Greil Marcus

Saloon

"I had a wonderful time with this book, reading it in two sittings. I found the writing strong, clear, occasionally electric. In some odd way it seems a sociological masterpiece. For the first time the American drinker has his Michelin, and for myself it would be unthinkable to start another journey without it."

Jim Harrison

"Toby Thompson found the place to study the country, and he got it down."

Thomas McGuane

"This book is a good place to get a drink."

Richard Brautigan

D0775498

The '60s Report

"A stunning book. Insightful, lovingly crafted. *The '60s Report* is at once a personal inquiry into contemporary history and a preview of the future. It tracks '60s survivors struggling toward the '80s, capturing their lives in haunted relief. I wanted to steal sentences, paragraphs—hell, whole chapters."

Tim O'Brien

"The '60s Report is nonfiction—well-written, and as readable as a novel. Toby Thompson recaptures the wild spirit of the sixties."

Jerry Rubin

"A brilliant guide to the generation that was the sixties, is the seventies, and will be the eighties and nineties."

Michael Halberstam

"Toby Thompson's writing represents the best of 'The New Journalism.' His new book, *The '60s Report*, is a catalogue of individual transformations that adds up to a definition of America's spiritual life. Thompson's portraits of people in change are vivid and revealing. In fact, *The '60s Report* is an American version of *The Canterbury Tales*."

Terence Winch

RIDING *the* ROUGH STRING
Reflections on the American West

TOBY THOMPSON

Montana
2012

RIDING *the* ROUGH STRING

The author and publisher would like to thank the following publications in which versions of these pieces originally appeared: "A Private River," *The Washington Post*; "Into the Light," "Ghost Alleys of Butte," "The Adventure Writer," "The Godfather," "Lessons from Fire and Ice," "Summer Wages," "The Sip 'n' Dip," "Montana Pickup," "Stacey's," "The Bridges of Yellowstone Country," and "West Boulder Runoff," *Big Sky Journal*; "The Art of Progress," and "Custer's Last Fight," *Western Art & Architecture*; "The Disappearance of Peter Fonda," *Esquire*; "The Man from Mountain Misery," *Outside*.

Published in the United States by

Bangtail Press
P. O. Box 11262
Bozeman, MT 59719
www.bangtailpress.com

BP

Cover photo and back cover photo by Lynn Donaldson.

To the Murray Hotel

"Riding the rough string...you get bucked off and you get back on. You understand what you did to make the horse scared. And you don't become a victim."

Gretel Ehrlich

TABLE *of* CONTENTS

Author's Note

There's a snapshot of me, taken in June, 1959, leaning wearily against a Northern Pacific railcar by the depot in Livingston, Montana. I am fourteen years old. I've ridden the Vista-Dome from Minneapolis, toward a ranch job near West Yellowstone, and I am bereft of sleep. In a moment, for a second photo, I will stand by a stone monument to Lewis and Clark, then enter the depot's café where I will order breakfast. But for the moment I'm staring at a turn-of-the-century hotel where, unforeseen, I would live intermittently for three decades.

That hotel was the Murray, where many of these pieces were researched or composed…stories that are but a handful of those I've produced in fifty-three years of writing about the West. The earliest were journal entries, scribbled during that ranch summer on the Madison's South Fork. Others were published as recently as this spring. I came to Montana a dreamer, a boy addicted to western comics and TV horse operas. The line between that kid who wished to be a cowboy and the writer he'd become is a straight one. Both youths were dreamers, conjuring

1

visions of an American West that were true and fanciful. Some of these stories concern writers who wished to be cowboys, or cowboys who wished to be writers. "Mama, don't let your writers grow up to be cowboys," Waylon and Willie might have sung. Or painters, or filmmakers, or actors and such. The West always has attracted artists. It is America's dreamspace, its hallucinogenic frontier. An afternoon drive between Buffalo, Wyoming and Lodge Grass, Montana, or from Elko to Winnemucca, Nevada will show that. As will an hour spent behind a good western novel or a finely crafted oater. Buy the ticket, take the ride, Hunter used to say. And stow your food: beyond here lie maneaters.

Toby Thompson
June, 2012

Preface: The Art of Progress

I am a native Washingtonian, and when I tire of that city's machinations, I walk eight blocks from Capitol Hill to the Smithsonian's American Art Museum—a Greek Revival temple high above the Mall—where hang two portraits of *The Grand Canyon of the Yellowstone*, each so vast as to transport one instantly to Wyoming. They are by Thomas Moran, an artist whose talent, more than any other's, was responsible for Congress declaring Yellowstone our first National Park in 1872. The more impressive canvas, 7 feet by 12 feet, was shown that year and sold to Congress for ten thousand dollars, then a gargantuan sum. A second, larger view, painted from 1893 to 1901, flanks it, as does his *The Chasm of the Colorado* (7 feet, 3/8 inch by 12 feet, 3/4 inch), painted from 1873 to 1874. These are the only paintings in the small Moran gallery, and to stand encircled by them is to be flooded by the water and space they depict.

I am a journalist who has covered the East, but I am also a wanderer who for many decades has summered and often wintered in Montana, not far from Yellowstone

Park. The pieces in this book are a result of those wanderings. On a recent Sunday, pining for the West, I entered American Art and rode to its second-floor galleries. To my left was George Catlin's Indian Gallery, ahead were Alfred Wertheimer's photographs of the young Elvis, but to my right was an explosion of light I knew to emanate from Moran's unique canvasses. Confronting their colors—rust red, yellow, rose pink, mauve—was like emerging from a darkened theater to the high desert at noon. A docent stood beside the space's circular stool, covered by a worn bison skin, or robe. I squinted against the paintings' brightness and watched as two children spotted the robe, then headed for it.

The docent was patient as they rubbed and tugged the robe's matted hair. She explained that the bison had been essential to Plains Indians' survival, and that they had wasted not a part of it. She took from her cart a small hide parcel she called a Bison Box. "This was the Indians' shopping mall," she said. From it she withdrew horns, sinew, teeth, soap made from bison fat, and even the bison's bladder, used as a canteen. The children cringed, but the docent explained that the bison had provided everything the Indians needed.

Except landscape, I thought. Those paintings before me, passionately orchestrated renderings of waterfalls, cliffs, and gorges, were not exaggerated but real. And quite necessary. The effect of Romantic Sublimity (Wagnerian rapture) they were thought to instill was for me, perhaps Moran, and certainly Native Americans, not an abstract theory but an accurate depiction of one's emotions in wilderness. One *became* enraptured. I stepped forward and was smitten by a 3-D vision of canyonland, a painterly lightshow evoking wilderness's splendidly erotic ambiguities: "a sort of delightful horror," as Immanuel Kant categorized the Sublime, "a sort of tranquility tinged with terror."

On another day, in a journalistic funk, I'd left the White House and its daily press briefing, and walked two blocks to the Corcoran Gallery. There, in a far alcove of its American Art wing, hangs Alfred Bierstadt's epic *The Last of the Buffalo*, a 6 feet, 2 1/4 inch by 9 feet, 11 1/4 inch painting completed in 1888 that dwarfs even Frederick Church's 3 feet, 6 1/2 inch by 7 feet, 6 1/2 inch *Niagara* and the canvasses surrounding it. Like Moran's 1872 *Yellowstone*, Bierstadt's is a painting that, in its time, was considered political. Where *Yellowstone* was seen as a broadside for westward expansionism, and a postcard both preserving wilderness and luring settlers to adjoining regions, *Last Buffalo* was viewed as a plea for conservation and a lament for the frontier's salad days. In its foreground it depicts a Native hunter as picador engaged in a Wild West showdown with a furious bison. Before them are skulls and carcasses spread against the plains fronting the Wind River peaks. For me it's the landscape, a Turneresque depiction of ocher grassland and snow-tipped mountains, that holds the power.

Minutes before, I'd been listening to commentary on trade imbalances, but now I was immersed in the "picture show" unreality of a carnival-like tour de force that for me was exquisitely real. Like Moran's *Grand Canyon*, it was meant to provoke sentimentality, yearning. (Cynically speaking, landscape was "the dreamwork of imperialism," in W. J. T. Mitchell's phrase.) Though both artists had toured the West, Moran painted *Grand Canyon* from sketches in Newark, NJ, and Bierstadt his *Last Buffalo* in New York City. I stood here in Washington, D.C. and felt their longing. Or as Bill Clinton might have said, their "pain."

Early in his administration, when the president was still jogging, I spent an afternoon at the National Gallery then drove my little sports car at a clip, past the rear gate of the White House. Black SUVs appeared, a runner darted out, and I hit the brakes, skidding. Before me was Clinton, his hands raised protectively, his great frame draped in sweats and his face ashen. I waved. He waved back. Quickly I was enveloped by Secret Service, and as they sent the president along I couldn't help picturing the Corcoran's *Last Buffalo,* and wondering if he wasn't hurrying to see it.

As a boy it was my luck to have a grandmother and great aunt who made certain I visited the icons of our nation's capital. These included the Washington Monument, the Lincoln Memorial, the National Archives' Declaration of Independence, the Library of Congress, the Capitol with Congress in session, and the Smithsonian. I don't recall whether I saw Moran's *Grand Canyon,* but in art books I studied Thomas Cole's 1836 *The Course of Empire* and Emanuel Gottlieb Leutze's 1862 *Westward the Course of Empire Takes Its Way*: the first cautionary, the second championing empire's limitless possibilities. That the latter would be hung in American Art, once The Patent Office, dotted with myriad inventions that sought to ease America's struggle to fulfill its manifest destiny, was not lost on me. I might have seen John Gast's *American Progress*, an 1872 painting that critic Alan C. Braddock considers "an allegory of technological conquest." In it, a goddess figure soars across the plains, in one hand a book of knowledge, in the other telegraph wires. "Progress was God," the governor of Colorado would write in 1873.

My great aunt worked at Patent, as had Walt Whitman, during the Civil War. He nursed wounded soldiers, bivouacked in its halls, and wrote, "It was a strange, solemn sight, the glass [invention] cases, the beds, the forms lying there...then the amputation, the blue face, the groan, the glassy eye of the dying." Whitman was employed briefly at the Bureau of Indian Affairs, housed at the museum, but was dismissed when *Leaves of Grass* was deemed by his superior "an indecent book."

Art was not held sacrosanct by government, though it might exploit it. This paradox was conspicuous on the museum's first floor. Removed from Moran's, Bierstadt's, and Church's ecstatic celebrations of landscape, stood a folk assemblage titled *The Throne of the Third Heaven of the Nations' Millennial General Assembly.* It had been made by a Government Services Administration janitor of African heritage, named James Hampton, who dubbed himself "Director, Special Projects for the State of Eternity." His was the premier piece of Washington art and it was junk; I don't mean that pejoratively. Constructed of found objects such as light bulbs, jelly glasses, old tables and armchairs wrapped in silver and gold foil and collected in alleys not far from the Capitol, it was inspired by the Book of Revelations, predictive of apocalypse, critical of bureaucracy, and magnificent. Often I contemplated its mysteries. "Fear Not," was written above its throne. In the garage where Hampton had constructed it hung a quote from Proverbs: "Where there is no vision, the people perish." Hampton was a visionary who claimed to have seen the Virgin Mary hovering above the Capitol, pointing him toward his goal. Which was to build God's throne from the detritus of empire. To me, back in the Moran gallery, Hampton's Virgin seemed a phantom not far in substance from Gast's muse in his *Vision of Progress*, shepherding the pioneers west.

My progress from a fourth-generation Washingtonian to a spiritual Westerner had been encouraged not just by the escapism of Roy Rogers comic books, Hopalong Cassidy TV, and summers in Montana, but by the psychedelically mind-altering paintings at hand. Even today their colors staggered. Destiny (call it progress) in my dotage may be to follow the path they've suggested. On this gray afternoon in the capital, Moran's canvasses, drawing me in, pointed the way.

Western Art & Architecture
2011

A Private River: Robert Redford

R obert Redford has a date. He steps through the door of Livingston's 1909 saloon, The Sport, in Levi's and a pearl-buttoned work-shirt. Then freezes, scouting a table. His companion is blond, slender. She wears a silk blouse and linen skirt—upscale for Montana—and fingers her hair anxiously. This must be a first date. She's leggy yet not so tall as Redford, who scans the room, his gaze never rising to eye level. He spots a vacant corner and the couple settles into period gamblers' chairs, beneath stuffed trout and an elephantine pair of button-fly jeans. Redford grimaces, orders wine. It is 9:30 p.m.; The Sport is hectic with cowboys, hay ranchers and fishermen, slumping conversationally at the mahogany bar, below elk and bison heads, or sitting at gingham-clothed tables wolfing blue-plate specials. Few heed Redford. He's been in Livingston since mid-June, when he began directing the film of Norman Maclean's classic Montana novella, *A River Runs through It.* And Livingston is accustomed to celebrities.

Jeff Bridges, Michael Keaton, Meg Ryan, Dennis Quaid,

Peter and Jane Fonda, Ted Turner, Brooke Shields, composer David Grusin, Glenn Close, Bruce Weber, Tom Brokaw, Thomas McGuane, author Tim Cahill, and painter Russell Chatham live or have lived nearby; Sam Peckinpah, Richard Brautigan, and actor Warren Oates, before their deaths, called Livingston home. Four previous movies have been shot hereabouts, including Tom McGuane's *Rancho Deluxe,* his *Cold Feet* (written with Jim Harrison) and his *The Missouri Breaks*, which brought Brando and Nicholson to town. A fifth McGuane film, *Keep the Change*, finished production in September.

The kidding of Redford has been primarily by business wags: "Welcome Wobert Wedford," reads Main Street Car Wash's sign, and "A River Runs through *What?*" demands Trower Drug.

The Yellowstone River runs through Livingston. Its blue-ribbon trout water lured McGuane here in 1968, and quickly he and its legendary angling drew other writers. Three sit at a neighboring table, two of whose publications are vying for Redford exclusives. As usual, he's stand-offish. "I want this film to appear just as it is," he told me, "without a lot of hoopla." Montana newspapers have received limited access (Redford's shooting on *The Livingston Enterprise* publisher's ranch), but national magazines have been discouraged. "I've had better luck with the local press," Redford added. "The national mags—and there are few I respect—would rather focus on what color my hair is than on what I have to say."

Redford's hair is a straw heap of reddish-blond, frosted with white; at the moment he has little to say. His date fidgets. He studies the menu. They sit close, like kids at a malt shop, sipping drinks and hardly speaking. She glances at his face. It's craggy, lined, and pitted with scars. The smile, when it flashes, is still brilliant. His chest and arms are powerful, but he's sprouted a belly. He's fifty-four years old, freshly divorced, a grandfather.

Like *Ordinary People* (for which Redford won a 1980 Oscar as best director), *A River Runs through It* concerns family; specifically familial communication. It was nominated for a Pulitzer in 1977, sold 275,000 copies and was called "an American classic" by Alfred Kazin, with passages "of physical rapture in the presence of unsullied primitive America that are as beautiful as anything in Thoreau or Emerson." A second Maclean book, *Young Men and Fire*—about the death of thirteen smokejumpers in 1949's Mann Gulch Fire—will be published next fall. But *River* highlights two brothers, one gently meditative, the other violently self-destructive, who share a passion for angling. "In our family," Maclean wrote in the autobiographical novella, "there was no clear line between religion and fly fishing." And to Maclean's father, a Presbyterian minister who alternated lessons in scripture with those in casting, "all good things—trout as well as eternal salvation—come by grace and grace comes by art and art does not come easy."

The Maclean brothers were first-generation, Scottish Americans who communed in sport. Redford is a Scotch-Irish actor who communicates best through physicality. He's told *River*'s publicist, Beverly Walker, "Scots have enormous difficulty in expressing feelings and emotions, and are capable of intense judgementalness, of punishing others by silence."

One patron who's noticed Redford's silence tonight is William Hjortsberg, the Montanan whose quirky novel, *Falling Angel*, was optioned by Redford before it became Alan Parker's film *Angel Heart*, starring Mickey Rourke. Hjortsberg worked with Maclean as a screenwriter, for Paramount, on the first adaptation of *River*.

"Norman was a salty old guy," Hjortsberg remembers, "whom I liked enormously. When I met him in 1978, his wife had died a few years before. That's why he started writing. He saw himself as this lonely guy retired from teaching at the University of Chicago, and what was he going to do with his life? He taught literature there for forty-five years. He was very quick to point out that he won the undergraduate teaching award not once, but *three* times. He was about seventy-five when I met him. We fished the Blackfoot River and afterwards he offered me a snort of whiskey from a Mason jar. He'd transferred whiskey from the bottle to this jar—I guess it reminded him of bootleg liquor during Prohibition, the era of his book."

Hjortsberg touches his glass. "Norman had this blunt way of speaking for a man who'd taught Shakespeare and Milton. But he was a guy who'd worked for the Forest Service and as a lumberjack in Montana. The word 'sonofabitch' came up a lot. And 'bastard.' One time he was talking about some faculty-friend's wife who'd run off with an undergraduate. I asked why she'd done it, and he snorted, 'Too much cunt between her legs, I reckon.'"

Maclean's brother, Paul, was a newspaper reporter and gambler who was beaten to death in a Chicago alley, presumably over debts. The bones in his right hand—the casting hand—were smashed. Paul is the brother in *River* that Maclean cannot save. "The book is really about loving somebody," Hjortsberg adds, "being unable to help them, and seeing them slide toward destruction."

When Paramount's option lapsed, William Hurt and Sam Shepard tried to gain the author's favor, but Missoulans William Kittredge and Annick Smith (creators of *Heartland*) won *River's* screen rights, forming a partnership with Maclean. They took a script to Redford's Sundance Institute, and Redford, according to Kittredge, said, "'But *I* was going to do this.' And," Kittredge adds, "when the steamroller starts moving, you get out of the road." He had spent two years on a screenplay for *River*, jousting with Maclean while writing several drafts. When their option lapsed, Redford beat Kittredge and Smith (who'd resigned from the board of Sundance to develop *River*) to the punch, purchasing rights. "If I'd have been Annick," Jim Crumley, the novelist and friend of the couple says, "I'd have sued the sonofabitch...the way he took it away was criminal."

Redford, in a *Premiere* article about Sundance unrest,

denied impropriety. "I wasn't aware of moving anybody out," he told Peter Biskind. But, he admitted, "I don't have a lot of success working with a lot of people." He was at the tail-end of a courtship of Maclean's family that required three visits to Chicago, an authorial visit to Sundance, and Maclean's approval of the final screenplay.

"I don't think this movie would have gotten made," Crumley says, "if Norman hadn't, unfortunately, expired."

He died last year at eighty-seven, cantankerous to the end. Redford's scenarist, Richard Friedenberg (*Dying Young, Promise*), met him in Chicago. "Norman disliked Kittredge," Friedenberg told me. "And he wasn't too fond of his screenplay." Maclean approved Friedenberg's script in 1990, but things never went smoothly.

"Norman obviously didn't much want to have a movie made," Hjortsberg says. "When he read *my* script, his reaction was, 'These are my family and you can't treat them like this.' I tried scrupulously to be faithful to the book, more faithful than the script Redford's shooting."

Maclean's sensitivity was not lost on Redford, whose own father was uncommunicative but through sport, and who died in April at age seventy-six. He was a Chevron accountant who'd been a milkman in Santa Monica while Redford was growing up. "Bob had to go down last month and clean out his father's things," Beverly Walker told me. "When he said that, tears filled his eyes."

Montana may be home to the Marlboro man (Philip Morris USA owns a guest ranch near Clyde Park), but Livingston has evolved as a kind of Boys Town for lost sons. Hjortsberg, McGuane, Brautigan, Chatham, Peckinpah, Fonda, and others were neglected by fathers or abandoned outright. Hjortsberg's died when he was ten. McGuane has spent a career writing of the twisted relationships, alcoholism, and "sadness for no reason," that comprise such sons' inheritance. For many, fishing, drinking, womanizing, and the blood sports were how they connected with fathers; what grew emotional tissue.

Redford's finished supper and is guiding his date toward the door. He looks distracted. The couple is outside when a waitress, waving her unpaid check, bellows. Redford reappears sheepishly, laying plastic on the bar. His date squints from the entryway. Time to settle up.

A 1920s motorcycle on high, thin wheels swims through gravel on Callender Street as a grizzled man in coveralls rides it past horse-drawn buggies, Model Ts, and a fat team of Percherons hauling a buckboard. The Panaflex swings as costumed extras cross an avenue dressed in fake balconies, gas lampposts and wooden sidewalks. This is *River*'s opening scene. Every trace of modern Livingston has been camouflaged. Redford's cinematographer, Phillipe Rousselot (*Dangerous Liaisons, Henry and June*), gauges the exquisite afternoon light before panning sky and mountains, then gliding to the Maclean boys scouting town.

They're supporting actors. Brad Pitt (*Thelma and Louise*) and Craig Sheffer *(Split Decisions)* will play the adult Macleans, with Tom Skerritt (*M.A.S.H., Top Gun*) as their father and Emily Lloyd (*In Country*) as Norman's wife. *River* is strikingly cast, but for the moment it's Redford's set that intrigues. It is perfect. Livingston's false-front buildings, wide nineteenth-century streets and surrounding Absaroka mountains—where Liver Eatin' "Jeremiah" Johnson killed over 300 Indians in 1847—have not required much doctoring. Livingstonians are happy to see *River* here; some speak of leaving its scenery in place, to lure tourists. Seven-to-ten million dollars will be pumped into a depressed economy by *River*'s crew. The civic center, rented for two thousand dollars per month, is now a sound stage. Merchants are being compensated for this shot's disruption. Locals have been hired as extras, grips, tailors, seamstresses, and carpenters. As Redford hopes to bring *River* in for ten-to-twelve million dollars, most are earning a bottom-drawer wage.

Redford slouches in a canvas chair on Callender's

sidewalk, his head tilted toward the sun. "Scots' reputation for being tight is well-earned," he's said. He's
conferring with Friedenberg and Rousselot when this
reporter's spotted. We shake hands, then face off in the
street like gunfighters. Redford initiates a diatribe against
magazine, television, and newspaper reporting, even the
Washington *Post*'s (whose Watergate coverage his portrayal of Bob Woodward, in *All the President's Men*,
eternalized) before conversation eases toward Montana
and Tom McGuane—a friend who introduced Redford
to Maclean's book in 1980. Redford's face brightens.
He's lunched at McGuane's, promising that *River* will
be dedicated to American Rivers, a foundation McGuane
represents. "Tom's got a great life," Redford says of that
rugged sportsman. "But I met him in Spain in 1966 and
he looked like a preppy then." I mention McGuane's
passion for cutting horses and the Zen of showing them,
and Redford says, "There's a lot of Zen in directing." He
pushes sleeves of his black T-shirt back. "There's competition in this film, like Paul throwing rocks to spook
Norman's fish. But directing's not about that."

He might have suggested "grace." His look is beatific.
He's won this slugfest for *River*, directing it for his own
company on a shoestring budget in an historical West
he adores. The past is Redford's territory. He wrote in
1976 that "As technology thrusts us relentlessly into
the future, I find myself, perversely, more interested in
the past." History is, colleagues suggest, one reason for
his avid preservationism: he cannot bear to see the past
erased. His mother, Martha Hart Redford, died when he
was eighteen. And of his boyhood haunts in Los Angeles
he's said, "I watched green spaces turn into malls, the
smell of orange blossoms turn into exhaust fumes...I believed California was a golden state, Los Angeles was a
golden city."

His boyhood was linked to Hollywood, if only its
studio gates. He remembers "the painted sky" of back-
lots "standing out against the real sky," and actors he

considered unmanly, even "girlish." His paternal grand-father was a vaudevillian, but Redford excelled only in athletics, competing in organized sports and immersing himself in the cult of Win. He had talent for sketching, which his father, Charles Redford, decried as futureless ("I was more of a dreamer than he'd hoped"), and talent for mimicry. Redford's stepbrother, William Coomber, told *Newsweek* in 1974: "He used to have a game called 'Guess who I'm walking like?' Bob could walk like any-body you knew, and you could recognize the person in-stantly." The capital of fantasy beckoned, and Redford found himself marveling at Brentwood mansions whose pools only servants' children or friends of children used. "I was the *friend* who used the pool."

At fifteen his family moved to Van Nuys, a communi-ty—in contrast to the Hispanic neighborhood he'd left in Santa Monica—that he characterizes as "a cultural mud sea." Yet the Valley's lushness moved him. He'd spent time at his maternal grandfather's ranch in Texas, and working summers at Yosemite National Park where he discovered the wilderness. But his real passion was for playing baseball; especially with his father. "Baseball was a strong connection between us...when we played catch his troubles seemed to go away." They talked while play-ing, a rare occurrence, for his father worked two jobs. "He was gone in the morning when I went to school and in the afternoon when I came home, so I felt like I never saw him." And true to Scotch-Irish practice, discipline was apportioned "by the use of silence as a weapon."

Redford's mother had been "a joyous person who found the positive in everything," he's said. Her death of a cerebral hemorrhage, during his freshman year at Colo-rado University, devastated him. He'd accepted a base-ball scholarship but lost it to heavy drinking. "I don't remember much of 1956." Even before, he'd had "dis-cipline problems" and "a lot of anger...I was a mess." He stole hubcaps, scaled theatrical towers and smashed their lights, burglarized Universal Studios and "those big houses in Bel Air, just to look around. I thought, 'What had *they* done to deserve all that?'" He and his stepbrother climbed mountains or shoplifted, training "to be soldiers of fortune."

He discovered painting at college, dropped out, then spent a year bumming through Europe—studying in Paris and Florence—as "that seemed to be where the Grail was for art." He liked sketching strangers in parks or cafés. His paintings were impressionistic, black-and-white washes: gloomy, disturbed. Disheartened by teachers' reactions, he returned home, bumming across America, sleeping in jails, carousing, but always sketching. He idled in Los Angeles, drinking hard, until he met Lola Jean Van Wagenen—a blond seventeen-year-old from Utah. He fell for her and her large Mormon family, who actually talked to each other. Lola encouraged him to pursue art while studying set design at Pratt Institute, in New York, to earn a living.

He auditioned for the American Academy of Dramatic Arts and was accepted. In acting he detected a sober outlet for his exhibitionism. The physicality of it pleased him. "Finding a place in the world had a lot to do with acting," he told Hilary De Vries. "The darker side is what interests me...it is the inability to express feelings in our culture, that's what's interesting to me."

He married Lola in 1958, joining the communality—not the religion—of her Mormon clan, praising its "incredible strength" stemming "from persecution and survival." The acting flowed. He worked extensively in television (*Alfred Hitchcock, Naked City*, others), landing his first Broadway walk-on in 1959's *Tall Story* because he could dribble a basketball. He starred in 1960's *Sunday in New York*, a comedy that ran on Broadway for six months. Though acting in four such plays, "it was the three intense years in television that really developed me," he told Hal Hinson. "Live theater and TV had that edginess about it that film doesn't quite have."

But not the artistic communality he sought. "He's

talked about that from the beginning," in-law Sterling Van Wagenen says. "He was too late for the heyday of the Actors Studio," or "live television and the studio system. He's always missed that kind of vital, giving, creative community of artists." By the mid-sixties, Redford noted, "movies were being taken over by men from food companies and tire companies and car companies."

His first film was 1962's *War Hunt*. He'd make four more (including *This Property's Condemned* with Natalie Wood, and *The Chase* with Brando) before fleeing Hollywood for Spain in 1966. "I'm damned if I'll be dumped on an assembly line," he barked. He'd built his own house in Utah's Wasatch Mountains—eventually he'd acquire five thousand acres—and starred for eleven months on Broadway in Mike Nichols's production of Neil Simon's *Barefoot in the Park*. But the art life called. He moved his family to Europe and spent half a year painting.

"He lived on the coast near Malaga," Becky Fonda, then Becky McGuane, recalls. "It was an artist's colony where Tom was writing *The Sporting Club*. What I remember is Bob's sense of humor—and those eyes! The only reason he came home was to star, with Jane, in the movie of *Barefoot*."

Barefoot in the Park became a major hit of 1967, making Redford a mini-star. He'd established "career momentum." *Butch Cassidy and the Sundance Kid* would make him a superstar, *The Candidate, The Sting, The Great Gatsby,* and *All the President's Men* solidifying his fame. He struggled not to abandon art, however. "When you are painting," he observed, "you are absolutely your own man. Nobody comes in and tells you that you can't use the color red. The decisions are totally your own."

He might have been speaking of directing.

Off Callender Street, Redford's moved to a shadowy alley—just below Russell Chatham's studio—where he's coaching actresses in a whorehouse sequence. Chatham is a world-renowned landscape artist and record-holding angler. He's so protective of Maclean's novella that he warned Craig Sheffer at a gallery opening, "I'll get you guys if you fuck up the fly-fishing scenes." Redford owns several Chatham canvasses, and the grace with which Chatham captures Montana's light in oil is, one presumes, how Redford dreams of rendering it in celluloid. The director stalks alley cobblestones, moving from camera to brick wall to pose a prostitute. For a second he becomes the girl, placing one arm against a roughened balcony, the opposite hand on his hip. He's posturing there when Chatham appears amid the garbage cans. Redford's startled. But smiling, he throws his arms round the burly painter and squeezes hard.

The legend behind the pulpit reads GOD IS LOVE. Redford sits in the front pew, a grayish skivvy tugged from his jeans, boots splayed out and his face corrugated with fatigue. It's 10:00 p.m. He's been directing since 9:00 a.m. The church is darkened, ghostly. A brunette masseuse kneads Redford's neck and shoulders as Tom Skerritt stands before a walnut lectern delivering Reverend Maclean's eulogy for his son:

"...and so it is those we live with and love and should know who elude us. However, it is also true that you can love completely without complete understanding..."

This is *River's* penultimate scene and Redford's determined to make it right. "Action," he calls as the white-haired Skerritt removes spectacles, pulls at his vestment and begins...then quietly, "Cut." Redford stares from his pew. He repeats this drill, suggesting minor variations to Skerritt and rising to check results on videotape. "Action..."

Watching this, one's reminded of that scene in *Downhill Racer*—the first film Redford produced—where as an Olympic skier he visits Colorado and his taciturn dad. His mother is conspicuously absent. The two men sit in a ranch kitchen without speaking until the father asks Redford why he skis, why he competes. Redford's take is one of utter surprise. "To *win*," he says. "To be a champion."

The old man sniffs. "Champions—the world's full of 'em."

Redford won big with *Butch Cassidy*, but soon questioned whether fame was worth it. "I'd walk down the street and see my face staring out at me from newsstand after newsstand and I just wanted to go someplace and hide." *Butch* was a buddy picture, "a love affair between two men," Paul Newman said, but *Downhill Racer*, with its James Salter screenplay and seamlessly photographed skiing, remains America's best movie about team competition, male or female. Like *The Candidate* and *Little Fauss and Big Halsy*, it weighs the cost of winning. "I think a winner," Redford observed, "doesn't have it as easy as a lot of people think. He is hit with a combination of the awe and hostility of those people who say: 'who are you to be there?'"

His father was not excused from slinging pebbles. In response to a *Life* cover-story on Bob, Charles Redford wrote, "We think of him whimsically as a combination of Tom Swift and Attila the Hun." Bob replied in *The Christian Science Monitor*, "My father is an old Irishman so I don't know whether it was his sense of humor or accuracy that prompted that remark...he thought I would be a little more solid...a lawyer is solid, a doctor is solid, an actor isn't. I wanted to become a painter, and he thought there was no future in that, either."

They were communicating, but through the media.

Redford's athletic grace, bemused self-deprecation, liberal reserve, and sensitivity toward the environment said much to his generation. As number-one box office draw, he personified the best attributes of seventies masculinity. He was its sex-symbol, yet he remained by most accounts faithful to Lola. "He flirted to the brink of conquest, though," a colleague reports. And his credentials as a liberal were unassailable, but for one issue: his ambivalence toward the press's right to know. "I owe the public a performance and a contribution and that's it," he argued. "I have no obligation to share my private life."

19

"He's always been *very* skeptical of the press," Bob Woodward says. The press were flacks, adjuncts to that studio mechanism which cost him privacy and his art. It was no longer possible to sketch strangers. The press (not stardom) rendered him the focus of public attention. Even while shooting *All the President's Men*, he quarreled with *Post* reporters and implored Ben Bradlee to yank his team off the Redford watch, to "let us work." Bradlee responded with a massive *Style* section story, which Redford lambasted as inaccurate, mean-spirited, and invasive. "I've seen some rank pieces in my time, but that was the worst," he told Pete Hamill.

Woodward does not find Redford's hostility inconsistent with his passion to make *All the President's Men*. "It's the shallowness of entertainment reporting he dislikes," Woodward confirms. "Watergate was about getting close to the bottom of something. Bob's skeptical about most press because it doesn't *care*." By 1978's *The Electric Horseman* (a cowboy corrupted by media), he'd inform Jane Fonda's character, a reporter: "I know what you want. It ain't answers. You just want a story—any story. Why don't you make one up? That's what you all do anyway."

A longtime associate says, "What interests Bob is that there's a surface and there's a reality. What you see on the surface doesn't always reflect the reality. He's really interested in secrets…what's hidden in an individual, a family, an institution, a culture…and what's hidden within himself."

"Sadness is inherent," Redford told Neal Gabler. "If you look a certain way, you're not supposed to be sad. You're not supposed to have nightmares."

By the late seventies he was digging inward. Repeatedly he spoke of quitting Hollywood: "I am retiring from films, definitely…by or before the mid-1980s I won't be an actor anymore." In fact he'd perform in only three movies during the eighties: *The Natural, Out of Africa*, and *Legal Eagles.* When his teenage son, Jamie, became ill with a physiological disorder connected to the stress of being Robert Redford's son, that heightened his introspection.

"Bob had no sense that it was hard to be his son," a family friend told me. "He was totally oblivious that well-intended, unconscious behavior can have an adverse effect on people close to you. There's a part of Bob that's naive, and this was a real wakeup call for him."

He retreated to the mountains of Utah, harboring plans to direct. He'd purchased rights to Judith Guest's novel, *Ordinary People*, and now he cast it with Mary Tyler Moore, Donald Sutherland, and Timothy Hutton. By 1979 he was ready to shoot. The final product astonished everyone. "It's no accident that he directed *Ordinary People* so effectively," a co-worker explains, "Because it's about inflicted pain within the family that's not intended." Redford told the *Times*, "I'd been interested in the challenge of keeping the family—my family—intact long before I read Guest's book. It's tough enough, but because of the nature of my business, it's even tougher."

Set in the Lake Forest section of Chicago, *Ordinary People* tracks an upper-middle-class family through its uncommunicative efforts to apportion blame for the death of a son—its favorite. Timothy Hutton plays the surviving brother, a seventeen-year-old who finds it impossible to reach his mother. Redford said, "I identify so much with Conrad Jarett, the teenager in this story. If I knew at seventeen what I'd learned by the time I was twenty-five, I would have had a much happier childhood. The feeling of not being heard—or not being able to make a connection—is one of the most agonizing things in life."

At Charles Redford's retirement party in 1979, friends presented him with a mock Oscar. The father quipped, "Maybe Bobby will win one of these." In 1980 he did. He took Best Director and Best Picture in a field that included David Lynch's *The Elephant Man* and Martin Scorcese's *Raging Bull*. He won the Director's Guild award as well. "I thought I'd lost my career in art or my way in art," he said. "I thought I would never see that again in my life." But, "when I direct I can really say I've *done* a film...I've created and completed a vision."

For a moment Redford abandons his pew, stalking the church's nave like a puma. He yanks at his shirt and chews gum madly. He stops, frames the shot, then disappears outside seeking isolation, but returns forthwith to accountability.

In 1972's *Jeremiah Johnson* he'd examined notions of frontier isolationism, but post-*Ordinary People* he explored them thoroughly within his life. He retired to Utah, spending primary energy on developing Sundance, a community that married his interests in art, environment, and sport. He pledged "to take some time to put something back in the ground." Sundance was named for his character in *Butch Cassidy*, but referred to a plains Indians' rite of purgation in which dancers commit self-immolation for the good of the tribe. Sundance Institute would nurture independent filmmakers, gathering them for retreats that honed technique and taught the brutal business of movies. A small ski resort was built to defray Redford's expenses, for as the Institute's major backer he diverted millions toward its operation. In off months it hosted environmental conferences, and in addition to his status as preservationist superstar, Redford soon became, according to *Newsday*, "the de facto godfather of the country's independent film movement." Sundance films would include *The Trip to Bountiful, El Norte, Desert Bloom, A Dry White Season,* and *Pretty Woman*, in a less-saccharine form.

What Redford wished for his mountain utopia was to "make art the core, and see if business can get around that." But like the family it aped, Sundance bred complexes. By 1990 *Premiere* charged double-dealing to the bone. Peter Biskind (a festival advisory-board member) reported poor decision-making, conflict of interest, mismanagement, staff unrest, backbiting and factionalism.

Institute spokespeople dismissed its report as "petty" and "vicious." But Redford met *Premiere*'s assault with a refusal to allow the magazine on future sets, and a cessation of business dealings with it.

The press had run riot over 1988's *Milagro Bean Field War*, which Redford directed, reporting mercilessly on script difficulties, conflicts with Chicanos over non-Chicano casting, disputes with his Hispanic co-producer over control, its budget inflating from eight to an estimated twenty-two million, and perhaps most disturbingly, the director's romance with his leading lady, Sonia Braga. The press had declared Redford's marriage on the rocks, and the openness with which he and Braga (*Kiss of the Spider Woman*) consorted, affirmed this. "I don't underestimate the target that I am," he told the Chicago *Tribune*. "The film had a very difficult karma...people in the community would say, 'Did you bless the ground before you started filming there?' Well, we should have." When *Milagro* wrapped its first season of shooting, locals burned Redford's set.

Milagro's conflict is between developers and the environment, but its focus is community as family. "I'm convinced one reason Bob speaks so much about the environment," Beverly Walker says here in this dimly-lit church, "is to avoid speaking about himself and his family. You know, the principals in *A River Runs through It* physically resemble Bob: Brad Pitt, the young rebellious Bob, Tom Skerritt, the older Bob. I think middle age is a tremendous relief to him. He's no longer handsome. We suggested air brushing his publicity stills and he said, 'Forget it.'"

Tom Skerritt's eulogy as Reverend Maclean at last seems spun. In a dozen takes Redford's muttered little more than "cut," his back bent and the masseuse kneading his shoulders. His fatigue is overwhelming. It's as if he were filming his own eulogy, or that of his dad. Skerritt makes some tiny adjustment in delivery and Redford stiffens. The girl's hands fall away. Redford straightens in his pew, and with a voice barely audible, whispers, "Nice."

It's lunchtime in Sacajawea Park: white cavalry tents shield crew and company from the mountain sun, as Redford sits alone beside his aluminum teapot of a trailer, a classic Airstream. Like *River*'s props, it might as well be vintage. He's so immersed himself in the Macleans' era, hanging photos of their family, reading Paul's newspaper columns, playing Norman's taped lectures, and studying his letters, that he's lived in their "world and life and time for several months now," he's said. "I've not read a paper or watched television, and I have only vague knowledge of what's happening in the Soviet Union."

Redford may be ignoring the world, but it hasn't forgotten him. *Esquire, Outside,* and *U.S.A. Today* are present, and sheriffs have been called to roust tabloid reporters from the shrubbery near Redford's rented house. His daughter and granddaughter have been here, as have Norman Maclean's children and grandchildren. Redford's longtime inamorata, Buffy Birrittella—a senior vice president at Ralph Lauren—has visited, and the *National Enquirer*, according to *Enterprise* publisher John Sullivan, entreated local reporters to do legwork on the romantic front, hustling photographs and misrepresenting itself in hornswoggling gossip from locals.

Rumors hatch about the set like caddis flies: Redford's drinking and philandering hard—"I hear he's worked his way through Bozeman"—producers are punching extras, male crew are fist-fighting cowboys and boinking cowgirls, Redford's quarreling with Forest rangers and not paying carpenters overtime, his complexion's poor and he's *shorter* than expected.

Reality is less colorful: The director's been out at night—for dinner; he attended a Bozeman arts festival on Sunday, complaining to Meredith Thompson of "not having a day off in nine weeks," but was alone. An "untrustworthy" stagehand attempted to file a complaint against producer Patrick Markey, alleging assault, but was not accommodated by Livingston's City Attorney. A bar fight occurred in the Hyatt House on July 19, but was broken up by crew members, to the barmaid's delight. Forest Service biologists refused permission to film on the upper Boulder River, a harlequin duck habitat, but producers complied graciously. And help, if underpaid, has not grumbled publicly.

The town genuinely likes this crew, an affection cemented when Redford offered *River's* vehicles to evacuate a Mill Creek ranch threatened by forest fire. On Wednesday he pedaled his mountain bike to the post office, where a crowd waited to assist Mayor Bill Dennis in presenting him with the key to the city. "You've been a great host," Redford called. "It was terrific!"

Now he sits on a metal folding chair, hands clasped behind his head, staring at the Absarokas. Off to his right, Tom Skerritt—in black trousers and braces—practices fly casting in a small lagoon. *River's* angling sequences have gone well, its actors coached by John Bailey, of Dan Bailey's Fly Shop, or George Croonenberghs, the Macleans' boyhood friend. Montana's native trout have been spared by hatchery and mechanical substitutes. Here behind Redford, on the Civic Center's steps, grips strum hillbilly tunes on battered guitars. Nearby, chefs distribute 120 desserts from a Winnebago as, due east, Brad Pitt squats on the riverbank petting his hound dog, Deacon, and smoking while he surveys the Yellowstone.

"Eventually, all things merge into one, and a river runs through it," Maclean wrote. *"On some of the rocks are timeless raindrops. Under the rocks are the words, and some of the words are theirs. I am haunted by waters."*

"It's that last line in the book that just rips me up," Pitt tells a reporter. "I identify with Paul in a lot of ways... people who have so much, yet somehow just can't get it together are very mysterious and compelling to me."

The Crippled-men's Movement seems to have captivated Redford's set. He's abandoned his customary lateness as an actor to strict hours of directorial focus. Skerritt's labored hard, admitting that "I see certain aspects of my own father in the Reverend. He had that same Anglo-Saxon stiffness and unwillingness to display affection...he never gave me a hug and I never heard him say, 'I love you.'"

In a season when *Iron John* and *Fire in the Belly* top bestseller lists, *River*'s crew are not the only visitors easing loneliness with obeisance to sport. At Big Timber's Sweetgrass Cutting (an event where riders "cut" cattle from the herd, with intricate explosions of beauty that Tom McGuane's described as "closer to the Japanese martial theater than to rodeo"), Michael Keaton and McGuane leaned forward in their saddles and spoke of Robert Bly. Keaton glanced around. "Can you imagine Bly conducting a workshop here?" he joked. "All these big cutters crying about their fathers?"

1984's *The Natural* was Redford's paean to his dad, and to the baseball they shared. It follows pitcher Roy Hobbs from a brilliant early career, where he succumbs to moral temptation and is lost, through a fifteen-year exile from which he rebounds to lead the New York Knights to a championship. Maclean accused Redford of turning Bernard Malamud's novel—"a sardonic replica of the quest for the Holy Grail"—into "an American-boy makes good movie." Nevertheless, Redford-as-Hobbs confesses painfully in one scene that he wishes his dad could have seen his last home run. "I made this movie in part as a tribute to my father," the actor told Gene Siskel. "My father and I have great affection for each other, but we don't see each other much anymore. Our lives have grown apart."

If *Ordinary People* concerned family, *Milagro* examined community versus development, 1991's *Havana* pursued a middle-aged gambler who taps unrealized idealism, *River* is about men: brothers, fathers, and their search for grace through sport. As Maclean suggests, neither fishing nor fish were what drew his family to the river. It was the dream of communication. *"Under the rocks are the words, and some of the words are theirs."*

Redford's moved to the parking lot where a blond woman leading a blue-heeler collie speaks with him. She's Pat Miller, co-owner of the Murray Hotel and an ex-rodeo queen who, as landlord, eased Sam Peckinpah through his last desperate years in Livingston. She's chiding Redford for not having visited the director's old suite, and he's smiling, thanking her repeatedly for the gift of a hotel T-shirt. But his gaze drifts above Miller's head to the mountains, river, and an antiquated bandshell at Sacajawea Park's center.

There Livingston residents perform a bi-annual variety show. Three years past—in celebration of Trout Unlimited's convocation—the bandshell was decorated like an underwater grotto. Papier-maché fish dangled from rafters, a riverbank graced the downstage wall, ferns smothered footlights, everything in vibrant color. Three hundred Livingstonians watched a tongue-in-cheek "Wooly Worm Review" free of charge, featuring a million dollar cast. Beau and Jeff Bridges (in a white toga, costumed as Neptune), Tim Cahill, William Hjortsberg, and non-fictionist Alston Chase mugged giddily in fishing attire. Poet Greg Keeler recited "Ode to Duct Tape" and "What to Do with the Butt of your Fly Rod," then strummed a few songs. Peter Fonda, who plays tambourine and sings backup in a local band, performed a monologue. And anyone with a smidgeon of talent was invited to join. Afterward, a cast party shook the rafters of downtown's Owl bar until two.

It's as if Redford can see this, somewhere in his communal mind's eye.

"Don't worry," he assures Pat Miller, "I'll be back."

The Washington Post
1992

Into the Light: James Lee Burke

The guitar James Lee Burke plays—no, caresses—is a classic Gibson J45 with rosewood back and sunburst top, the model that countless Nashville musicians have owned, and that he bought in Lexington, Kentucky, on installment in 1965. Credit plans for the bestselling novelist are things long past, but the songs he's been picking, "That's Alright Mama" and "Wildwood Flower," spring from the guitar's body with familiar resonance.

"I'm one of those guys who's played forty-five years every day, and never gotten any better," Burke insists. "When I start, you hear doors closing, people leaving, my kids driving away." He mugs. "I don't know what that means."

We're at his house near Missoula, in his study actually, where the sixty-nine-year-old Burke sits behind a desk, his warm face and laser-point eyes capped by a George Strait Resistol ("If it's good enough for George, it's good enough for me"), and framed by photos of his Louisianan and Texan ancestors. A 1990 Edgar Award (mystery fiction's Oscar) for *Black Cherry Blues* rests on a shelf near his guitar picks and fly rods, and surrounding him are hundreds of his own books in every sort of domestic and foreign edition.

Music is crucial to Burke—it saturates his fiction—and thumping out bass runs to "Folsom Prison Blues" he abandons himself to Cash's familiar lyrics: "*I know there's rich folks eatin' in a fancy dining car...*" But he pauses, strumming to a halt.

"I signed three books for Johnny. But get this—one day the Governor of Louisiana, Kathleen Blanco, called our house and said, 'Mr. Burke, Johnny Cash, June Carter Cash, and Robert Duvall are in New Iberia making this picture, *The Apostle*. Johnny wants to ask you all to dinner.' I said, 'Miss Blanco, I have never in my life hated to turn down an invitation worse than this one. But we're in Montana.'"

This is weeks before the Gulf Coast devastation wrought by Hurricane Katrina, and the thought of Blanco's call is wistful. He eases back toward his music. Burke and Pearl, his wife of forty-six years, now live most of the year in Montana. In fact they've just celebrated the construction of a log house on 120 acres up a canyon at Lolo, with a huge party. "We got The Revelators," Burke says, "the best rockabilly band in Missoula. We invited all kinds of people: musicians, photographers, writers, a lot of working people. The whole choir from our church came. And a lot of twelve-step people."

Like the Cajun detective, Dave Robicheaux, hero of Burke's recent novel, *Crusader's Cross*, and thirteen others in that Louisiana series, he's both Roman Catholic and a recovering alcoholic. "I'm CIA," Burke jokes. "Catholic, Irish, and Alcoholic." And as for Robicheaux and Billy Bob Holland, the ex-Texas Ranger and Missoula attorney at the heart of his newer western series, great music and the legal system trot in double harness.

Burke explains: "In 1961, another guy and I did some recording of the inmates in Angola Prison. There'd been three twelve-string guitarists, Guitar Welch, Robert Pete

Williams, and Hogman Maxey. Only Maxey was left. But what we got was quite extraordinary."

Readers of Burke's fiction know the Louisiana State Prison at Angola to be his and Dave Robicheaux's Buchenwald, a heart-of-darkness enclave that, through much of the last century, saw brutality, murder, and the worst kind of social degradation. Hiring inmates to plantation owners, it was a perpetuation of the slavery system. Burke's research there horrified him, but fueled interest in the dark side of human nature.

"It was a terrible place. We interviewed guards who spoke openly about beating men, putting them on anthills, and didn't give it a second thought. One ex-convict told me he knew of a man who'd been put in a cast-iron sweat box for over three weeks. He said, 'When they took him out he had molded to the box.'"

For real-life Angolans like Leadbelly and Hogman Maxey, or Burke's fictional Junior Crudup, in *Last Car to Elysian Fields*, or Iry Paret, in *The Lost Get-Back Boogie*, music was the only escape. "Here," Burke says, "I learned these guitar runs from Hogman. Let me get this in tune."

The Lost Get-Back Boogie—Burke's 1986 novel set in 1970s Missoula—concerns a country-western singer, Korean vet, and ex-Angola-inmate who has accidently killed a man in a bar fight and struggles to finish a song, one about his childhood in "a more uncomplicated time," the completion of which somehow would redeem him. Violence punctuates *Boogie* and most of Burke's other fiction, and its victims are often musicians: Dixie Lee Pugh in *Black Cherry Blues*, Tee Bobby Hulin in *Jolie Blon's Bounce*, Junior Crudup in *Last Car*. In *Crusader's Cross* a mandolinist and "hillbilly singer" named Ida Durbin is beaten, then forced into slavery as a prostitute. But not before she rescues a teenaged Dave and his half-brother from sharks in Galveston Bay, inspiring a reverie of "pink Cadillacs, drive-in movies," and "stylized street hoods," that seems a paean to Burke's own boyhood.

Earlier, Burke offered thumbnail sketches of his Texas relatives—photos of which hover behind him as he strums—that indicate his family was no stranger to violence. Or to alcohol, which plays a Lucifer-like role in both the Dave Robicheaux and Billy Bob Holland books.

"My grandfather was a gunfighter, and his name was Sam Morgan Holland. I use his name in the Billy Bob books. Sam supposedly shot and killed nine men in duels, and had a violent temper. And he had his troubles with whiskey. He took a herd of two thousand head up to Wichita. And that should have made him a rich man. The night before the sale, he had the cows bedded down outside of town. He was going to take 'em in the morning to the railhead in Wichita. And there was dry lightning. The cows got loose on him, and he said he chased cows all over south Kansas and Oklahoma, and he lost everything. He said they trampled his camp into strips of canvas, pieces of splintered wagon, and he said he cursed God for his bad fortune. He said, there were only three words that went through his mind: 'whiskey, whiskey, whiskey.' And he got drunk and he stayed drunk all the way back to Texas."

Burke is a cheerful man, even funny. And he's been so today, despite a bout of sciatica and discomfort from "some bad food" eaten at the Western Montana Fair. He's enjoying this picking and looks forward, tonight, to an outdoor concert at a park beneath Missoula's Higgins Street Bridge. "They always have great music." He's also heartened by *Crusader's Cross*'s ten-spot on the New York *Times* bestseller list, and by the movie nibbles it's received. But dark forces have been gathering. There's the Iraq war, to which he's unequivocally opposed, there's an administration in Washington he feels is "Machiavellian," at best, there's this moment in history, "worse than ever, and I lived through the Depression," plus talk of alcoholism and family shades.

"I believe ghosts are out there," Burke says. "There are agencies working around us that we don't see. As Dave

Robicheaux puts it, 'The dead lay a strong claim on the earth.'"

The major death in Burke's youth was a violent one—that of his father, "a very gentle, genteel man"—from an automobile accident in 1955, when Burke was eighteen. Like Robicheaux's father, Burke's (an engineer) died while working the pipeline. Yet he seemed possessed of an ethereal prescience: "My dad believed that history perhaps was not sequential. In fact, he believed that perhaps all of history occurred simultaneously in the mind of God. He said, 'It's we who impose sequence on time. But God is not bound by past or present or future, and in reality we are already inside eternity. We fear death, but we are already dead. The dead and the living still live simultaneously in the mind of the deity.' And this would maybe explain the fact that on occasion people think they see ghosts."

Ghosts filter through Burke's work, as both angelic and demonic forces. Robicheaux, in *Jolie Blonde's Bounce, In the Electric Mist with Confederate Dead,* and other novels, meets transcendent figures, and Billy Bob Holland, from *Cimarron Rose* through *In the Moon of Red Ponies* is haunted by the walking, talking ghost of his Ranger partner, L. Q. Navarro, whom he killed accidently in a Mexican drug raid. Burke feels his own talent originates from supernatural forces. As he reflected in a 2002 *New York Times* essay, "Early in my writing career I came to believe that the stories I wrote were already written in the unconscious by a hand other than my own," and citing Jack Kerouac, "'Your art is the Holy Ghost blowing through your soul.'"

He adds here, "Every artist feels that. It's as though another hand was at work. And those who claim credit for it are about to lose the talent."

Burke has written at least one novel, *White Doves at Morning*, that concerns ghosts of his Louisianan ancestors. His father's family has lived in New Iberia since before the Civil War (Burke keeps a house there), and though he visited often as a child, he grew up primarily in Houston, where his ninety-eight-year-old mother's family, the Hollands, retains its Texan roots. And though Burke, with New Iberia Parish, has fashioned an environment as precise to readers as Faulkner's Yoknapatawpha County, his work is without geography.

"All narrative art, for it to survive its own time, needs to represent a story that is larger than a regional one," he says. "The story of both Montana and Louisiana is very similar. Their old way of life is disappearing, for good or bad. The family farm, the family ranch, is going under. In Montana, the life of lumberjacks and people who ran small mines—that's all gone. There are vestiges of it, but the extractive economy today is run by enormous international corporate interests. The consequence has been that the area's under great environmental stress, and the same is true of Louisiana. The Cajun world that Dave Robicheaux grew up in is quickly vanishing."

Burke has admitted that Robicheaux is partially his alter-ego. "The character defects are mine, none of the good qualities." Like Robicheaux, he worked the Gulf Coast oil patch as a young man, but also as a truck driver for the U.S. Forest Service, a teacher in the Job Corps, a newspaper reporter, a social worker in Los Angeles's skid row and professor at four universities and a community college. He went thirteen years between hardcover books, mid-career, and drank alcoholically during that period. "But I never stopped writing," he says.

The telephone rings, and Burke answers in a soft, tentative voice. "Oh, hi," he says, recognizing the name. "What's up?" It's a twelve-step friend who says that his motorcycle has been vandalized, and that he thinks he knows who did it.

"Call the police," Burke advises, "they'll come and fill out a report. Don't speculate and don't lie—we don't lie in the program, and lying to the police is a felony." His manner has shifted from reticence to pure efficiency. He offers procedural guidance like a cross between Bishop Sheen and Detective Robicheaux.

Burke's hesitant to speak of his drinking years, other than to characterize them as typical. "All forms of alcoholism are expressions of the same personality," he says. "There's no difference in alcoholic behavior. And every active alcoholic is one drink away, not simply from a drunk but from a seizure—of becoming a wet brain."

The Neon Rain, Burke's first Robicheaux novel, was the first he wrote sober, and several unpublished novels formed its genesis. Burke cocks back his hat. "One novel was titled *Heaven's Prisoners,* about a young Cajun boxer—he's twenty-one, he's a Marine Corps veteran, a Golden Gloves boxer, and he falls in love with a girl named Bootsie from Spanish Lake, outside New Iberia. I thought it was a failure. I wrote another one that dealt with the Giacano family from Orleans. It was called *Before the Hills,* and it was an allegory about the search for the Grail in modern times. Then Rick DeMarinis, my writer friend, said, 'Jim, you've tried everything else, why don't you try a crime novel?' We were fishing in the Bitteroot River. We laughed, and Pearl and I left for San Fran. Up there on North Beach, there's an Italian café that has tables outside for espresso. I had a legal pad, and in longhand I started writing *The Neon Rain.* I used the character from those two failed novels. I made the young Cajun prizefighter older, a Vietnam veteran and an officer for the New Orleans police department. And I had these great characters from the other book, Didi Giacano and these other thugs. That's how I wrote *The Neon Rain.*"

The novel would redeem Burke's career. "Three companies bid on it. I almost fell down. I couldn't believe it, after all those years. And I learned a lesson: never say something's a failure. Failure's just an increment in success."

In Dave Robicheaux, Burke met a character he could relate to: a deeply flawed Everyman, haunted by his alcoholic past yet driven to atonement through an often secular religiosity. What religiosity suggested to both men was a code of conduct—that oft lamented perk of older novels—which included the strong's protection of the weak, the rich's protection of the poor, a responsibility to one's community and its environment, and an embracing of what Burke calls Jeffersonian liberalism, "founded on the notion that ultimately the individual deserves the protection of his government, and that the government has to give power to and protect those who have no voice, who are disenfranchised." That is Robicheaux's role as homicide detective. That and a broodingly relentless self-inventory, rare in crime fiction outside Dostoevsky's, rendered with gothic humor and irony's lack.

An average day for Dave Robicheaux might begin with his awakening early in New Iberia, noting that "on East Main, in the false dawn, the air was heavy with the smell of night-blooming flowers and lichen on damp stone and the fecund odor of Bayou Teche," where "the antebellum homes...loomed out of the mists, their columned porches and garden walkways and second-story verandas soaked with dew, the chimneys and slate roofs softly molded by the canopy of live oaks that arched over the entire street." It might continue with his opening his bait and boat shop, run in partnership with a Creole named Batist, "well into his seventies now, his attitudes intractable, his hair the color of smoke, the backs of his broad hands flecked with pink scars from a lifetime working on fishing boats and shucking oysters," and offer Dave, over the next twelve hours, interaction with various criminals, high and low born, causing him to struggle with his alcoholism, hit a meeting at the Insanity Group or leave a votive candle at the tomb of his dead wife, Bootsie...before ending comically with his ex-partner, Clete Purcell, in "blue silk shirt with huge red flowers on it, a porkpie hat, and Roman sandals and beige slacks," his arms with "the girth and hardness of fire plugs," chaining a wrecker to the trailer of a child molester named Bobby Joe Fontenot and ripping it off its cinder blocks, Bobby Joe inside, then skidding it down the road "across the steel grid of a drawbridge, geysering roostertails of sparks in the darkness," before its propane tanks explode.

"Clete's the trickster," Burke says, chuckling. "He and Dave are opposites sides of the same personality. It's Clete, this merry prankster from the Irish Channel, and Dave, the idealist running at windmills in rusty armor."

Though Burke quit drinking in 1977, it would be years before he found a recovery program. "But when I started *The Neon Rain*, I was a twelve-step person. And my work became much more positive when I started writing the Dave Robicheaux stories. They're about hope, recovery."

The first response to Robicheaux "was huge," but *Black Cherry Blues*, third in the series, would be Burke's breakout book. "It was 'Paradise Regained,'" he says. "Its success allowed me to quit teaching, and to write full time." It was also the first Robicheaux novel to be set, partially, in Montana. And it proved a mash note to the state, becoming simultaneously a bestseller and Burke's ticket back to Missoula.

He'd taught at U.M. during the 1960s, and has said that when he first drove through Hellgate Canyon, "I decided right then this was where I was going to kick the bucket." The Burkes moved their family (four children) to a modest A-frame up Grant Creek and settled in for the long haul. Since then he's published sixteen novels, six of which have been bestsellers, and has had two movies made from his work.

Most of this has been on the shoulders of Dave Robicheaux, though the Texan/Montanan, Billy Bob Holland, earned Burke his second Edgar Award in 1997 for *Cimarron Rose*. Possessed of a dicey past ("The Hollands were violent people," Billy Bob says. "The penchant in our family for red-black rage...lay as strong a claim on our souls as a genetic desire for alcohol"), Holland, in absolution, has proved a less chaotic figure than Robicheaux—perhaps because of Burke's own metamorphosis. And he's yet to attract the same breed of rabid fan. "Dave's an unusual character," Burke allows. "I can't really claim credit for him. A character comes out of his own seminal bog." He laughs. "And Dave's a better writer than I am."

Despite chronic insomnia, which Burke calls "the Tiger," he writes every day, aiming for one thousand words, and this morning has wrestled with his next Robicheaux novel, *Pegasus Descending*. "It deals with Dave working in an exchange program with Miami P.D.," Burke explains. "But it's really about the gambling industry—the casinos and the horse tracks in Louisiana. Dave's an old gambler and he's kind of got caught up with his nemesis." Burke smiles. "He's still Dave."

The Burkes' daughter Pamala arrives, with her son Jack—whom Burke calls Pachyderm—and he breaks to say hello. Pamala's had dental surgery and Pearl quickly puts her to bed. Burke's much the patriarch, here to provide counsel, and today, phone calls seeking it have been fielded from Jim, Jr., a Justice Department lawyer in Arizona, and daughter Alafair, a law professor and mystery novelist in New York City. Burke's fourth child, Andree, a psychologist, has not checked in. Alafair (who shares the name of Robicheaux's daughter) seems stressed. "We're really proud of you," Burke says, "but you can't teach, tour, and write a book a year. It's too much." He listens a moment, tells her he loves her, then rings off.

Now he's back at his music, slipping into it like a bath. It's both a balm and an essential filament to his work. "A person who writes about blue collar America, about the Southeast," he's said, "ultimately is going to have to write about the music of the people...Elvis, Jerry Lee Lewis, all of those guys came out of the same background, the Assembly of God church...their lives were like cultural vessels filled with all this great stuff: music and religion and cultural desperation and poverty."

Within a few weeks, Katrina will slam New Orleans, and friends—including his twelve-string partner, Murphy Dowey—will have evacuated to the Burke compound in New Iberia. But for now, in this new house set on "eighty thousand pounds of quarried rock," things are stable. Burke picks the antique Gibson, singing softly in his high Southern tenor:

"*I saw the light, I saw the light, no more darkness, no more night...*" He stops. "Hank Williams used to sing this song, and there's a famous story that Minnie Pearl told. Hank went on stage at the Opry, shortly before his death, and he sang it. When he walked off, Minnie said, 'That's the most beautiful rendition of that spiritual I ever heard.' Hank said, 'Thank you, Minnie. But there ain't no light. There just ain't no light.'"

Burke stands up. He lifts the guitar strap from his shoulder. "The only thing I've learned about age," he says, "is that if a person does not deal with his character defects earlier in life, they will define him. And they will consume him." He sets the J45 back in its case. "If he's made some inroads, got 'em in a cage at least, he's probably going to have a pretty happy last three innings."

Big Sky Journal
2005

Ghost Alleys of Butte

If you're a fan of alleys, as is Jim Jarvis, Butte-Silver Bow's historic preservation officer, you might stare from your fourth-floor apartment in the 1922 Finlen Hotel and marvel at a striated snapshot of Butte's fabled Uptown. And if a generous host, you might descend to Wyoming Street and go hands-on. "The best things in alleys are the ghost signs," Jarvis says of those hand painted advertisements for products or businesses, signs that have faded from sunlight or weather but which endure in the passageways' dimness. "This one, for Wrigley's Spearmint Gum, has survived because it's always been in the shadow of that north face of the building." The sign is exceptional, covering the south wall of a tall brick structure with faded green, red, yellow, and white pigment—the gum pack rendered in trompe l'oeil. "Imagine painting that right on the side of a building," Jarvis says. "Which is not the most uniform surface to begin with. Imagine some poor guy on a scaffold, clinging there for days. Like Michelangelo in the Sistine Chapel."

Jarvis owns the scholarly creds to compare Butte's

alleys to the Vatican sanctuary, but he also has enough street sense to admire the skill of a semi-truck driver backing his huge rig into the Spearmint alley. "At 5:00 a.m. every Wednesday, a semi will back all the way in here to unload at this little furniture store. The first time that happened, I couldn't figure what the hell the guy was doing. He was quick about it, and it was pretty amazing."

Though seemingly vacant, "The alleys are well-utilized," Jarvis explains. "With the coming and going of materials to these large buildings, they serve a valuable function. And the locals use them quite a bit as shortcuts. Even though they can be scary-looking. During the day, they're a lot of fun. In the evening, the alleys associated with bars tend to take on a more seedy quality."

It's then that Jarvis and his wife can watch from their perch in the Finlen, as the sun sets over Uptown, stars flicker in the eastern sky, and a thousand lights ignite the city. "This alley is the best view you get from our apartment," he says. "You can see the historic side of Butte's buildings here, which on the streets are often covered with stucco or another facade. The industrial architecture in alleys is lovely, as are the fire escapes, original cobblestones, and granite foundations of the town." He turns. "In addition, this alley lines up perfectly with the facade of the M&M Saloon, and that big old neon sign. There are lights and shadows throughout the day, but at night you get this *reddish glow* at the end."

Alleys are the backs of things, containing much of what citizens wish hidden, but which often reveal more of a city's character than do its facades. In Montana, fine alleys survive in Missoula, Miles City, Billings, Bozeman, and Livingston, but as Peter Brown, of the state's Historic Preservation Office, tells me, "Of all Montana's alleys, Butte's have the least amount of updating." That's true of the alley between Gamers Café and the M&M, and it's celebrated for it. There, a scene from Wim Wenders's 2005 film, *Don't Come Knocking,*

starring Sam Shepard and Jessica Lange, was shot. Lange
plays the M&M's manager, and Gabriel Mann her son.
They argue vehemently, and their verbal jousting is significant, for innumerable such disputes have been settled
by Butte's alley doors. As have romantic comminglings.
Historian Ellen Crain, Director of the Butte-Silver Bow
Public Archives, says, "People do all sorts of things in alleys: pee, drink, smoke pot, make love."

But mostly they idle, alleys having become urban commons...quiet spots where a city dweller may escape the
bustle, walk, smoke, or watch the sunlight change on
the scored brick. In an alley off Granite Street, an artist
sketches in watercolor the pastels of a nineteenth-century building, as a young mother pushed her stroller toward Montana Street and a cook idles on wooden steps,
meditating. Traffic is audible from Broadway but here,
with flowering weeds growing through cobblestones and
bricks cooling in the shade, they might be in an English
country mews.

Despite alleys' utility as commons, pedestrian thor-
oughfares and delivery ways, their integrity in Butte is
marginally threatened. "People are always trying to block
off, widen, or get them closed," Crain says. "But they
rarely are successful." Police remain edgy and hyper-vigi-
lant about their after-hours use. Yet alleys endure.

This morning, a brown-bearded man in an M&M
T-shirt had stood behind the saloon, on break. He was
Rick Dolittle, chef and waiter at its café. I asked what
habitually occurred here, and he said, "Just about everything. Bumping uglies, smoking pot." He had grown up
in Butte, and as a kid had swung off the transverse walk
across the M&M Alley, near Broadway. When asked
about alleys as underground he said "the tunnels were
the underground"—for wealthy notables to walk in privacy to the whorehouse district. Though Jarvis negates
this belief ("there are steam chases and pipe galleries
that might have been used for that purpose, as well as

connected basements") there is a persistent myth about this underground history of Butte.

The M&M Alley, as most locals call it, extends two blocks from Park to Granite, with an elbow above and west of the saloon. This afternoon, its pavement is bisected neatly by shadow and light, and puddles glisten from a recent shower. The west wall shines dark red from the movie's repainting, but effluvia of steam ducts, coal chutes, and industrial wiring hangs from the east. Ghost signs for the "Bronx Lounge" and the "Leggat Fireproof Hotel" are visible, and an ancient steel door to "Cannon's" shows a graffiti-like death's head. A cast iron vat labeled "For Grease Only" squats behind Gamers, and the stone foundations of another building and its zigzagged fire escapes hold the feel of lower Manhattan.

There was a deliberate effort by Butte's early planners to emulate Chicago and New York. These were *the* twentieth-century American cities, and though Butte was built above claims of nineteenth-century gold and silver miners, its copper boom shrieked modernity. Copper was the metal that would electrify the era, and Butte's skyscrapers—its Finlen, designed after the Hotel Astor in Times Square, and its Metals Bank Building, designed by architect Cass Gilbert of New York—were bold statements on the prairie. Town princes like William A. Clark, Marcus Daly and F. Augustus Heinze wanted the mix of theatricality and commerce that city architecture suggested. Butte was a boomtown, the largest city between Seattle and Minneapolis, and it wanted class. With an undercurrent of naughtiness, to be sure.

Venus Alley, with its Dumas Brothel, is the last vestige of Butte's redlight district, one that employed hundreds of prostitutes in elegant parlor houses, moderately priced brothels, and inexpensive cribs: tiny rooms with doors that opened directly onto the alleys. Earlier, proprietor Rudy Giecek gave me a tour of the Dumas. It operated as a brothel from 1890 until 1982; for a while Giecek ran it as "a Museum/Antique Mall/Old Time Photography

Studio," but closed its doors in 2005. "Rudy is a character," says Jarvis. "But historically the Dumas is a very significant building. It was specifically built as a brothel, and that's just unheard-of."

Giecek is a sharp dresser with a croupier's mustache who, in an effort to save the Dumas, briefly partnered with the California group, ISWFACE, "International Sex Workers for Art, Culture and Education." He showed me both the interior cribs, constructed on a central hall or alley, where girls would pose behind windowed doors, and the cribs that opened onto the alley.

They'd been sealed since 1943 when Butte prostitution was made illegal, though it continued inside the brothels. The alley cribs were too blatant, however (in 1903 prostitution had been relegated there), and not until Giecek and his son tore off walls concealing the cribs were their interiors revealed.

Giecek took me downstairs and showed me one. The narrow room held a small gas stove, a simple chair, a white porcelain sink, a bureau, and the head and foot railings of a gold-painted bed. A window and door faced the alley. "See that path worn in the linoleum?" Giecek said. "It leads from the alley to the window, where the girl stood, to the door where she greeted her customer, to the stove where they negotiated services, to the low sink where she washed him, to the bed, where you can see wear marks where its feet moved."

The room was a time capsule; it belonged in the Smithsonian. I could almost smell its cheap perfume.

Giecek is convinced ghosts inhabit the Dumas. He's written a novel, *Venus Alley*, based on a madame's diary he discovered in the Dumas, and claims to have channeled the woman's voice in composing his book. She was Elinore Knott, a prostitute who started in Venus Alley cribs. Giecek has numerous tales of ghost-whores appearing in windows, moving furniture and making strange phone calls. Images of their auras appear on the Dumas's website.

Photographs in Butte histories show prostitutes lounging in Venus Alley (also known as Whore, Pleasant and Piss Alley), but all that physically remain there are wooden cutouts of "girls of the line," and part of a fence that, after 1943, sheltered them from view. Asked if prostitution thrived today, Giecek said, "If so, it's pretty well hidden."

A man who fondly recalls Venus Alley is Curt Buttons, a retired gandy-dancer on the Butte, Anaconda and Pacific Railway, who frequented the Dumas. I meet him at an Irish pub called Maloney's. Buttons is a hyper-intense grayhaired fellow with a wildly unkempt manner and a persistent cough. "I think I'm dying!" he says. He stutteringly admits that he began frequenting Butte's redlight district "about 1962 or '63," and paid from two dollars to five dollars a trick at the Dumas. "The girls there would treat you right—and I've been to whorehouses from Livingston, Montana to Wallace, Idaho." He didn't enter the Dumas from its alley, but exited through that door many times. About prostitution, Buttons waxes sentimental. "Butte had the largest redlight district except for New Orleans'," he says. "Its girls made you feel you were the best-hung guy in the world." An advocate, he has written editorial letters to the *Montana Standard* about the Dumas's closing, has donated over one thousand dollars to its restoration, and as Giecek says, "volunteers to help save the Dumas in any way he can."

Not all memories of Butte's redlight district are salubrious. Journalist Wesley Davis, as quoted in the Montana Writers Project's 1943 book, *Copper Camp*, recalls Galena Street, off Venus Alley, thus: "It seemed like a street leading into hell. Young men, boys, old men... Girls in the doors and windows soliciting in honeyed words. Young girls, some looking as though they should be in school...Beauty, withered hags, Indian squaws, mulattoes, Japanese, Chinese...Noise. Ribaldry. The shrill shrieks of a police whistle...."

Bars were accessories to vice, they benefitted from it, and even today follow a good-neighbor policy toward alleys. Many have doors opening upon them, not for secrecy but for air, light, and a glimpse of urban space. One such is the Club 13, a blue-and-yellow-tiled "saloon moderne" at 13 West Broadway, on the M&M Alley, with upstairs remnants of an infamous speak called The Alley Cat. I duck in at 4:30 and sit before a fifty-foot-long wooden counter and statuesque back bar from which hangs the sign, "Viagra: An Exciting New Drug That Increases Blood Flow to a Man's Brain." One other customer is present. A lovely barmaid, with a resemblance to Isabella Rossellini in *Blue Velvet*, approaches.

"What will you have?"

My heart flutters. "A Diet Coke," I say, and think, here is a patch of light where I can take notes and watch the sun cross alley bricks, as a mountain breeze courses through the door and cools my ankles.

I've hiked Butte's alleys from Montana to Wyoming Streets, marveling at their architecture and observing how citizens use the spaces; I photographed signs, artifacts and the stray pedestrian. In an alley facing the County Courthouse and behind the Carpenters Union Hall, I met a girl named Candace, a brown-haired, tie-dyed, tattooed youth, her arms speckled with white. She'd been laboring as a housepainter, wore a Rastafarian cap, jeans, and enormous shades, and was cutting to the public library, "away from the street." She explained, "I just feel more comfortable in alleys." Near a ghost sign that read, "Main St. Lounge—Let the Good Times Roll," carpenters played rock on a boombox, which leant the space a back street air. In China Alley, behind Pekin Noodle Parlor and near the Silver Dollar Saloon, Asians smoked cigarettes where once gambling and opium dens had flourished, tong wars raged, and red gilt posters with Chinese lettering hawked services. Colorful graffiti decorated alley walls of the Blue Luna, a hip coffee shop off Venus, and omnipresent were ghost-town vacuity and the aura of history.

The Club 13's barmaid, Tanya, takes me outside to view the alley, toward which she holds a proprietorial air. "I keep it clean," she says, "sweeping it regularly." Across it are beautiful steel doors, at least one hundred years old, ancient brick arches and a ghost sign reading, "Post No Bills First." Above it is a "Creamery Café" ghost, and remnants of the transverse walk Jarvis had mentioned. I ask Tanya what sorts of things occur here. "People hang out, talk, smoke," she says. "And," smiling, "one night I saw a couple having sex across the street."

The Alley Cat was famous during Prohibition, and Tanya takes me upstairs to see how its artifacts are being restored. There's a front and back bar set, with stained glass inserts, two pool tables, and boards across the second-floor windows, "for the idiot factor," she says. The Alley Cat's entrance had been on the alley, and like Club 13 the bar had a softer, plusher corner "for ladies."

I ask her what appeals to her most about Butte. "Its sense of community," she says. "I never leave Uptown. I never go below Front."

Downstairs, the Club is getting crowded (five people are at its bar), and Tanya lays before me an elaborate book of black-and-white photographs, titled *Saloons, Bars & Cigar Stores*. I leaf through its pages as customers discuss the latest rash of Butte friction fires—"where the mortgage rubs up against the insurance policy"—and drink beers. A swamper carts a bucket of ice to the men's room urinal. A younger fellow, a student at Montana Tech, enters on crutches. I ask how he's injured himself. "I broke my ankle when I fell off a bicycle," he says. "Turning into an alley." He shrugs. "I was leaving here."

I'm reminded of Jack Kerouac's remark that, "a short walk around the sloping streets (in below-zero weather at night) showed that everybody in Butte was drunk." Or eccentric. This was a city where, the *Standard* recently reported, a man was arrested for running down the street naked, and a woman for permitting her cats to defecate six inches deep in her living room.

Light on the alley bricks shifts from ochre to rose, and in the warmth of fine company and Tanya's womanly care I relax to a mood of equanimity, *samadhi* if you will, a near-mystical state endemic to bars on a good afternoon in the magic of twilight. Tanya is speaking of ghosts—like Giecek and other Butte residents, she accepts their presence—and tells me of those she encountered in a previous lodging. "It was at 103 Dakota, the St. Francis building, in rooms that had been used for prostitution. There was a 'johns' tunnel' in the alley there." Ghosts frequented her apartment, music was turned on for no reason, doors opened, etc. "I took a picture of a ghost. Let me show you." She lifts from the bar a pink laptop, with a matching pink mouse, and searches for it. "Dang, not there."

Outside it's nearly dark, and in the gloaming I see ghosts queued up for the Alley Cat like homeless on a shelter line. They stand in homburgs or bowlers, carrying lunch boxes or beer pails, their hands stuffed into pockets. Wind roars, snow swirls, but the alley cloaks, coddles, and comforts. They're waiting for the night to happen. In the Club 13, we're already there.

Big Sky Journal
2010

The Adventure Writer: Tim Cahill

"That's Livingston Peak," Tim Cahill says, pointing. "In August, I'm planning to go from the door of my house on Callender Street, swim across the Yellowstone River, walk across this field to that road, and go about five miles to the peak, then hike back, swim the river and finish at my door. That's about a six-thousand-foot change in elevation, and maybe twenty-five miles. I plan to do it in a day."

We're standing at the edge of Harvatt's Flats, an expanse of Montana ranchland bisected by Interstate 90, framed by the Absaroka and Crazy Mountains, and dotted with electricity-generating windmills. Cahill's dogs—Grace, a forty-pound Brittany spaniel, and MacGregor, a rangy Great Schnauzer—study an antelope that pogos against a far ridge line. Cahill digs behind the front seat of his truck and hauls out a weighted exercise vest. With effort, he slips into it. It's Kevlar black; but for muddy paw prints, it might be taken as bullet-proof.

At six-foot-one and 215 pounds, the white-bearded Cahill looks grandfatherly. Yet his rocking gait and self-effacing manner ("You have a mountain like that with Superman at the bottom, and where's the conflict...you have that mountain with *me* at the bottom, you've got conflict") suggest a clumsiness that's not there. He's an accomplished athlete who set NCAA records in swimming at the University of Wisconsin, competed in Olympic trials, and has hiked the diciest corners of the planet. And despite an ingrained competitiveness ("I hate to lose"), modesty and faux-inefficiency have become hallmarks of his adventure pieces—which include swimming with great whites, kayaking between calving glaciers, exploring toxic-air caves, hunkering among mountain gorillas, air ballooning across Rocky Mountain peaks, partying with Irian Jayan chiefs in feathered headdresses, body paint, and penis sheaths. These are collected in seven of his nine books, including his most recent, *Lost in My Own Backyard,* a chapter of which received a 2003 National Magazine Award.

"If you read my stories, you can see that I don't suggest that I'm the only one who can do this. Somewhere embedded in the story is the suggestion that just about *anybody* can do this."

We're hiking south, on an ice-age terrace by the great bend of the Yellowstone River, and despite a thirty-pound vest, Cahill steps off cockily. As a co-founder of *Outside* magazine and editor of various travel anthologies, including *Best American Travel Writing, 2006,* he has every reason to feel cocky. "Tim's brilliant at what he does," *National Geographic Adventure* editor John Rasmus has said. And fellow adventure-writer Kira Salak notes that, "Without a doubt, Tim Cahill is one of this country's most accomplished narrative-nonfiction writers." Critics have called him "A "rock 'n' roll philosopher-jock" who writes "with the precision of John McPhee and Joan Didion tempered by a Monty Pythonesque sense of the absurd." His books are bestsellers, and he's among the highest paid magazine writers in America—earning as much as $25,000 per article.

And he's funny. Collections have titles like *Jaguars Ripped My Flesh, A Wolverine is Eating My Leg,* or *Pecked to Death by Ducks.* His pieces are idiosyncratic. In one, he's kayaking the northern Pacific, tests his balance and flips, hanging there underwater—he breaks, relates the expedition's history, and only in the last scene manages to roll upright. In another, he's rappeling down El Capitan some 1,500 feet above California, breaks, and hangs there practicing blues riffs on his harmonica.

He often risks his life for these stories, "but the scariest I've done," he says, "are not the ones with cannibals or headhunters, but those with fourteen-year-old soldiers carrying AK-47s in unstable countries like Sierra Leone."

We've been speaking of the changing nature of his craft: "My job as an adventure writer is to go to an extremely remote place. What 'remote' means these days is not 'distance' so much as 'political instability.' You got to get by a line of guns and you've got to be able to talk with your hands in the air."

And you've got to be in condition, which explains this hike. At 62, Cahill is impressively fit. Despite a lifestyle that once included too many cigarettes and still is fueled by the odd cocktail in Livingston saloons, he race-walked the Dublin Marathon in over six hours last year ("placing 109th in my age group, out of 11,000 runners") and spent two weeks of hard backpacking in the Bob Marshall Wilderness. "I hope never to turn down a story because it's beyond me," he says.

This trail is not one in the Himalayas or Andes but a prehistoric footpath that's a two-track circling 3.2 miles around a brushy plain resplendent in wildlife and in its view. The sky is azure, the air crisp, and the dogs course out before us, flushing curlew, which scold from above. "The first nonfiction piece I published," he says, "was for the *San Francisco Chronicle Examiner*, about vultures on Mount Tamalpais. I was getting an MFA in creative writing at San Francisco State. What I liked to do was find a field and lie down and then watch vultures circle overhead. We didn't have any vultures where I grew up."

That was Waukesha, Wisconsin, where Cahill's father ran a small lumber yard/coal company; his mother clerked at Montgomery Ward. "In high school, our camping out would be a summer night, we're sixteen years old and somebody has scored two cases of beer." He wasn't interested in adventure sports, "because I was involved very heavily in school athletics. The coaches were hell on not doing things like skiing or even ice skating, which tightens up your ankles."

What he did do was read. "Somewhere in the basement were books by L. Frank Baum, the guy who wrote *The Wizard of Oz,* and the Edgar Rice Burroughs *Tarzan* books. I thought to myself, this is what I'd like to do for a living, to write. But I kept it to myself." He smiles. "To aspire to do something so godlike would be immodest."

He majored in history at Wisconsin and spent a semester at its law school, but left for San Francisco State in 1967. "It was the winter of the summer of love." After writing a novel for his MFA thesis and freelancing, he began working at *Rolling Stone.* He became a key figure there, and when staffer Michael Rogers convinced editor/publisher Jann Wenner that *Outside*, a magazine about hip adventure-travel, might fly, Cahill was onboard. "When I'd moved to California, I started rock climbing and camping on weekends. I was a great outdoorsman by *Rolling Stone* standards. What we did was say, 'Why don't we do a magazine that will cover outdoor things that will have good writing in it?' That was considered a stupid idea by the publishing industry, because people who go outdoors were considered to be knuckle draggers."

Outside was launched in 1977, and it revolutionized the outdoor-magazine industry, mining a demographic that had been thought interested only in sex, drugs, and rock 'n' roll, and launching careers in literary adventure writing for not only Cahill, but John Krakauer, Sebastian Junger, David Quammen and many others.

All this spiked Cahill's competitiveness. He sought *Guinness World Book* records, on the El Capitan climb, "the second longest free-fall rappel," and his epic drive with Garry Soweby (memorialized in *Road Fever*), from Tierra del Fuego to Prudhoe Bay, Alaska, in under twenty-four days, "which still is a record." In trekking he also "wanted to get to the most remote place, to find people closest to the stone age." And to take glee in the "sure knowledge that, throughout all of time, no other human being has stood on the same spot." Such adventures pushed him toward risk and risk's payoff: "a kind of euphoria...a biochemical reward edge workers of my acquaintance strive to achieve." He's described risk takers as "Two drinks short of par...that means two jolts of adrenaline below par. Some of us need a little bit of excitement to just feel normal like everyone else." Riskers are interested in "concentration, control, ecstasy, and tranquility." But for Cahill, the *calm,* the *tranquility,* after danger was the true addiction. "And so it was that I came to understand that risk is a form of therapy," he wrote in *Wolverine.*

It was therapy he required after writing *Buried Dreams*, his 1986 bestseller about the serial murderer, John Wayne Gacy, who entertained small children in clownface but tortured and strangled twenty-nine teenage boys, burying them beneath his house. Cahill became obsessed with Gacy, and calls *Buried Dreams* "a study in human evil," noting that his response to its intensity was to became engaged with risk. To heal his obsession with Gacy, reason demanded that his escape "be equally intense."

So not only did Cahill risk his life trekking, climbing, and diving, but almost Biblically sought out dark places—"hearts of darkness," or "jungles of the mind." Where most authors visited such places literarily, Cahill did so literally. "They scare me," he wrote of triple-canopy jungles. "I find them dark and mythic. I have felt the sheer weight of indifferent animosity, of some vast, humid hatred."

After cult leader Jim Jones led nine hundred acolytes into suicide at "the necropolis of Jonestown," Guyana, where "the stench of decomposing bodies sent bile rising into my throat," Cahill reported on it brilliantly. Jim Jones "had been deluded...even before he moved to the jungle," he later wrote. "But the jungle tore at his mind and fed his paranoia." When Livingston friend Paul Dix's son was murdered on a jungle river in Peru, Cahill accompanied him there to confront his son's killers. And when another friend's daughter had life-threatening surgery, he wrote the dog story, "Trusty and Grace," an allegory of faith and redemption that proved one of his strongest works.

Cahill pauses by a cairn of fieldstones, watching Grace bound toward the foothills. Raised a Catholic, he's not now conventionally religious. Yet he's written of Grace that she "attends me on my jaunts into the steep mountainside wilderness...I am led by Grace up the steep hillsides," and "sometimes, when Grace leads me through the forest, she maketh me to fall down beside running water...in the evening, Grace accompanies me to bed, where she tends to fart a lot."

Why the scatology? "Humor undercuts the seriousness," he says, "which in turn gives the story depth." He looks off toward the Crazies. "Just as you can evoke sorrow with prose, so you can evoke laughter. It's the same thing, and it's all serious."

He moved to Livingston in 1978 (where he lives with wife, Linnea Larson), intrigued by its coterie of writers and artists, and because it was a town of seven thousand inhabitants. "I grew up in a small town and feel most comfortable in one. Also, *Rolling Stone* and *Outside* moved their offices to New York and Chicago, respectively. I didn't want to live in either place. I wanted to try freelance writing and thought knowledge of the wilderness would infuse me here, as if by osmosis. But I know mountains halfway around the world better than I know the ones I can see from my front door."

He's done his best to remedy that. He wrote *Lost in My Own Backyard* in 2004, and has taken various assignments in the Montana outback. "But writing about home, where I feel comfortable and want to be, is difficult. Certain excursions here are not really dangerous— at least, not for me—and are therefore harder to write about. So I'm looking for a way to write about familiar and nearby places in a manner that does not always involve adrenaline."

We push on briskly, past a site that prehistoric humans inhabited nine thousand years ago. Cahill taps a painted fence post for luck. "I've exhausted my interest in risk," he adds. "The important thing is the story—if risk is involved, fine. What I found out is that there's a certain point in doing something risky that you *train* for. When it comes, you're not really thinking at all. You're in the flow. Some people can get there sitting cross-legged in their rooms, others of us need a bit of a harder bump."

But some assignments require risk. Last fall, he dodged drug smugglers and desperate immigrants in the Cabeza Prieta desert of southern Arizona, and, in places like the Sahara of Mali, has hired armed bandits to protect him.

"No story is worth a human life," he says. "But here's the problem: twenty-five years ago, I could go to places in Peru and elsewhere, and they literally had not seen gringos before. Now, in those very same places, sometimes actually following footsteps and roads that I've written about, adventure-travel companies have said, 'That sounds like a neat trip, we could arrange one just like that and take paying customers.' So I've got to be looking at politically unstable places these companies would not take their clients to—because they can't guarantee anyone's safety."

We're on this hike's back leg, and Cahill picks up the pace. I nearly sprint to keep up. "Uh-oh, the dog's in the mud," he says, and whistles up Grace. MacGregor follows reluctantly.

Cahill's been inching away from adventure travel, and has been looking for a different type of book to write.

"But it's harder to pitch. I wanted to do one on business and greed, and the editor said, 'You don't write those kind of stories, you write about cannibals in Irian Jaya.' I said, 'It's not that different.' I'd like to do more of the meditative pieces, too. I've been privileged to go many places and see many things, and it's time to figure out what it all means. Maybe I can manage some fingernail-paring-size figments of clarity."

But for thousands of readers he's still out there, fulfilling their dreams on impossible journeys. Such dreams, he's written, "are, in fact, adolescent in nature, which I find an inspiring idea...when we allow ourselves to imagine as we once did, we are not at all in our right minds. We are somewhere in a world of dream, and we know, with a sudden jarring clarity, that if we don't go right now, we're never going to do it. And we'll be haunted by our unrealized dreams and know that we have sinned against ourselves gravely."

So Cahill trains—religiously. We've reached his pickup, MacGregor pants at the cab but Grace trembles beside her master. He bends to the floorboards and removes an odd-looking pair of circular weights. "Kettle bells," he says.

They're thirty-two pounds of cast iron each, with handles. He spreads his legs and with one bell starts a ritualized ballet of curls and presses. MacGregor scurries back, but Grace remains constant. The mountains hover ambiguously. Like Goliath, or a Buddhist temple guard at the gates of the wilderness, Cahill woofs and grunts, hardening himself against the contests ahead.

Big Sky Journal
2006

Custer's Last Fight

During the summer of 1972, I was embarked upon a four-year search for the Great American Bar, a trip that took my VW Bug thirty thousand miles across this nation's roughest roads and myself into its oldest, most colorful dives. That quest resulted in a book, *Saloon*, published to cork-popping effervescence in 1976. One afternoon I visited the Idaho Hotel bar, in the ghost town of Silver City, an emporium reached after a two-hour drive up twenty-five miles of mountain road that was a spike strip of stone and shale, and that deposited me before the 1863 structure, parched and crabby. I entered the hotel and in its once-elegant saloon found ten customers (the town's population) arguing neither politics nor baseball but whether the Seventh Cavalry's uniforms were accurately depicted in the lithograph that hung before them.

It was Otto Becker's *Custer's Last Fight*, an 1896 print distributed by Anheuser-Busch to scores of bars across America, seen repeatedly by me in my travels, and touted, by mid-twentieth century, as the piece of art viewed by more Americans than any other. "If not the best liked of all American pictures," noted Professor Robert Taft, who published his "Pictorial History of the American West" in the *Kansas Historical Quarterly* in 1946, "it doubtless has been the most extensively examined and discussed of any."

Inspired by an 1885 painting of the battle of the Little Bighorn by Cassilly Adams, the lithograph was splendid in its violence, dubious in its historical accuracy and in its portrayal of a golden-haired George Armstrong Custer, romantic to a fault. Yet as my experience affirmed, its presence in saloons across the United States caused a ceaseless spate of chatter. It had been created before television, yet provided comparable entertainment as promotion for Anheuser-Busch beers. This was the Pleistocene of subliminal advertising. Art such as *Custer's Last Fight* created in the drinker a trance-like reverie easily infiltrated by the sponsor's product. Patrons stood hypnotized by the lithograph's gruesome battle scene, glanced at its Anheuser-Busch logo, then ordered a Bud.

Depictions of the 1876 massacre of Seventh-Cavalry troops, at a time when the flamboyant Civil War hero, Custer, may have been planning to run for president, and Indians were considered not just America's enemies but bloodthirsty heathens, already had captivated viewers. No less a critic than Walt Whitman characterized the popular 1881 painting, *Custer's Last Rally*, by John Mulvany, thus: "Swarms upon swarms of savage Sioux, in their war bonnets, frantic, driving through the background, through the smoke, like a hurricane of demons... deadly, heroic to the uttermost; nothing in the books like it, nothing in Homer, nothing in Shakespeare...I could look on such a work at brief intervals all my life without tiring."

He and many Americans would, as Mulvany's 20 feet by 11 feet *Rally*, containing forty-odd figures, toured this country and undoubtedly Europe, as a kind of Wild West Show on canvas. Its impact was huge. William Merritt Chase admired Mulvany's painting to such a degree that

Toby Thompson

he traveled to Europe to study with his teachers. Frederick Remington saw *Custer's Last Rally* and was inspired to sketch his version of the subject. Another artist who undoubtedly saw Mulvany's work was Cassilly Adams.

He was a Civil War veteran, like Custer, but descended from the John Adams family of Boston. He had been trained in painting, and by the late 1870s was employed in St. Louis as an artist and engraver. Members of that city's Art Club commissioned him to recreate the battle scene "for exhibition purposes," Robert Taft wrote, "stimulated no doubt by the success of the Mulvany picture." Adams's rendition was large: 9 feet, 6 inches by 16 feet, 5 inches, and included end panels that portrayed Custer "as a small boy in his father's shop playing with toy soldiers," the second showing "Custer dead on the field of battle." Adams's son recalled that figures "were posed by Sioux Indians in their war paint and also by cavalrymen in the costumes of the period." There was little attempt at historical accuracy as no army participant had lived to verify it. The painting was finished about 1885, and toured widely. It did not realize a profit, however, and was sold to a St. Louis saloon, where it hung for years. Anheuser-Busch obtained it after the saloon keeper's death, and a Milwaukee artist, Otto Becker, was hired to make a chromolithograph of it, which would be copyrighted in 1896.

We depend upon Professor Taft—a Kansas University chemist as well as a historian—for details of the artist's life. Becker was German by birth, had studied at Dresden's Royal Academy of Fine Arts, and so far as an interpretation of Custer's death went, was independent of mind. His daughter, Blanche Becker, told Taft that her father had painted for the Milwaukee Lithographic and Engraving Company, specializing in western scenes "after the manner of Remington." Becker understood the art of advertising. He must have been struck by Custer's plight, though, for his interpretation of the battle, "Taken from [Adams's] Sketches," the original lithograph noted, is more classically framed and far more dramatic than its predecessors. As Taft wrote, "It is indeed a picture that tells a powerful, if melodramatic and horrendous, tale... Troopers are being brained, scalped, stripped; white men, Indians and horses are dying by the dozens; Custer with flowing red tie and long ringlets is about to deal a terrible saber blow to an advancing Indian who in turn is shot by a dying trooper; and hundreds of Indians are pictured or suggested in the background. A careful survey of the lithograph is enough to give a sensitive soul a nightmare for a week."

Yet the print's subtler message was cautionary, as Custer's hubris was an issue. By dividing his regiment and not waiting for reinforcement, he had insured defeat in a skirmish thought unloseable. "Custer was a fool who rode to his death," Sitting Bull said. Comments like his inspired endless commentary before Becker's print—and at times fisticuffs.

In its celebration of war, the print was meant to incite passions, chief among them rage at the killing of a white hero by Sioux, Northern Cheyenne, and Arapaho warriors: racial "others." In two years America would invade Cuba, then the Philippines and Europe; during WWII armed forces would enter the Pacific theater, decimating Japan. Thousands of *Custer's Last Fight* prints had been shipped by the Defense Department to US service folk.

The lithograph's main purpose was not jingoistic, it was to sell beer. And that it did. It stands as one of Anheuser-Busch's most successful ad vehicles. By 1946 the company had produced over 150,000 copies of the lithograph; it is still producing it. A 1933 letter from Becker to his daughter states, "I painted *Custer's Last Stand* in 1895. The original painting is still in my possession, but unfortunately I was forced to cut it into pieces so that a number of artists could work on it...making the color plates." Becker died in Milwaukee in 1945, at age ninety-two. His painting hangs at Anheuser-Busch headquarters, in St. Louis. Cassilly Adams's canvas, upon which it had been based, was presented to the Seventh Cavalry at Fort Riley sometime between 1888 and 1896. It was lost in various moves, restored by the WPA, and rehung at Fort Bliss by 1938, then destroyed by fire in 1946.

Copies of the lithograph still exist in taverns ("Keep this picture under fly-netting in the summer time and it will remain bright for many years," Anheuser-Busch advised), and I recently purchased a 36 inch by 27 inch print from the Custer Battlefield Museum. Spread across my desk, it is a vivid reminder of my travels. Its colors are Technicolor bright, and while not so classically rendered as Mulvany's *Custer's Last Rally*, it is more grippingly dramatic in its rendition of Custer, shown in buckskins and holding both saber and a pistol wielded as a club. The horror of the battle is plain, with Indians tearing scalps from troopers' bloody skulls and stabbing them where they lie. Mutilation would follow. Taft, who hung a copy near his University of Kansas laboratory, wrote: "The reaction of those who have never seen the picture before is always interesting to observe. Incredulous first glances are always followed by study of all the gory details. 'Holy H. Smoke! Was it as bad as that?'"

It was the battle that had been horrific, and the lithograph—no gorier than war paintings in museums round the world—makes no claim to high art. The 1890 massacre of Lakota Sioux at Wounded Knee, by a Seventh Cavalry troop near Pine Ridge, South Dakota, had been, in part, payback for Little Bighorn, and one Saturday, during 1985's Crow Fair, I entered a saloon in Hardin, Montana, near the battlefield, that was crowded with Native Americans. To the back bar's left was Becker's print, defaced with pen and pencil, and bearing colorful epithets. I wore my blond hair Custer-long, and this was a frightening place. I did not linger, but I did ask the bartender why he kept the painting. "So we don't forget," he said. At the American Legion down Center Avenue a friend's band was playing, and when I entered the packed room I saw we were the lone Anglos. What the hell, I thought, and invited a girl to dance. Thereafter I was asked by Native women to jitterbug at least fifty times, and no one disapproved.

Custer's Last Fight was not on display.

Western Art & Architecture
2012

Lessons from Fire and Ice: Gretel Ehrlich

"I hate the heat," Gretel Ehrlich says, as she has for much of this ninety-degree afternoon. We're hiking the glacial moraine behind her Wyoming cabin, flanked by a boulder-strewn meadow stretching to the western face of the fourteen-thousand-foot-high Wind River range. And though clouds rile and thunder booms, the temperature remains high. "We're at eight thousand feet," she says. "This is subalpine. We've never had ninety-eight to one hundred degree heat up here."

Ehrlich's last two books, *The Future of Ice* and *This Cold Heaven*, have examined the problems of climate change, and she's at work on a third, *Farthest North*, for which she's spent a year studying glaciers—from Alaska to Greenland to western Siberia to the eastern Canadian Arctic. "These kettle ponds," she says, pointing, "were scoured out during the last ice age. Usually they fill up in spring with rain and snow melt, and provide great water for wildlife and domestic animals—and also a habitat for birds and ducks. But they're all dry. The big ones have *never* dried up."

Rain sprinkles and thunder sounds, closer this time. In

August, 1991, Ehrlich was struck by lightning on a hike at her former ranch near Shell. She barely survived, then spent years in recovery, during which she wrote a memoir of her experience, *A Match to the Heart*—a stunning examination of body, mind, and nature, and how they are intertwined. "To be struck by lightning," she wrote, "what a way to get enlightened." It was not the first time she'd been hit, and after the second, objects began to combust around her: a hotel lobby, a plane, a forest. Ehrlich's favorite dog, Sam ("a kelpie…a herding dog") had been with her, and though he survived until 2003, today is the anniversary of his death. Gaby, Sam's sole-surviving relative, trots beside us. She is deaf, and arthritis causes her to move stiffly. Yet she yaps at an antelope in the dry pond. Ehrlich smiles. "Those are your seal barks," she says, ruffling Gaby's fur.

For Ehrlich, and in various mythologies, dogs are "spirit helpers," standing "for the guardian who carries the human spirit forward." A favorite expression of hers is, "God is dog." She elaborates: "I'm not a theist. There's godliness, there's divinity, the divine in every square inch, every atom. But to ascribe it to a single point or persona is missing how complex it all is."

She sees a similar complexity in weather, which for her is analogous to consciousness. She's noted, in *The Future of Ice*, that this "mixing of mind and space," for Greenland's Inuit "is called *sila*. The two are one…lightning can make scratch marks on brains; hail gouges out a nesting place, melts, and waters the seed of an idea…" These clouds and the light rain may reflect Ehrlich's current pessimism about climate change, world and local politics, but I hope lightning won't make her point emphatically. I ask if she's worried. "No," she says, "I'd always go out in a thunderstorm if my dog were lost."

But the meadow through which she and Gaby move is threatened by more than lightning. "There's a mandate to the BLM to drill gas and oil wells as fast and as furiously as possible, through the million acres between these mountain ranges. It's part of a big migration corridor for elk, grizzlies, wolves, coyotes, black bears and swans and sandhill cranes and every kind of duck. Our road's closed in the winter, so you have to snowshoe or ski three miles in. The highway doesn't go anywhere, so we don't have through traffic. It's very secluded." She stops, catches her breath. "We're working on a case to save it. When I bought this place I thought, 'This is great, this is home.' But I have no interest in living here, even if there's an oil well forty miles down the road." She sighs. "It would be the final desecration."

We've enjoyed a lively supper, and now breakfast with Ehrlich's husband, Thomas Kearns—a retired philosophy professor from Amherst—but Kearns has left to study the drilling case at his house in Pinedale, fifteen miles southeast, and we're alone. "Our postmistress, my old friend Pat, introduced us," Ehrlich says. "Because we subscribed to the same magazines!"

They've been married three years, but the simple log cabin where we sit is one that, in 2003, Ehrlich designed and built for herself. "I had sorted out my life to live the rest of it basically alone," she explains. "Pat told me Tom was a professor, and invited me to dinner. I said, 'No Pat, anything but that.' I expected some drooling idiot who didn't know his way around a piece of sagebrush. But when I walked into the room and saw this bright-faced, intelligent being, I just started laughing, because I could see that this was a wonderful person."

Kearns has been more than congenial at dinner, helping Ehrlich pick Swiss chard and tomatoes from their garden and assisting in the grilling of buffalo burgers. Conversation ranged from questions of free will to those of the presidential debate, and there was not a moment when Ehrlich did not smile. Their wedding had been a Buddhist ceremony, with prayer flags decorating the cabin. "The priest said, 'Do you want me to wear my robes, or blue jeans?' I said, 'Robes.' We had ranchers, writer friends, just really hard core. It was fantastic."

The leis they wore hang by a French door, near a padded bench and high windows that cause the room to float on a landscape of thick sagebrush, erratic boulders and scoured meadowland. "I wanted a space that would in some way acknowledge the beauty of this landscape," she tells me, "without calling attention to itself." She's written, in *Islands, the Universe, Home,* that "I want to break down the dichotomy between inside and outside, interior and exterior…a house is not a defense against nature but a way of letting it in." Her study, where I've slept—with screened windows ajar to sagebrush, hummingbirds, and chipmunks—is even more one with nature.

"Power wise, I'm off the grid. The cabin is solar heated. I do have a little propane stove that gets turned on when it starts getting to twenty below."

In this heat Ehrlich wears khaki shorts, a brown shirt, and her blonde hair in pigtails. She's sixty-two and, while beautiful, looks older than in photographs from the 1980s, when a stunning cowgirl gazed sexily at us from book jackets. Her face is tougher, reflecting a life outdoors. Yet her personality, aloof and mysterious in print, is wise-crackingly funny. Its edge is rough as the eight-foot-high boulder, "lion colored and dappled with lichen," forty yards from the house, where Sam is buried and about which Ehrlich has repeatedly written. "This is the landscape that's become my heart's home," she says.

It's been so since 1976, when she traveled to Wyoming to make a documentary about sheepherders, "an ethnographic film about lonely people in lonely places." She returned during the terrible winter of 1978-1979, when temperatures plummeted to sixty below. Her first great love, David Hancock, a partner on the film, had succumbed to cancer. She was grief-stricken, isolated, and camped in a one-room cabin near Yellowstone Park, performing day-work "for meat" on ranches. "I had suffered a tragedy," she wrote in her first, groundbreaking work, *Solace of Open Spaces.* And here adds, "I didn't care if

I lived or died. I cut my hair off with sheep shears, and I burned all my clothes in a burn-barrel back of a sheep wagon. It was tabula rasa time."

But that winter and the next she read "the entire western canon," wrote a book of poetry, *To Touch the Water*, journaled, and found her voice as a writer. "All art, all expression, all of living is perceived through some sense of stripping everything away," she says. "And I believed I needed to live before I wrote." Eventually she produced *The Solace of Open Spaces* (1985) and *Islands* (1991), about those ranching years, establishing herself, with Edward Abbey, Barry Lopez and Peter Matthiessen, as a new intelligence in the literature of place.

Time called *Solace* "the sleeper of the year," and it won the H. D. Vursell Award from the American Academy and Institute of Arts and Letters, and a Whiting Writer's Award. One critic remarked of *Solace*, "Her essays, delicately combining interior and exterior exploration, are as spare and beautiful as the landscape from which they've grown." Another said, "Ehrlich's best prose belongs in a league with Annie Dillard and even Thoreau." She had written of the Wyoming ranch country and the people who work it with lyricism and deep affection. "I think writers are lonely people," she says. "You're always embracing and struggling against being an outsider." The ranchers proved "instant community, instant family," she says. They "gave me a life. I was just this little wraith, living like a coyote. I had nothing."

Though Ehrlich grew up near Santa Barbara in privileged circumstances—her father was a plastics manufacturer who invented, among other items, the seeping garden hose—she did not have a trust fund. "My parents insisted that my sister and I go out and meet life in any way we chose, but get out and make it on your own." She wasn't close to her family, "Probably ever. Later they'd say, 'what have you done this year?' and I'd hand them a book. They visited Shell, which was pretty hardscrabble for them. They'd say, 'It's a shame you didn't buy a ranch in Jackson.' I'd say, 'Give me the money and I will.' We led very different lives. But we talked about everything before they died."

I ask what killed them. "Martinis and cigarettes," Ehrlich says. "That's what they die of in Santa Barbara."

She adored animals as a child, rode horses and sailed, and felt more akin to the Mexicans and Asians of coastal California than to her parents' country-club set. "I wanted to live in remote places with animals," she says. "But I loved Japanese and Chinese poetry. And I was fascinated by things Asian." In 1978 she would spend time in a Tibetan Buddhist monastery, but by age twelve (when she left Montecito for boarding school) she'd discovered Latin poetry and the writings of Zen master, D.T. Suzuki. "The basis of meditation is that, between each breath, is death," she says. Latin strengthened her sense of language (she still reads in it) and Zen helped her cope, leading to the study of art, dance, and avant-garde theater at Bennington. She nearly completed film school at UCLA before being offered her first job, as a film editor for NET in New York. She took it.

"Once I discovered film I thought, 'Oh my God, this has all these visual elements, it has music, it has movement, it has stories, it has...' because before then I had hardly seen any movies in my life. Our family just didn't go to movies. You read books, you painted, you sailed, you rode a horse, but you didn't go to movies—unless it had been raining for two weeks."

We've been chatting at her dining table, over tea and the remnants of breakfast. Gaby pants and Ehrlich says to her, lovingly, "If you're too hot, maybe you should go outside." Gaby complies. Ehrlich watches, then blurts, "Antonioni died today. Bergman yesterday." I'm surprised. I ask if her art films were in any way Bergmanesque. "Yeah, also like Antonioni's. The first one I did was called *Autopsy*." She laughs. "The second was called *By Pass*. They were about these fractured, alienated, devastating relationships between men and women.

And about death. They certainly were a reflection of how I was feeling about life and love."

By 1979 she'd left her cabin and moved to Shell, Wyoming. At a John Wayne film festival in Cody, she met Press Stephens, her first husband, an outfitter with a Ph.D. in art history, who had grown up comfortably. "Like me, he was a culture straddler." Their relationship is characterized in *Solace*'s "Just Married" chapter; she and Stephens were separated when Ehrlich was struck by lightning, and the marriage did not survive her ordeal. That Stephens wasn't there seems to rankle her. "I don't want to talk about it." Ironically, it was her distant father who "saved my life completely," by hiring a plane to fly her from Greybull to Santa Barbara, and a competent hospital. She'd been passing out, "And if I'd stayed at the ranch, the cardiologist said I would have been dead in twelve hours."

During that treatment she had an experience akin to witnessing her own death: "I was in a coma and I could hear the nurses counting down my heart rate and saying, 'We can't find a pulse.' I knew that I was dying. I could feel my mother stroking my hair. And I could hear the cardiologist saying to her, 'Gretchen you better call Grant. I don't think she's going to make it.' But I was completely awake in my mind. I was pissed off! I thought, God don't let me die! I'm fine, I'm completely awake... there's nothing wrong with me! Just because I can't see or talk or move, I can hear.' Afterward, I would lose consciousness many thousands of times, and had to be resuscitated in the hospital three times...so I really lived day to day with the prospect of death...the fearful part is leaving, the goodbyes. I didn't want to leave my dog, and I didn't want to make my parents suffer."

She would survive, but "lost everything" in her divorce. "I'd hired a crappy little country lawyer, and he hired a Harvard lawyer from Jackson. I thought, 'I don't care.'" But by losing her ranch, she "lost the font from which everything was coming," she says. "My world was taken away, totally. It was like another 'David' situation. And I was hit in the middle of where I thought I was coming into being as a writer."

She'd published a novel, *Heart Mountain* (1988), about a Japanese internment camp in Wyoming, and previously a short fiction collection, *Wyoming Stories* (1986); within six months of starting *Match*, she had finished that book. "My editor had come out and I said, 'Of course, I really want to write another novel. But my body is trying to heal.' So I just wrote *Match* every day in the mornings. And I was exhausted."

The result was a unique nonfiction work, part memoir, part treatise on neurobiology, cardiology, and lightning, part spiritual meditation on death and near-death, part ode to love and other injuries of the heart. It's both a paean to home and to her dog Sam, the spirit-helper, who led her back from the underworld. Above all it's confirmation of her belief in *sila*, the Inuit notion that weather equals consciousness. As the *Chicago Tribune* wrote, "Ehrlich is a compulsive connector of the physical to the mystical," and the *Rocky Mountain News* added, "The Buddhist in her gives us a thoughtful meditation on the state of suspension between life and death." The *London Review of Books*, said: "*A Match to the Heart* is a tale of solitude. There is no one to share Ehrlich's ordeal intimately...Her solitude is almost never commented on; it is just a truth about her."

The book seemed to purge Ehrlich of fire, however, and to nudge her toward ice. She began journeying to the Arctic. "It was just too painful to come back to Wyoming," she explains. "And in the Arctic I saw this amazing culture that was threatened. Because the ice is disappearing. So that other part of me, 'the trained ethnographic film maker,' came into being."

It's afternoon and we've moved to her study, where my rumpled sheets on the window seat contrast with the order of her talismans, notebooks, and mementos from

Greenland. The one-room cottage has plank floors, high windows, and a simple desk at its center. Ehrlich gives a tour: "That's a Siberian reindeer harness, that's the *National Geographic* map of Greenland I carry, those are my handmade sealskin mittens and boots, my field notes in Ziploc bags, that's a knife made in Alaska, my collections of Asian poetry and books by the transcendentalists, a Jackson Pollock print—'Action! Do something!'—a piece of Siberian tundra...." The list continues.

I ask if she has a writing ritual. "Absolutely not. If somehow you can't *do* that ritual, then you say, 'Oh well, I guess I can't write today.' If you're lucky enough to wake up and not be dead, then you can write." We move to her desk, decorated with a piece of Mali cloth from Zimbabwe. "I've been writing this section of *Farthest North* about the Koni people, nomadic reindeer herders in Siberia. I put in stuff about tundra ecosystems and what's happening to that, in terms of melting permafrost. And things about the Bering Sea. It's really a book about the effects of climate change on indigenous Arctic people. Because they're the first climate refugees."

I ask about the brush sketches on her desk. "They're doodles. I do them when I'm thinking about Greenland and ice. I hate to say it, but I've spent more time there, in a more intimate way, than I have here. I keep dreaming of hunters carrying these huge panes of ice and putting them back down on the water. Greenland's the most beautiful place in the world."

By 1993 she had begun the years of travel that resulted in *This Cold Heaven: Seven Seasons in Greenland*, published in 2001. She wrote in its preface, "I first traveled to Greenland...not to write a book but to get above tree line." Her weakened heart could not function at an altitude "where I felt at home," and she learned that "tree line can be a factor of latitude...it's a biological boundary created by the cold." She lived with the Inuit and Koni, crossing ice by dogsled at sixty below, the snow by reindeer sled, and backpacking through the Arctic where no human had ventured.

Greenland was another remote place with a strong community and hunting culture that wasted nothing, was in sync with nature and Zen-like in its existence. "I feel totally at home there. Living with the Inuit, you see people in whose eyes and faces you see the isolated world into which they go. They haven't been jaded by Starbucks or convenience stores. *Nothing* is convenient...but to me it's like a cow camp. I tell them, 'This is Wyoming, with ice instead of sagebrush.'"

Seasons took years to finish. "My parents were dying, and I told them I would help them, because they'd saved my life." But after their deaths she returned to the Arctic. Cold seemed to obsess her. And she soon learned that not only were the glaciers receding, but the humans and animals who depended on them were seriously threatened. "They're real depressed about it. They're extremely aware that nothing they have done has caused this." She's quiet a moment. "It's like having your world taken away, for no reason. Here we can blame ourselves. But they live the *real* green life."

Ehrlich has written so extensively about Greenland that I coax her back toward Wyoming, the home (this forty acres) she's struggling to save, and to her marriage. She laughs about the latter. "It's as hard as it ever was," she says. "To be with a person...in your twenties there's so much excitement about how you're going to make your life. But we're sort of at the end of the line, here. So you think about what it is you still need to do to make a contribution to the world. We're working on climate change, and indigenous peoples things, and legal issues and justice issues and land use issues. It requires more tolerance and compassion than a young relationship, which is fueled by lust and by excitement about what's coming up in the future. Now it's the Buddhist commitment to do the best, and to be compassionate." She frowns. "It's about forgiveness and taking care of each other in the last years of your life. None of us is perfect, especially me.

And Tom has a writer's sense of despair and desolation and darkness."

She looks off. "We've really been depressed over the drilling issues. This land is his heart's home as well. I've lived sort of a bum's life—I mean, I have nothing, no family...and there's the whole issue of loneliness." She snorts. "It's nice to think that there's somebody around who might notice that you're dying."

Gaby needs a walk, so Ehrlich leads us through forty yards of sagebrush and heat to the enormous boulder by Sam's grave. It's marked by a white stone from the meadow. She studies it, then points to a piece of ground near the erratic. "This is where I want to be buried."

I recall a passage she's written, in *The Future of Ice*: "The place where Sam is buried is a view of the world without end. It is the center and the edge of time; it's the place where eyelids fall away."

Not a bad spot, I offer.

"Yeah." She grins. "One friend has said, 'Stop being so *depressed* about everything, Gretch. Just think, we get to witness this enormous change. As enormous as the beginning of an ice age.'" She touches the boulder. "And from a geological point of view, of course, it's all a phase. It's just humans and animals. Megafauna's going to crash and the planet will survive. Then something else will happen." She turns toward the cabin, but hesitates, gesturing. "That's all there is, stripped-away life. This sage doesn't expect to become a pine tree. The pine trees don't have an expectation that they should live one hundred years. Coming home, to live here and write about it, I had to actually *understand* that I was part of the natural world. There were no inalienable rights attached to my existence. There was just bare-assed existence."

Again she laughs.

"Everything is about learning to see."

Big Sky Journal
2008

The Godfather: William Kittredge

"That's Ross Dollarhide," William Kittredge says, indicating a tall man wearing leather chaps and a tweed cap in a 1943 black-and-white photo of four buckaroos at the MC Ranch in Warner Valley, Oregon. "Ross is on the left, then Shirley McConnell, Hugh Cahill and… goddamit, what's that other guy's name?" The photograph, in Kittredge's Missoula apartment (cramped space for an heir to what was the Northwest's largest ranch) is prominently displayed. It anchored the cover of *Owning It All*, his first collection of essays, and was taken by his mother on a cold day "during a lull in the branding," on the thirty-three-square-mile MC ranch (with grazing rights to fifteen hundred square miles more) that Kittredge's family owned and where he grew up. He's described the MC as "a feudal kingdom," that "could have been a paradise; maybe it was, maybe it still is." This photo, this *movie* of that paradise, in Kittredge's mind, stars Ross Dollarhide, the MC's wagon boss, a storied horseman and "my main vaquero model in matters of grace and manliness." Buckaroos like Dollarhide,

Kittredge has written, "knew better than to imagine you could ever own anything beyond a coherent self."

Kittredge owns few possessions and no land. "I feel no need to. The world is there anyway." He believes stories, not property, define selfhood. Without stories, "We do not know who we are, or who we might become." And this morning he's told great ones, of how he and Annick Smith, "my true companion" of thirty years, contracted with Norman Maclean to film *A River Runs Through It*, then capitulated to Robert Redford, taking associate producer credits on his movie ("I said, 'If they need me, I'll be on the golf course'"); of how in 1988 he and Annick edited the 1,164-page anthology, *The Last Best Place*, and how Kittredge imagined that title ("I was into my second glass of gin at Chico and thinking about Hugo's 'the last good kiss' and Lincoln's 'last best hope of mankind'"); of how there may be responsibilities for coining such a phrase, and for writing too lovingly about place. And, with prompting, of how he's published eight major books, plus nine Western potboilers "with Steve Krauzer," during the eighties...and of how this year he's won an Earl A. Chiles Award "For illuminating the changing culture, landscapes, personalities, and possibilities of the Intermountain West," and a *Los Angeles Times* Book Prize for Lifetime Achievement. In October, 2008, "dead or alive," he's also to receive a lifetime achievement award from the Western Literature Association.

For such a paragon of Montana lit (one of few who grew up on a ranch), he's dressed like the golfer he is, in yellow polo shirt, tan slacks, and leather sandals. "I used to wear cowboy boots, 'endangered species boots,' I called them," he says. "They were like foot binding. My size, since I stopped, has increased by one and a half." He coughs, stubs out a cigarette. "And I play golf every day I can."

At seventy-five, his hair has grayed and the once-bear-like physique has shrunk. He and Annick (author of the memoir, *Homestead*, and producer of the film, *Heartland*) have returned from Vermont's Bread Loaf Writers Conference, where each taught a class. They travel widely, Kittredge having retired from the University of Montana as Regents' Professor of Creative Writing, where he taught "thousands" of writers, including several he's anthologized in *The Last Best Place, The Portable Western Reader, Montana Spaces,* and *The Best of Montana's Short Fiction* (with Allen Jones). Most readers consider Kittredge the godfather of Montana prose, an honorific earned through his poetically thoughtful essays, but also through his three collections of short stories, *We Are Not in this Together, The Van Gogh Field,* and his *Best of...* As David Quammen wrote, "If there's a literary New West, growing crazywild and green and true right there out of the Old one, Bill Kittredge is it. Compared to him, the rest of us are pavement."

The story he's exploring now is that of being a literary novelist. His first such, *The Willow Field*, was published in 2006 to fine reviews (its paperback is due in October), and though he'll publish *The Next Rodeo: New and Selected Essays,* in November, his mind is enveloped by fiction.

"When I'm writing, I get up pretty early and make a cup of coffee, turn on the computer, and go into that room," pointing at his study, "practically in a dream state. Once I get people," his players, "it's all about character and not about concept. I got to the point with *Willow Field* that I dreamed about these people. Like they were real."

In a sense they are. *The Willow Field* is a historical novel—Kittredge drawing on experiences and friends (the protagonist is named Rossie), for male and female characters, including a passionately independent one named Eliza. "I think there must be some of me in Eliza," Annick will say. "And the novel is all Bill, of course." It starts with a 1933 horse drive from Nevada to Canada, where the buckaroo Rossie falls ruttingly in love with Eliza, whose father (a Scottish intellectual) owns a ranch in the Bitterroot Valley. "He's looking for a mom,"

Kittredge says, "someone to hold him together. And God knows I've done enough of that." Rossie follows Eliza to the Bitterroot, they marry, suffer through child rearing, parental deaths, and the political upheavals of the 1960s. It's a novel about family, horses, and the fickleness of sex. "It's about loneliness, really," Kittredge says. "About people trying to connect...with each other, the world, with something psychically actual and not terrifying. And that probably goes back to being five years old in that hospital room in Portland screaming for my mother."

In 1937 Kittredge endured a year of treatment for polio—first in Portland, then at the Shriner's Crippled Childrens Hospital in San Francisco. "It was terrifying. An absolutely crucial experience for me, I think. My father went back to the ranch, and my mother would only come an hour a day, in the evening. She'd leave and I'd scream in the room all by myself for three hours." In his 1992 memoir, *Hole in the Sky*, he wrote of being "hypnotized by loss," and of "not being allowed even the solace of my only love." He was "a broken thing, forced to live in make-believe." His memories of his family, "of things being whole," and of the Warner Valley ranch, had become his stories. Through loss, he'd acquired "an understanding that the world can be lived in as one act of the imagination after another..." And connecting through stories, he says, is "the theme that's been through practically everything I've ever written."

"Dis-ease," is a term Kittredge uses to describe a psychic discomfort and "catatonic fearfulness" that, in his case, bordered on crackup. By April 11, 1961, he was boss of farming operations at the MC, and aching to become a writer. He'd taken a fiction seminar at Oregon University, while studying agriculture, and it had intrigued him. But he was on a career path in Warner that had compromised his grandfather's and father's lives—and that, through modern farming, was ruining the land. That path would drive him through "frantic years of trying to name what was real, and figure out which story was mine," he wrote in *Hole*. That morning of April 11, he felt an "instant of oncoming panic," and that "the world was meaningless." Years of struggle followed, in which he "saw booze as a fence against my fear that nothing was real, and sex as a doorway into something that might turn out to be." Leaving home was a problem, as was having succumbed to his grandfather's dream of property. Kittredge's father, Oscar, had suffered thus. "We never understood that you have to save your life by making up a new one." Eventually he realized (as do many authors) that by composing stories related to the wholeness he'd felt in childhood, he could leave home physically without doing so emotionally. "I had indeed found my life," he'd write, "the freedom and chance to turn my obsessions into a profession." He applied to Oregon in creative writing, and later was accepted at Iowa University's Writers Workshop.

"My dad approved of it," he remembers. "I'd broken up with my first wife and was living in a little shack on the Klamath Marsh, and he drives in to meet me in a yellow Mercedes. I give him some Jack Daniel's, and he wants to know what the hell I'm doing. 'I'm going off to graduate school,' which is clearly the most dubious thing he's ever heard. 'I'll just say one thing,' he said. 'I've done shit I hated all my life, and I sure as hell wouldn't recommend that.' That was the end of it."

"He was a character, Oscar Kittredge," Annick says. "I really loved him. He had those courtly cowboy manners, and was just a charmer. A great guy—and a very funny man."

We're at her ranch—163 acres above the Blackfoot River, 25 miles east of Missoula—in the 1890 log house she wrote about in *Homestead*, where she raised her four sons, two of whom are filmmakers, and where her husband, Dave Smith, died of a heart attack in 1974. Kittredge lives here four to five days a week. It's on high ground overlooking the valley, and seated at her dining table, he looks at home.

Annick is seventy-one, with a head of cascading white hair. Kittredge calls her "the luck of my later life," and "a good deal less flighty than I am when anything like the ultimate chips are falling...she'll take care of you if you take care of her." They became involved on Halloween, 1977. "We'd fenced around, but that night I went to a party with someone else and went home with her. I asked once whether she wanted to get married, and she said, 'If it ain't broke, don't fix it.' We have an endless conversation—disagreeing, arguing, getting pissed off, getting together—it's very volatile."

Annick has been speaking of efforts to protect the Blackfoot and its valley—"She's a lot more active than I am," Kittredge admits—and they've been discussing storytelling and the responsibilities of artists to place, Annick being the producer who first convinced Maclean to make a film of *River*. "I think you do have some responsibility," she says. "I remember being at a meeting about recreation on the Blackfoot, which is out of control, and this guy practically jabbed me in the chest, and said, 'It's your fault.' To some degree I suppose it is."

Kittredge shrugs. "To some degree you're responsible, to some degree you're not. I mean, the world's changing anyway...what I believe about all that kind of rigid defining is that probably both sides are sort of wrong and both sides are sort of right..."

"But Bill, you're not being concrete at all..."

They argue good-naturedly, and conversation turns to Warner Valley and Kittredge's family. "My dad enjoyed himself, he had a hell of a time," Kittredge says. "Movie stars and politicians came to the ranch hunting, and there was lots of joviality and good times where he was around. My mother Jo, after their divorce, was in the state legislature in Oregon, but she also was interested in the arts. I probably wouldn't be doing this if not for her." He wrote, in *Hole*, that "she never lost her belief that art and music could survive the ranching life she had come to when she married my father." But, he says here, "about the age of seventy-five she went into an old folks home and literally went to bed. She had some kind of real crisis—her will broke, and she had been an extremely strong, willful woman."

Annick interrupts, says, "Look at those birds outside— blue on their wings, a white bar around their neck, a red- dish breast." Kittredge nods, continues: "After I got out of college, and most of the time I was in the Air Force—I tried to write. And I read philosophy: Whitehead, Kant. I kept waiting for somebody to explain the world to me. Nobody could and nobody would. I agreed with Kant that the world's a construct. We invent it as we go along. Except on the other hand it's always out there, too—you can stub your toe on it. And that's a devastating idea. I had my flip out over that, I had a major anxiety attack. And it lasted three or four years—I kind of wrote my way out of it. "

"Drank your way into it," Annick says.

"Oh, blah, blah, blah. I was trying to *write* during that period. But not much."

"It was a *very* long period."

"Lighten up!" Kittredge says. They laugh.

"But anyhow," he adds, "trying to connect through that impasse that Kant plays out is what my writing's really about." The creation of stories, in fiction or nonfic- tion, can provide direction. "Somebody comes to a recog- nition, a moment of insight, a moment of understanding. That moment gives them leverage to control their life for a while. But it never really works. Because we can't really understand things too well, we have to keep redoing them. Every morning we wake up with 'What am I going to do today, how am I going to do it? How am I going to act, who am I going to be?' And as the day goes by, you discover the answers. That's a model for human decision making. We're continually involved in those questions: how to resolve this, how to make sense of it, how to or- der things, how to get through this, how to put things together. Before they fall apart again."

Earlier, over lunch by the Clark Fork River in Missoula, Kittredge had spun stories of the poet and UM professor Richard Hugo (whose life fell apart repeatedly), but offered paternal guidance, as had Ross Dollarhide and Oscar Kittredge. In *Hole*, Kittredge wrote, "More than anyone, he helped me convince myself that I wasn't crazy, and that my anxieties were quite usual." Kittredge reached Missoula on a fall day in 1969, with a teaching appointment. He knocked on Hugo's door. The poet "studied me like an anthropologist," he'd later write. "'You're very drunk...I'll join you.'"

Hugo was a widely respected poet and English Department star. "Dick kind of spirited us through the academic world around here. We all hung out in a roving entourage of drunks." That group included James Welch, Jim Crumley (whose job Kittredge inherited), Jon Jackson, James Lee Burke, Rick DeMarinis, Dave Smith, and Annick, who would make a film, *Kicking the Loose Gravel Home*, about Hugo. This group, with a comparable one of Livingston-area writers, actors, and artists, would comprise the nexus of Montana's cultural renaissance.

Right now, Kittredge and Annick are weighing that renaissance. "My feeling," he says, "is that twenty-five years ago, when we were doing *The Last Best Place* and other projects, I thought we were going to see a literary boom in the West. And in certain ways it's been disappointing. I don't think it's quite materialized."

Annick demurs, listing a number of recognized authors, "and of the younger writers there's Maile Meloy, Allen Jones, Debra Earling, Florence Williams, Mark Spragg, Craig Childs..."

"And Rick Bass," Kittredge says, "but he's about fifty."

Conversation moves to *The Willow Field*, and the degree to which its characters' personalities and themes reflect those of Kittredge's nonfiction. "Maybe all of them," he says. "Because the book comes of what I think, what I believe." Rossie's dependence upon Eliza is mentioned.

"That's also kind of true to our relationship," Annick offers. "I know that I'm always struggling to have Bill be less dependent. 'Get out of here and do your own thing.' Which he does. Also, there's a certain amount of passivity in all of Bill's fictional characters. And that must come out of Bill."

"Yeah," Kittredge says. "You know, I never got in a fistfight in my life. I was decked once, but I didn't strike back." He smirks. "On the dance floor of the Indian Village in Lakeview, Oregon, dancing with this guy's wife—whacko."

Further commentary is superfluous, so a drink is suggested. Kittredge brightens. He loves the camaraderie of saloons, and in the next few hours will conduct a tour of, or a drive past, Missoula's best—Charley's ("They sold twenty copies a night of *The Last Best Place*"), the Depot ("where Crumley hangs out"), the Oxford, the Missoula Club, and the Milltown Union Bar, near where Hugo had lived—"It was real handy for Dick, this ramshackle two-story working man's apartment-hotel, only fifty footsteps away"—and about which he wrote a poem, "The Milltown Union Bar (Laundromat & Café)": "You need never leave. Money or a story brings you booze… you were nothing going in and now you kiss your hand." Kittredge, admiring its eccentric fixtures and roughneck clientele telling story after story, will exclaim: "I could sit here all night."

But he's not there yet. "Remember," Annick says, affectionately. "You have to play golf tomorrow."

"I know," Kittredge mutters.

"Don't have too much fun."

Big Sky Journal
2007

Summer Wages

The picture shows me at five, standing on a pier in New York's East River, slapping leather with one finger extended beside a white, double-holstered gunbelt. I wear a blue-checked shirt and jeans, a black Hopalong Cassidy hat and scarf. My boots are red as Howdy Doody's and my grin is wide as the Queensboro Bridge.

The boots were borrowed from an actor's daughter upstairs, but those in another snapshot—taken at age fourteen on my first day working at the Madison Fork Ranch near West Yellowstone—were purchased in Montana and are black with green and red intaglios. They are complemented by a red gingham shirt (white-fringed with pearl snaps), stiff Levi's and a white Stetson two sizes too big, that my uncle had given me. I'd bought clothes for ranch work that someone raised on the costumes of Roy Rogers might have chosen.

Madison Fork's mistress was Maggie Meyer, the middle-aged scion of a privileged Long Island clan, who oversaw the family ranch, with its one hundred cattle and fewer annual guests—tolerated to maintain the property's dude-ranch status. The place was perhaps one thousand acres. Guests were mostly anglers who paid high fees to fish Maggie's stretch of the South Fork. In her middle fifties, she was bronze-blonde, weathered, and fit. She worked each day in Levi's and cowboy shirt, but at the stroke of five, she emerged from her cabin in Chinese pajamas, silk turban and Arabian slippers with the toes curled up. Her foreman had been hired not for his ranching abilities but because, as a bartender, he mixed the best martini in West Yellowstone. Maggie would knock several back then grab a .22 armed with birdshot. On the porch, cigarette holder askew, she would blast incoming swallows that nested in the ranch house eaves—leading their darting shapes, in her silk pajamas, expertly.

As a child raised on theatricality, I found this conduct fitting. Like that generation which by century's end would repopulate Montana, I grew up in the false dawn of television—Hoppy, Roy, Gene Autry, Tex Ritter, and the Lone Ranger were my heroes. My uncle was a television producer. When I'd been five, Boris Karloff leant me the prosthesis he wore as Captain Hook in *Peter Pan*, and when I'd been one he tickled my toes to make me walk. If Maggie wished to transform herself from Annie Oakley to Auntie Mame in a costume change, that was acceptable.

She was the cousin of friends, who by considerable effort talked her into hiring me and a pal, John Holland—later a producer for NBC's *Nightly News*—to work that summer. They knew that Maggie, raised in boarding school or with servants, was not "good" with kids. She suffered fools poorly. But we would sleep in the bunkhouse, dine in the kitchen, and hang with the wrangler—an odd drifter I'll call Ray—who was thin as lodgepole and ornery as spit, but who crooned Appalachian murder-ballads as we worked.

In 1959 West Yellowstone was funky, with vestiges of old Montana surviving—notably in its saloons, to which Maggie dragged us immediately. Doc's, the Frontier, the Cowboy—like movie sets, they filled me with hope, an emotion bruised by our three-day trip west. Maggie ordered a drink, then spoke: "This is a real job. You'll be expected to work and you'll be paid for it." Her accent was Long Island lockjaw, familiar yet intimidating. Though she added that our wages would be fifty cents an hour, I felt easier. The whiskey in that battered room, and on the ranch, smelled like home.

Maggie was representative of an old phenomenon in Montana, the wealthy remittance person who—black sheep or dreamer—fell for the country and stayed. She had graduated from Foxcroft, ridden to the hounds, made her debut, studied painting at the Arts Students League, had two failed marriages. Yet she loved the ranch and was primarily a New Montanan, that transplanted Easterner or Californian whose presence would transform the region.

Our log bunkhouse was named "the Martha," and its ranchyard companion "the George"—after the Washingtons, we presumed. In 1895, the ranch had been a stagecoach stop on the two-day drive from Monida to Yellowstone Park, before West Yellowstone was developed. The Martha had been Dwelle's Grayling Inn. Its owner guaranteed trout for breakfast. The railroad put Dwelle out of business in 1909 and the Meyers bought his property during the 1920s. In 1959, John and I slept apart from our wrangler, beds snugged with wool Navajos or Amish quilts, their brass frames polished. It was cold at 6,666 feet. We shared a clawfoot tub.

We had come to work, and work we did. Each morning the foreman, Bob, drove us to an ancient fence line collapsed with brush. Our first task was to rip barbed wire from the undergrowth, twist it into portable loops, then stack those for pickup. Far from my fantasies of roping and riding, it was dull work—comparable, I thought later, to that of migrant onion toppers. Bend and pull, swat a deer fly, bend and pull. It lasted weeks. We switched to roofing, then weeding larkspur, where at least we could recline. We killed time by reciting plots of every *Alfred Hitchcock Presents* we could muster.

Occasionally we rode, but mostly on weekends and in the corral. There were eight or ten horses; none were permitted out by us. The Madison flowed past our window, frustrating on bug-thick evenings, as we had hoped to fish. Its waters were forbidden, saved for Maggie and her guests. We might cast in the lake, which to kids raised on whitewater, was comparable to fishing an aquarium. No one drove us to town.

A first job is a kid's rite of passage, but so is his fifteenth summer. Half boy, half billygoat, his psyche darts from make believe to making out, as his body creates a perfect storm of hormones. Add ranch life's isolation, and that storm rages. Afternoons, a fellow might be mastering the hard trot; evenings, the hand gallop.

Though we worked arduously, in slack moments we read the Beats and for school Jane Austen. The distance between Wrangler Ray and ourselves widened. Thomas McGuane, who as a kid worked on ranches, wrote of that time: "A lot of us read Jack Kerouac, and if you read Jack Kerouac and were an American of a certain age, you felt you owned the whole place...He trained us in the epic idea that the region was America...It was called *On the Road*." I was prepared to meet our wrangler as Neal Cassady, but when we lobbed Jack's Zennishness at him he stared like we were Communists.

We had drawn Ray and we stuck by him. As Kinky Friedman says, "You can pick your nose and you can pick your friends, but you can't wipe your friends on your saddle." Ray mostly fiddled with horses—he was quite gentle with a new colt—but when Maggie decided she wished a corral built, with loading chutes for steers, we began working alongside him.

I've downplayed Ray's attractiveness. To start, he was nineteen, an unimaginably advanced age; he wore perfectly faded Wranglers with knife-edge creases, billowy plaid shirts, a gray felt hat and stovepipe Tony Lama's.

He was six-one with a sharp-featured, Scotch-Irish face and close-cropped reddish hair. He had a pencil-line mustache. His legs flapped like a marionette's and his posture resembled a boat hook's.

Ray drove us on the tractor to the foothills above Madison Fork, where we cut timber and stacked it on a trailer. He knew things we didn't. He taught us how to sharpen an axe, run a chainsaw; he spoke little of his Wyoming childhood, but was swarming with paranoia. There were conspiracies by the foreman, Maggie, and even the cook. "They're agin' us," he'd whinny, or, "we can't last." In every photo, his head is ducked or his face averted. Obviously he was wary, even jealous—perhaps sensing how thoroughly his way of life would become threatened by our sort—but sang his songs sweetly: "Pretty Polly," "I Wish I Was a Mole in the Ground," or his favorite, "Knoxville Girl," with its "I met a little girl in Knoxville, a town we all know well, and every Sunday evening, out in her home I'd dwell / We went to take a little walk, about a mile from town / I picked a stick up off the ground, and knocked that fair girl down / She fell down on her bended knees, for mercy she did cry / 'Oh, Willie dear, don't kill me here, I'm unprepared to die...'" He killed her anyway, and I've always remembered the lyric.

It was obvious someone was shorting us wages. We would work forty hours, which should have yielded twenty dollars, and the check would come for eight. Later we understood what was happening: Ray told Bob we had slacked and Maggie docked our pay. No one spoke to us about it. We were frightened to complain, and it was characteristic of Maggie's class, during that era, not to discuss "family" difficulties. Also, "She hated to spend money," her daughter-in-law would say later.

Gradually we were permitted more time horseback. We patrolled the upper reaches of Maggie's fork, shooing fishermen from its waters. "You own the land, not the stream," they would argue—but always retreated. We hid on a ghost ranch at the top of her property, awaiting trespassers. I felt like a vigilante.

One Sunday we built a raft from ghost-ranch lumber and floated the river's curlicues. At each bend hung the most immense browns I've ever seen. A dozen to a pool, they passed beneath us salmon-like. A week later, a guest angler landed a twenty-five incher, which Maggie dismissed as minuscule. There's a picture of me measuring its length against a sledgehammer.

The daily reality was back-breaking labor, and I've often laughed at the appropriateness of Dylan's line, "I ain't gonna work on Maggie's farm no more." The reality sobered my notions of the West, comparably to when, as a tyke, I'd met the Lone Ranger. He was scheduled to visit a Washington, D.C. arena and my father took me; I might have been six. After his performance the Lone Ranger rode around the perimeter, shaking people's hands. My father held me forward and the Lone Ranger shook mine. Except it wasn't Clayton Moore's Lone Ranger. An actor other than the actor I expected shook my hand. I gasped in betrayal.

That same emotion gripped me in ranch work. For kids raised on that hardship, I doubt there's a comparable letdown. But for Easterners it was the romance of the West. My grandfather came out in 1890 because he was good with horses and because he'd read dime novels, penny tabloids, and Horace Greeley ("Go west, young man"). My father watched Tom Mix and Hoot Gibson in the movies and he eventually came. I watched Saturday TV, which gave me Roy, Tex, Gene, and Hoppy, and strangely I would not feel at home in Montana until the 1970s, when movie stars infiltrated Paradise Valley. When I shook Warren Oates's hand I knew I was touching *The Wild Bunch*.

The more time I spent horseback, the more I appreciated our wrangler's cowpokeishness. He'd become a hero to me. I rolled my hat like Ray's, lost my baby fat to his leanness, and when not riding, labored with him building Maggie's corral. Cut, stack, and lift, cut, stack, and lift.

I'd not had a haircut for months and was deeply tanned. We had to move cattle from one acreage to another, and I drew a white gelding named Smokey. Rank under the best circumstances, Smokey blew up once we were in cows. He snorted, bucked, fishtailed; with no hope of staying aboard, I bailed, flipping high and landing hard. Something twisted in my right arm. I stared at the shattered wrist: both ulna and radius were broken, one pointing up, the other down, both pressing hideously against the skin. Ray gawked, then spurred for the house. I sat in my fringed shirt, breathing dust as the cows milled about me.

The cook had codeine, and Bob fashioned a splint from two shingles. When he cinched them together I almost fainted. There was no doctor, so we drove 88 miles to Bozeman, where we couldn't locate proper treatment. I remember climbing stairs to offices of various sawbones, until one told Bob, "Get this kid to an emergency room." We drove the 88 miles back to West Yellowstone and another 107 miles to Idaho Falls, where I was admitted to a hospital.

It was Catholic; I recall flirting with the nuns. An orthopedist was called off a trout stream and took seven hours to reduce my fracture. I lay anaesthetized during that time, my physician father calling every thirty minutes to scream, "What in Christ's name is wrong?" Weeks later, at home, an X-ray showed the arm to have been wrongly set. I had to have it rebroken.

On the drives to and from Bozeman, sailing on codeine, I'd cradled my ruined arm and thought, "What is the sound of one hand clapping?" Trees shimmered as the Gallatin slid past. Only recently had I mastered the hand gallop, and now my right arm was smashed. Could I switch hit, or was this Buddha's warning that *satori* lay not with pleasures of the flesh? I recalled fantasizing, in that claw-foot tub at the Martha, about Dolores Hart in *Love Me Tender*. I'd imagined her in tight jeans and blouse, moving languorously among us ranch hands. I'd seen her comforting Elvis in her cotton nighty, clutching greasy sideburns to her breast. The title song played. Then, as if my insides were being extracted by pliers, I'd seen Maggie's shapelessness in her ridiculous pajamas, her gaunt figure and yellowed teeth, her cracked and leathery face. This was reality—I came like a freight train.

Days afterward, I flew home and bought an electric guitar. On August 17, our new corral and the Martha were wrecked in Hebgen Lake's earthquake, as we might have been had we lingered. Back East I played in bands, finished prep school, joined the Merchant Marine and forgot cowboys awhile. Then in the summer of 1962, my father met my ship in San Francisco with a new Corvette and we toured the mountain West. We stayed with Maggie at the ranch. Her cousin Jack raced grand prix and we had a memorable afternoon skidding toward Yellowstone Lake, he at the Corvette's wheel. A night of drink ensued, during which Maggie confronted me, aired a few secrets and cried. Through the boozy haze, I felt absolved.

She died in 1983. She had loved Montana, and eventually I realized the gift she had given me: the chance to experience, as a spoiled Easterner, some small truth about ranch life, about labor—the unfairness of the workplace, its spiraling jealousies, its craziness—and some vision of the future, where the reality of Montana would be transformed by our pompous ilk.

I saw Maggie once more, during the summer of 1976. I drove down from Paradise Valley, where I was staying, and showed her my book about saloons. I sat in her log cottage, bragging on new friends—actors, movie stars, some of them cowboys—all notorious.

She crinkled her leathery smile. "I hear it's mad up there," she said.

Big Sky Journal
2001

Sip 'n' Dip

The business of business, in Great Falls, is dampened. A cruel norther has kept shoppers off Central Avenue this afternoon, and but for a few dawdlers clustered before a turquoise counter, the Sip 'n' Dip Lounge is vacant. Its backbar window, with Polynesian frame, opens like a porthole to the motel swimming pool, which splashes patrons with broad strokes of aquamarine. It's a heartless season, with tourism and wheat prices down, and Mel Mantzey, Sip 'n' Dip's proprietor, takes comfort in the prating of regulars: Duane Work, a Chinook cattle trader, Fred Saunders, a Grassrange feed salesman, and John Goggins, a Billings columnist for *Western Livestock Reporter,* who photographs seed bulls for breeding ads.

"Capturing a seed bull's conformation," John exclaims, is "harder than shooting a *Playboy* bunny." Mel laughs. Each of these wanderers has patronized the O'Haire Motor Inn for decades. "My father stayed here," John says. "If Mel knows you, you've always got a room."

Built high-tech in 1962, the O'Haire is a time capsule

of space-age modernity. Duane cocks his Stetson. "It's too modern, if you ask me. One night I drew that honeymoon suite and the vibrating bed kept me up all night. I couldn't *find* a plug."

His gaze drifts to the pool. "Folks can't see that window from the deep end. It's underwater. And what you get is their headless bodies floating." His brows arch. "All manner of things happen."

Vern, a bartender, says, "Once I had the entire Chinook girls' softball team—no player less than 160 pounds—pressed bare chested against that backbar glass."

Duane, the Chinookian, snickers. "You'll see some sights—honeymoon couples petting, exhibitionists. One time an airman flashed the barmaid, came downstairs in his skivvies and asked her what she thought. 'Hell,' she told him, 'I've seen hemorrhoids bigger than that.'"

The entourage guffaws. Then drifts to meditative silence. Sandy Johnson, Mel's petite stepdaughter and manager, breaks it. "Western's flight teams used to have a tradition that any new stewardess must swim a naked lap to join Sip 'n' Dip. And they did."

Mel snorts. Then turns. "Don't forget those mermaids," he says, wistfully. "Ones we hired New Year's." He studies the vibrant depths. "I liked those mermaids."

The O'Haire was six in 1968 when Mel Mantzey, shopping for a business to help support his Clyde Park ranch, purchased it. The slight but rugged Mel (now seventy-one) was a horse breeder, wheat farmer, ex-Marine, jockey, and rodeo cowpoke who'd made his money building A&W Root Beer franchises throughout the West. He owned three A&Ws in Great Falls. Elsewhere, antiwar protesters stoned police, psychos gunned presidential candidates, and inner cities burned. But Great Falls was flourishing. Malmstrom Air Force Base purred with SAC and ICBM activity, oil, copper, zinc, steel, livestock, and grain prices were high, and there seemed no cap to prosperity. Tourism was up; there were burgeonings of the Lewis and Clark phenomenon. Its Corps of Discovery had mapped the region in 1805, dallying a month by its five waterfalls, and travelers liked that notion. It was a great year to enter the motel/bar business.

Ed O'Haire had been a visionary who saw the new Corps's pounding of America's interstates, and its revamping of sexual mores, as hard cash. "In sixty-two," Mel recalls, "Ed was in construction, so he thought he'd build this place." To accommodate his Corps, Ed created a quintessentially modern motel; romance and privacy would be its cornerstones. The O'Haire was downtown, yet celebrants parked their Bonnevilles roomside in a covered lot hidden from the street. Ranchers and Air Force pilots landed choppers on a rooftop helipad. Each room had two telephones, queen-size vibrating mattresses, a television and radio, bathroom speakers, a wall-mounted ironing board, and pink Formica vanities with overhead lighting, controlled bedside. O'Haire hung double-thick windows and poured sand into his Treasure-lite building blocks. Soundproofing was crucial. "Especially for politicians," he told the *Tourist Court Journal* in 1966. "The loser can go behind this sand-filled wall and cry away his blues." Little could O'Haire have foreseen the countless political trysters whose cries of ecstasy would fall muffled to his largesse.

"Lots meet their girlfriends here," Sandy confirms, "but we don't tell."

Ed's stroke of genius had been Sip 'n' Dip, the motel's magic gate. "He'd been to Hawaii," Mel says, "and came back thirsty for a tropical motif." It was the era of Trader Vic's, "when people still drank," and Samoan Fogcutters, Suffering Bastards, and other nine-shot rum concoctions were popular aphrodisiacs...but to O'Haire, insufficiently romantic. So in 1967 he lined Sip 'n' Dip's walls—then "locker room green"—with straw matting, while inserting a grass-hut ceiling, Polynesian war canoes, flower drums, tiki torches, fake orchids, lemon trees, banana-festooned lamps, palm fronds, nautical murals, Formica tabletops with tiny seahorses, and a wall-mounted aquarium. The sunken lounge already was complementary to his romantic mandate, but with the Hawaiian design, O'Haire created an erotic dreamspace irresistible to Montanans in the bleakness of a Great Falls winter. Its nucleus was O'Haire's heated, indoor pool where semi-nude swimmers could be ogled like butterfly fish on a reef. His idea was not far removed from that which nineteenth-century backbar manufacturers employed in creating saloon dreamspaces. Carved nudes, or caryatids, often framed such mirrors, heightening romance and inspiring fantasy. At Sip 'n' Dip the caryatids were living, bikini-clad wahines.

It was homey, in a Hefneresque way. "Guests tell me," O'Haire boasted, that "'when we're away from home, we're lonesome.'" Like waifs at the *Playboy* mansion. Such hominess was beguiling to Mel Mantzey, a handsome cowboy and only child who'd left his parents at age ten to break horses for a rancher in Clyde Park. Mel owned several businesses and was something of a ladies' man. "He made good use of Sip 'n' Dip," Sandy says. Mel's extravagances were curbed on December 5, 1979, when he and two women, driving to a birthday celebration in Great Falls, hit black ice near Ringling and flipped into Sixteen Mile Creek, where they lay three hours in its icy shallows. "I broke my back in twenty places," Mel says, "and I've had two hip replacements. I recently stopped walking with canes."

He coddles his Bud Lite. "How did it affect me? I'm down to one business, where I probably would've had ten. I had to sell my horses. I'm with the same woman, twenty years." He stares toward the healing waters. "I thought then I could control the world."

It's 10:30 p.m. and Duane, Fred, and John are still kibitzing. The Sip 'n' Dip is jammed. Patrons swill fishbowls ("Something to Sip While You Watch 'em Dip"), Pink Squirrels, Tahiti Martinis, Doll-Fins, Grass

Skirts and other brightly-hued cocktails, elbow-to-elbow with livestock traders, ranchers, missile technicians, and corporate lounge lizards. Organist Pat Spoonheim croons "I Wish You Love" from her perch, the mike stand hung with Day-Glo parrots. She has the soulful, husky delivery of a Peggy Lee. Pat, sixty-three, has torched here for thirty-eight years, yet she's fashionable with the younger set. Two twenty-somethings neck in a far booth as a blonde country-rocker, Georgia, explains why she's brought her pianist teen, Heidi, to hear Pat sing: "It's her first live music in a bar!"

The lounge craze explains only part of Pat's *fin de siècle* allure. "I know thousands of songs," she says. "If you request it, probably I can play it." Over the years, a bizarre assortment of stars, including TV's George Gobel, bluegrass's Allison Krauss, and outer space's Leonard Nimoy have sung along. Whether performing show tunes, pop classics, soft country, or swing. "What I do is the hardest job in show business," Pat claims. Her following contributes mightily to the O'Haire's success—which motel chain and miracle mile incursion threatens.

"Great Falls is how Montana *used* to be," a salesman yips, "before that franchise crap." But downtown classics like Tracy's Diner, the Club Cigar saloon, and Sip 'n' Dip are barely profitable. "Thirty years back," Mel says, "those Cut Bank oil men would party here a week." He sniffs. "The oil business, big steel, and Anaconda Copper all went down in the seventies. And five thousand new rooms have been built since we opened."

"It's tough for a family motel in the nineties," Sandy adds. "But Great Falls's economy looks bright. We're in competition to be the X-33 space-shuttle site, and the new Lewis and Clark Center is drawing visitors." She nods toward the motel. "Once we get a customer, we keep him."

The Delta pilots, hoisting Parrotheads, concur. "We've had a contract here for nineteen years," one says, "but Delta cancelled it for the Holiday Inn. We petitioned and won back the O'Haire." Pat swings into "Copacabana," as the pilot grins. "There's no place like the Sip 'n' Dip."

Mel, eyeing this morning's financial news, carps about tractor prices as Barry Taylor, a John Deere salesman, sips his Clam Digger and passes slices of roast beef—from a company party—to the assembled few. Mel tells Barry, "I paid more for that yard mower you sold me than my first ranch tractor."

"You beat me so bad," Barry counters, "I hardly made a commission." Mel studies the Dow. "How and where we advertise is a big problem," he mutters. "It's hard without a franchise."

But promotion is as promotion does. "We had that mortgage-burning party poolside," Sandy says. "The banker lit Mel's papers while he ran a little motor boat 'til they burned. Let's see—we're having Dean Martin Night for New Year's ninety-nine, with a five dollar cover if you don't wear polyester…"

Mel shrugs. Sinatra crows "That's Life" from the backbar stereo.

"And we've got mermaids…"

A curvy blonde, cinched into a green satin sheath with flippery feet, a gold lamé belt, bikini top, and a half-dozen strings of gold beads, waddles across the barroom, modeling a photo shoot. Mel studies the blonde, brightens. "Maybe we can use her for that new brochure! Redo the old one, heck, throw it out." A photographer barks orders, directing the shot.

Mel and his Stetson are posed facing the pool; the mermaid will swim past the glass, beckoning. Barry Taylor and a concrete salesman named Gary Prugh move their drinks near a wall of "autographed" photos-of Clint Eastwood, Beau Bridges, Bill Clinton, and other celebrities who've never visited Sip 'n' Dip. They stand at the bar. Mel freezes as the photographer cries "action" and the mermaid submerges, sending kissy moues toward Mel. They repeat this a dozen times. Barry and Gary watch.

"You know," whispers Taylor, "I think she's mouthing the word *Bar-ry.*"

"No," says Prugh, "it's definitely *Gar-ry.*"

A deliveryman enters, stocks Mel's cooler, then grunts, "Mermaids in the pool today, huh."

"Yep," Mel says. "Mermaids." But he's faded to reverie. Between shots, he manages, "That oughta get her." But his spirit's elsewhere: surfing Diamond Head, perhaps, or galloping the beach at Bali Hai, or walking the shipwrecked shores of youth. Anywhere but Great Falls in winter.

The turquoise pool shimmers. The mermaid contorts, shrimplike, thrusting herself glassward. "Needs to pay her lawyer," someone says of a regular, "so she can get her babies back." Who? It hardly matters. The business of fantasy booms, earning heady dividends. And it's a fantastic business.

Mel bathes in the recuperative waters.

Big Sky Journal
1999

Montana Pickup

Dan Lucy was set to haul a load of junk so formidable that his dinge-red, rust-flecked Dog Truk squatted on its haunches like a sumo wrestler. There were full garbage cans, stuffed Hefty bags, stacked appliance cartons, and trash lumber that hung a dozen feet off the tailgate. The pickup was angled near an immaculate Lincoln Town Car that Lucy also owned—or had, until he sold his Classic Limo service, with its forty-foot, disco-lighted stretches and staid Excursions, the previous week. Emotionally he was focused on this Dog Truk. "It's a 1969 Ford F-100 Custom—very custom," he said. "It has air conditioning through the floorboards, an eight ball on the gearshift, a quartz knob on the four-wheel-drive transfer, and rack and pinion steering that will break your arm. It has steer horns on its hood, above the Dog Truk plates, and a custom gun rack, where I keep an assault rifle for all the people moving to Montana who shouldn't." He laughed. "Like me."

Lucy moved to Bozeman from Colorado in 2001, and for a young businessman—he's thirty-four—had the bachelor gear down: a hilltop house with a Tiki Hut entry to his bedroom, a sixty-two-inch video screen in the parlor, guitars, motorcycle, weaponry, and a switchbacked driveway with signs warning, successively, "Respect Our Privacy," then "You Have Gone Too Far," then "You're in My Sights Now"…plus this dinge-red Dog Truk, which despite its wretchedness had exceptional style. "I bought it about three and a half years ago. The glasspacks had been removed and it had no catalytic converter, so I kind of went for it. I was driving Suburbans—my dogs were destroying their interiors."

A Lab and a weimaraner hovered, anxious to load up. "I could have bought a nice new truck," Lucy added, "one with brake lights and turn signals. But there's not as much art in driving that as in driving an old piece of crap." He indicated the Dog Truk's wheels. "Fact that it has off-color rims, one orange and one red, really did it for me. The body paint was dilapidated. And it had cab lights on the roof—that was *so* seventies. I feel like every time I get in the thing I'm in a big rig. And every boy wants to be in a big rig."

I'd spotted Lucy's truck in Bozeman. It was truly enviable, a vehicle that, with its steer horns, seemed like it should hang mounted in some dusty saloon. It got me puzzling over Montana trucks. What I knew I'd learned driving a forties-vintage, bottle-green Chevy pickup, on a ranch job the year I turned fifteen. Its pedals had been rusty and its interior wrecked, but my hormones had kicked in and I sensed its lurching power reflected my own. It had a stubby short bed, rusted grille, and split windshield, and I drove it around the ranch with the cockiness of a bridegroom. As an Eastern kid, the only pickup I'd noticed was *The Roy Rogers Show's* Nellybelle, a 1946 CJ-2A Willys Jeep customized to resemble a ranch vehicle. It had been driven by Roy's sidekick, Pat Brady, and compared to the palomino, Trigger, was decidedly unsexy. But modern cowboys drove pickups: in 1961's *The Misfits*, Clark Gable drove a flatbed sufficiently alluring for Marilyn

Monroe to sleep on it. In 1963's *Hud*, Granddad Melvyn Douglas drove the pickup but hellraiser Paul Newman, who wanted out, drove a Cadillac convertible. By 1969, in movies and real life, every hippie had his VW bus.

I returned to Montana in 1972 and found a thriving truck culture. The archetypal vehicle was a Ford or a Chevy long bed, chaps and lariats hung from the headache rack, a blue heeler in back and .22 shells in its heater vents. Perhaps its ideal was the white Ford that Jeff Bridges drove in 1975's *Rancho Deluxe*, a movie Tom McGuane created about hipster/outlaws' reinvention of the West. Bridges's truck—which he owned "in partners" with Sam Waterston's character, had cab lights, a roll bar, roof spots, wide side mirrors, Montana mud flaps, a rifle rack for the .50 caliber Sharps, oversized tires, and spoke wheels. A lot of nifty driving was done, and McGuane wrote a pickup truck sermon for Waterston's dad that has become classic: "I've seen more of this state's poor cowboys, miners, railroaders, and Indians go broke buyin' pickup trucks...as soon's they get ten cents ahead they trade in on a new pickup truck...there's a sickness here worse than alcohol and dope. It is the pickup truck death. And there's no cure in sight."

I pondered this as I toured Montana, a region dominated by the $50,000 Dodge Ram and $35,000 Ford Super Cab, wondering if the low profile ranch truck had run its course. Junkers were everywhere, but lovingly restored pickups proved scarce. The newer ones carried messages: a neighbor's tailgate, in enormous hand-painted letters, read: "Hey Osama, Kiss My American Ass." Mudflaps urged me to "Cowgirl Up." Bumper stickers asked, "If We Shouldn't Eat Animals, Why Are They Made of Meat?" Every truck seemed a billboard. Then someone told me of a fellow in the Gallatin Valley, a verifiable artist, who restored old vehicles. He sketched, sculpted, and worked from a Quonset hut stacked with tools, parts, and automotive detritus. There I found him buffing a baby blue, seventies F-150 Ford, small dogs yapping at his feet.

Let's call him Gil. He owned the reputation of an eccentric, spraying cars wearing just a thong, so I was pleased to see today he wore jeans. He had graying hair and few front teeth. I asked about restored pickups. "I got nothing to say," he barked, adding that he no longer was in the business, having been often cheated by customers, but that he'd continued restoring vehicles to sell on his own. I asked what people were looking for in a Montana pickup, and he said, "Same as anywhere—something great for nothing."

Gil showed me scrapbooks of cars he'd customized, of bicentennial parades he'd driven in, and indicated two trucks he'd restored: a fifties Chevy and this seventies F-150, which he'd sanded himself. The Ford was spectacular. He extended a muscular right hand. Fibers from brushes were embedded in his palm. "I sanded the skin right off," he said. "Who else would do this?"

I was moved by Gil's question. Who else *would* do it? His pickup reminded me of another artist's: a 1949 Chevrolet, "the Cosa de Llama truck," driven to Livingston from San Francisco in 1972 by the painter Russell Chatham, who'd been so broke that for two years he'd lived in it. One night he'd been driving down Deep Creek when he spotted an unusual convergence of moon and mountain. Not having a sketchpad, "not being able to afford a sketchpad," he scratched the scene onto his fender with a rock. That sketch became the basis for one of his major canvasses: the 50 inch by 60 inch "Moonrise over the Absarokas."

I meditated on this. A truck lived with for art that became art...that seemed the paradigm.

I hit the road in July, driving north on Highway 89 through White Sulphur Springs, Great Falls, and Fort Benton, on to Chinook then south through the Missouri Breaks to Lewistown.

Everywhere were giant pickups, Fords, Chevies, Dodges, with the F-150 remaining predominant not just in Montana but in America. *Business Week* reported that, despite gas prices, "Americans still bought 1.2 million more trucks than cars." Pickups were a national trend, in part due to bellicosity (Ford bragged of the F-150's service in Iraq) but also from an ethic that had its roots in populism but thrived on middle-class pretension.

According to Mike Mueller's book, *Pickup Trucks*, it was "Ford's Model T Runabout with Pick-Up Body that is commonly identified as this country's first true light-duty pickup." That appeared in 1925. Barebones vehicles had been manufactured earlier, "some as large as their buckboard forerunners," but not until after WWII did production explode: "Dodge and Willys took what they learned building bulletproof military machines," and took off "in the burgeoning off-road, four-wheel-drive field." By the 1950s, Ford and Chevy had "user-friendliness" and two-tone elegance—the El Camino and Ranchero hybrids combining truck efficiency with passenger comfort. And by the sixties (another war decade) Dodge offered the first true muscle truck: a 426 wedge V-8 which scorched the tarmac. Then during the seventies fuel crunch, Japanese pickups exploded, with gas-swilling SUVs just behind…and by the nineties, the goal in pickup design had become "to transform common transportation," Mueller reported, "into an uncommon fashion statement."

Behind the Super 8 In Lewistown I spotted a business called The Pickup Guy—"Cool Stuff for Your Truck." Its sign was red-white-and-blue electric, its facade sleek, and inside, it was a pickup junkie's dream. It sold bed liners, tonneau covers, louvered tailgates, bug shields, rocker panels, grille guards, running boards, chrome steps, tool boxes, towing hitches, mud flaps, seat covers, accessory lights, stainless wheels, custom logos, audio gear, detailing services and more. Its owner was a fifty-four-year-old, retired CEO named Tom Balek, who wrote for trucking magazines and had created an elaborate website for The Pickup Guy. He'd opened it five years ago because, "Everybody's driving a truck," and chose central Montana's Lewistown because of nearby relatives, and because

"People from all over the country visit." His business had grown forty percent *a year* since 2001, because it filled "a niche," pickup accessories being "an underserved market." Balek's motto was "protection, personalization, and better performance," and he saw no reason why he couldn't take Pickup Guy national.

For relaxation, Balek was having "a 55 Chevy pickup with banana-cream-pie finish," customized. For work, he drove a 2005 Ram 5.7 Hemi Magnum, for which he'd paid $37,000 ("a deal"), and which he'd tricked out with $3,000 worth of extras.

We walked outside to look at it. Snow white and grand, his Dodge seemed the ultimate status toy. Exteriorly, its steel and chrome extras screamed stylish tank, but interiorly, its four-seater, climate-controlled, luxury accouterments purred limo. I studied it. It seemed the pickup equivalent of Dan Lucy's Town Car. But was it hip?

"Depends on your frame of reference," Balek said. "Both city and country guys can get into a truck like mine. But city guys don't want the smoky old wreck with chewing tobacco running down the door. To me, a cool truck is one that doesn't look exactly like every other." He added, "My '55 Chevy will be 'cooler' than my new Dodge."

I told him I'd composed my own criteria for Pickup Truck Hip. A vehicle was hip if it suggested the randier side of its owner's nature; if it resembled more a quarter horse than a Clydesdale; if it was driven by a cowgirl; if it was pre-crew cab and not diesel; if it skipped the camper top, or was a restored piece of art.

Balek and I agreed on about half of this. He admitted that many of his services were status oriented, and much of his clientele middle-to-upper-middle-class. But he also valued practical customers like the seventy-two-year-old Harold Donaldson, who drove a red 2000 F-150 Lariat Super Crew, and with his wife June lived thirty-four miles west of Lewistown on a 1,149-acre wheat farm in Denton—population 288. I found the Donaldsons in a house built by Harold's grandfather, near a shed that Harold told me housed tractors, a combine, and five trucks: two oversized GMC s for hauling wheat, and three pickups—the Lariat, "my good truck," Harold said, an immaculate steel-blue 1986 GMC long bed, and a classic 1967, dinge-red Ford.

The Donaldsons had a new grandson, and after lunch we rode to an adjacent field in the luxurious four-passenger Super Crew. Where the wheat was waist high, Harold and June stood holding their grandson as their daughter, Lynn, photographed them. Afterward, we drove past Hoosac, a ghost town on the property with a false-front mercantile where Harold and June had once attended dances, but eventually we parked back at the truck shed.

I inquired whether I might see the '67 Ford. Harold's eyes brightened. "I thought you'd never ask."

It stood outside, and but for a white roof, resembled Dan Lucy's Dog Truk. Its finish was ruined and it carried a large fuel tank on its bed, but was otherwise unadorned. "I bought it the fall we were married," Harold explained. "It was both our good and our work truck." I got in and Harold pointed it back toward the highway, then veered through rutted wheat fields. Where he'd appeared stiff driving the Lariat, formal, in the '67, he was all relaxation. Rifle by his leg, he gunned the Ford's engine. "Good power," he said, happily. "I hope we see a gopher—you can shoot one." Windows open to the one-hundred-degree heat, wheat fields in every direction, mountains ahead, .22 shells in the heater vents, Harold and his '67 were like a Remington sculpture of man and horse. Except this was *man and truck*.

Here was pickup rapture: an old Ford and an old man, bouncing across land they'd worked together, in synchronicity.

Still unsatisfied, I wondered how Harold's and Dan Lucy's trucks—iconic as they were—might look restored. On July 2, in Livingston, I'd spotted a flawless '56 Ford at the rodeo parade, and had gotten the owners' number. I was intrigued by this F-Series, and one Sunday in August, drove south to the chalk cliffs below Emigrant to examine it.

Phil and Betty Anderson greeted me in the living room of a house they'd built themselves. Both Andersons were handsome people in their late sixties. Phil was retired from the Smithsonian in Washington, where he'd been a director of lighting and multimedia design. He admitted his impetus for restoring the '52 was "nostalgia." He'd grown up in the teen-car-culture of the 1950s, and his first car had been a 1950 Ford club coupe. He's drag raced various rods, but he admitted, "this is the first truck I've owned."

He'd wanted a 1950 Ford, in memory of a buddy who'd owned one, but settled on this '52 when he saw its meadow-green finish, "what my friend's truck had." He'd spent two years restoring it. "It had a '53 bed and the running boards were cut in half, it had holes in the roof, it had big turn signals up on the fenders, it had a tire mount on the side, and I didn't like any of that. I pulled the engine down, stripped the frame, the springs, took the motor out. I repainted and redid the firewall, and spent endless hours sanding it down. I put all new glass in it, new weather stripping, new shocks. It was a labor of love."

I asked Phil why. He sat back. "For my friend, but also because old cars and old trucks sort of remind me of... some world famous painting." He paused. "If you love old cars and love old trucks, and customs, some of the things that people have created, to me it's really artwork in itself. I've got a piece of artwork in the garage that I like to look at."

I remembered Gil and Russell Chatham.

We talked a bit about Montana pickups, and eventually I asked if I could again see the truck. Anderson said, "Let's take a look."

We walked downstairs to a space that was less garage than bedroom. *A truck lived with for art that became art*. That was my paradigm. Phil's '52 sat there as pretty as I'd recalled. The finish and brightwork glowed, the creamy grille work was like a smile. And it was perfectly lighted. A small truck, it was almost toy like; I wanted to play with it. Instead, I walked round it, admiring the polished oak short bed, the stainless hubcaps, headlight rims and trim. Anderson popped the hood, showing me a 238-horsepower flathead V-8. It was an intimidating flame-red.

I opened the driver's door and patted the bench seat.

Anderson studied me. "Why don't you get up and sit in it?" he said.

I did, and as I held the bus-wide Bakelite wheel and toed the clutch pedal, I was transported to that ranch pickup I'd driven in 1959. The feel of the gearshift, the lowness of the cab's roof, the rifle-sight narrowness of the windshield carried me instantly to that first Chevy. I was fourteen again, horny as a toad, with a life of hard driving before me.

Phil was rifling the dash, searching for original documents, when I sputtered, "It's the truck's *feel*. Everything from that first time."

A grin split Phil's face. "For me it's the *smell*," he said. "Of how a flathead processes the gas. When I put this truck back in the garage, and later come down, it hits me as soon as I walk in the door." He whispered, "It's my '50 Ford."

Big Sky Journal
2006

Stacey's

The first night I danced at Stacey's was in August of 1985, a blistering Saturday when truck engines ticked in the neon and perhaps three hundred revelers crowded about the horseshoe-shaped bar. I'd arrived with a pal from New York and Jamie Jean, a singer who fronted a local band and was the toast of two valleys. We elbowed through cowfolk, Jamie in snug Levi's, a Hawaiian shirt, and shorty boots, I in buckaroo vest and bulldogging heels, and my friend in a tweed sportcoat and corduroy trousers—no doubt the squarest outfit ever seen at Stacey's. Jamie's hair was roached into a rockabilly pompadour, and her smile was bewitching. Quickly I had her on the floor, twirling, two-stepping, the scent of her hair in my face and her belt buckle tapping mine. The band played shuffles, swing tunes, Cotton-eyed Joes, the crowd whooping at familiar intros, dancers packed tightly as we spun round the saloon. Smoke blanketed its stuffed animals and rodeo portraits, and the fragrance of spilled beer rose from its duckboards. We danced, drank, danced again. Near closing I ducked to the Gents, bobbed out, and there she sat, enveloped by tweed, her head on my buddy's shoulder. He'd stolen her heart.

I like to think Stacey Crosby watched this, his lank frame curled over a Schlitz, a Lucky Strike in hand, and his angular face split by a grin. He would have been fifty-nine, myself forty, and like him, I'd grown up around saloons. His father had been a bootlegger, mine a contentious tippler, and I was a decade past my four-year search for the Great American Bar—a journey that had floated me from Key West to Seattle, and resulted in a book that somehow missed Stacey's Old Faithful Bar, fourteen miles southwest of Bozeman, in tiny Gallatin Gateway. I'd never meet its proprietor, though in the years before his death, I boogied many a mile across his dance floor.

On another Saturday, this in 2006, Stacey's daughter, Toni Donnelly, greeted a stranger toting a canvas sack with, "What's that you got for me, a bag of money?" She's a feisty ex-emergency room nurse who, with her two sisters, inherited the bar, but owns majority interest and runs it. "A chip off the old block," her sister Marti Klette—a waitress at the restaurant—told me. "Very much like our dad." The barroom was cheerful in the afternoon light (with that razor clarity peculiar to Gateway) and idlers sat by the picture windows as a Chilean fashion model posed near an upright piano. Commercial shoots occur periodically at Stacey's. "They just did scenes here for *Plumm Summer*," Toni said, of a film being shot around Livingston. The space holds a cowboy legitimacy difficult to recreate—it has long been a hangout for Flying D hands (icons of Montana ranch culture)—and on every foot of the barn-sided walls hangs some memento: a wilderness scene painted on a moose antler; another on canvas above the piano; signs reading, "If you feel the need to carve your name in our bar, you might need to pull a boot out of your ass," and the ubiquitous photographs of rodeo greats (Benny Reynolds, Larry Mahan, Walt Linderman) inscribed to Stacey, himself an ex-bull rider and roper. The bar is fashioned from barn siding, and though stylistically plain seems rugged as a stockade fence.

"They had some fights," Toni said of oldtimers. "Dad would holler, 'You come here and you're breaking my glasses and busting my barstools and you're using good air I could keep breathing!' Mae Ping, the first owner, was famous for shutting off the lights whenever a fight broke out. 'There's no glory in the dark,' she'd say. But when she shut them back on, one night, somebody'd slit the piano player's throat. So much for that theory."

Toni is an attractive, middle-aged Montanan, a brunette, but Mae Ping was a comely four-foot-eleven-inch, redheaded French women, "just a little firecracker," who founded Old Faithful about 1926, when Montana repealed state Prohibition. Its building was two-story brick and built by "the Anceney Station people," Toni said, as a kind of company store. It had a bank, and butcher and clothing shops, and "it was mostly for the people who worked on the Anceney Ranch," now Ted Turner's Flying D. The town was called Salesville, for Zach Sales, who owned its sawmill. "A lot of people here were farmer-ranchers, but we had loggers back then, and mill workers too."

The men wanted companionship, and Old Faithful kept prostitutes upstairs. "Mae always denied that," Toni recalled. "She said she rented those rooms to those girls, and what they did was between them, God, and the IRS. But a fellow met my husband and said, 'I have a token from the Old Faithful that was my great-grandfather's.' Because Mae didn't trust the girls with money. If someone wanted to go upstairs they had to pay the bartender and get a token."

Salesville was a lively town, but nothing like what it became in 1927 when the Milwaukee Railroad built Gallatin Gateway Inn, a posh stopover for tourists en route to Yellowstone Park. Visitors arrived by train, rested, visited Mae's saloon, then toured the Park by bus. The inn survived until the early fifties, when automobile travel killed it. The town, now Gallatin Gateway, retreated to its sleepy status.

"The Inn was grown over when we were kids," Marti told me. "And that was our playground. They had left everything—tables still set. Every family in town had tablecloths and dishes from the Inn."

Though Gateway today has a ghost town air, it kept its population through the late seventies. "Every house that you see had kids in it," Marti said. "R.G. Roberts had his cabinet shop there and the cheese factory was still functioning. We'd get cheese curds every morning. The café in town was open." And as children the Crosby sisters had their run of Stacey's. "Mae always said, 'This isn't a bar, it's a community center,'" Toni added. "The Gateway kids sang with the band, they played pool, they'd have a Hershey bar here and a pop. You could sit on the bench and watch everybody dancing and having so much fun. It was a wonderful way to grow up."

Stacey's wife, Phyllis, who died in 2003, was raised in Ashton, Idaho. But Stacey was a castoff kid from Butte, whose hardscrabble father shipped him and four siblings to Great Falls's Ursuline Academy after their mother committed suicide. "Dad said, 'You can put a fancy name on it, but it was an orphanage.'" A Bozeman family took him in, and by age seventeen he was bartending, first at West Yellowstone's Stagecoach, then at Bozeman's Eagles, which he managed. He seemed to find a home in saloons. He and Phyllis bought Old Faithful in 1963 ("Dad might have been the personality, but Mom was the backbone that held it all together"), and moved with their daughters upstairs. Mae's prostitutes were gone, but the quarters had no kitchen, so Phyllis cooked downstairs and her family gathered in the saloon galley to eat. "One night," Marti remembered, "my mother told Dad, 'These girls are hearing too much! I want them out of here.' So we moved up Wilson Crick, past Broken Heart Ranch," where all three daughters live today.

Toni learned much at her father's knee. "He was an

entertainer," she said. "He was a storyteller and very quick-witted. People were just *drawn* to him." She laughed. "That's not to say he wasn't wild. Us kids would wake up and there'd be rodeo cowboys sleeping on the floor. And I'm sure it wasn't easy being married to him. One fellow said, 'I was at the bar when your dad got his divorce papers served.' Because my mom tried to divorce him many times. "He said, 'Your dad crumpled them up and threw them on the counter, then he got thinking about it and spread them out and says, *Jesus Christ, pard. Perry Mason couldn't get me out of this one.*'"

An article on the far wall describes a reporter's visit to Stacey's in 1987, during which the 150-pound Stacey bragged of out drinking 240-pound bulldoggers in five-day marathons, and "went through several cases" of beer, during the interview—"enough to bury a normal human."

Toni admits, "He'd go on these binges. But he was fun to be around. He'd keep telling stories. And he drove up Gallatin Canyon a lot. When he took his old black horse we knew he was going to the Corral Bar, because that horse was trailer broke. If he took another we'd think, 'He's really going to the cabin riding.'"

Hard drinking is a Montana tradition, and Old Faithful's regulars did not stint. Some, like the Flying D's cattle boss Johnny Flowers, wintered at the bar ("'Til the grass got green"), and lawmen, like one eastern Montana sheriff, made Stacey's a must-stop while transferring prisoners to Deer Lodge. "He'd hit the top of the hill with his lights flashing," Toni said, "and us kids were going, 'Mommy, are they going to take daddy away?' He'd bring his prisoners in and handcuff them to the poles. He'd look at us and say, 'Don't take any checks from that guy on the end.' He'd give him a bottle of Jack Daniels and say, 'Pard, where you're going you better drink up now.' Another night, they caught a young man stealing equipment out of the musicians' pickups. So they set him on the bench and said, 'Get a rope, we're going to hang him.' A bartender called the sheriff and he said later, 'Toni, I've never met a person so happy to see me. He said, *Take me away, these crazy bastards mean to hang me!*' Dad said, 'Pard, we could have had it done but none of us could remember how to tie a hangman's noose.' That would have been right around seventy, or seventy-one. They were pretty crazy about then."

It was a period when hippies weren't welcome at Stacey's. A long-haired cannibal named Stanley Dean Baker had been arrested for a murder by the Yellowstone River, with two finger bones in his pocket, and hair-trimming parties had become popular. "Hippies were the bad people," Toni remembered. "We were the cowboys, the good people. One day a bunch of hippies thought they were going to take over Gateway. Dad said, 'Phyllis, you better get Dell on the phone,' and half the MSU rodeo team came barreling round this corner, just as the hippies were converging on Stacey's. These big old bulldoggers said, 'We hear you want to take over Gateway. You think you're gonna start here in Stacey's?' And there were ponytails and asses and elbows flying everywhere. The hippies didn't even make it in the front door."

Fights used to be expected in Montana saloons, and one test of a Great Bar, I'd found, was how well it processed this manner of chaos. One required *form* to frame or isolate chaos. Stacey's had form (and Plexiglass in its pool room windows), but since Toni had taken over, she said, "I haven't had a single darn fight in here or anything. No trauma, no nothing. I think, 'Come on guys, just a little trauma.' Things have mellowed some." One reason might be that in 2005, she refurbished Stacey's, adding a steakhouse at the eastern side of the building, and following Gateway's lead, a nod toward gentrification. "We redid the bathrooms, we took out the false ceiling and put the plank floor in. And did lighting for all the pictures. This used to be a horseshoe bar, but now it's not. People were very angry with me. We got calls from California: 'When's the last day it's going to be Stacey's?'

We had one fellow come in and say, 'Your dad would be rolling over in his grave.' I looked at him and said, 'That's precisely why we had him cremated.' I thought, 'How dare you...my mom and dad would have been proud of anything us girls would have done.'"

Stacey died of stomach cancer in 1990, and 500 people attended his funeral. "It was wonderful," Toni said. "We had it at that Catholic church by the MSU field house, and it was so full people were standing outside. They loved him so—he was always for the underdog, always helping people. We came back here, and everyone who had ever worked for us got behind the bar. People were throwing down money, and it paid for all Dad's hospital bills. Afterward we had one can of beer left—it was non-alcoholic."

It was late now, a Western band played and visitors from all over the valley were roistering with locals. One group of twenty-somethings, in snug Wranglers and kilt-toed packers' boots, stood by a picture window. The girls were lovely, the boys stout and apple cheeked. I asked one why he liked Gateway. "'Cause I can live fifty yards from the river and one hundred from Stacey's," he said. He rodeoed, but was loading hay for the summer, and his girlfriend grabbed him before he could say why, and they muscled toward the dance floor. Toni had been joined behind the bar by a stylish blonde, Michelle, but Toni was the star, joking and kidding with regulars. "When I'm tending bar," she'd told me, "I'm definitely my father's child. I can't believe what comes out of my mouth. I grew up here and I've watched them all perform. And of course, I sang with the bands for years. I remember my dad saying, 'Well, Phyllis, we've got her out of her shell, now how are we going to get her back in?'"

People often ask me if I'd ever found the Great American Bar, and I say no. During the seventies, Montana saloons were at the top of my list, and the Montana Bar in Miles City, Luigi's in Butte, and the New Atlas in Columbus were candidates for best-in-show. If I'd found

Stacey's it would have ranked—but in my leathers and longish hair, I might not have been welcome. Tonight I was just another boomer dodging jitterbuggers from Gateway and swing dancers from Bridger Bowl, as they celebrated a spirit that seemed undiminished. Ghosts lingered, it was said—of Mae Ping, her soiled doves, her slain piano player—and even that of Stacey. As I watched the rough cowboys and urban partiers, I thought, nothing substantive has changed.

At the electronic poker machines, my sweetheart was gambling. I walked over as a grizzled mountain man slipped a five into her dollar slot, negotiating a pick up. She flipped it back, not missing a deal. I glanced toward the bar, but Toni wasn't watching. I liked to think Stacey Crosby was.

Big Sky Journal
2007

The Bridges of Yellowstone Country

The hood of our vehicle is canted at a thirty-degree angle, and Jon Axline—historian for the Montana Department of Transportation and expert on archaic steel bridges—peers through the cracked windshield of a government loaner and says, "One problem with this bridge is that you can't see somebody coming from the other side." Then we are up and opposite a black Trans Am that's snarling its engine at the far reach of the 480-foot deck.

"That car, I think, would have to back up," Jon says, uneasily. Which it does, and we are inching across the 1904 single-laner, a "three-span, pin-connected, Pratt through-truss structure," Jon's told me, "with a queen post approach span on the west and a timber stringer approach span on the east." All this in Craig, a sleepy hamlet north of Helena with a bait shop, two bars and, on a clear morning, dozens of SUVs trailering drift boats, antsy to cross the Missouri.

"Craig doesn't have much going for it," he adds, "but it's got a great bridge."

Jon's a big man and he likes a big bridge. In fact he

prefers a *solid* bridge. "I was kind of afraid of some of them when I was a kid," he says, of Montana's steel bridges. "With good reason I found out afterward." Yet he's passionate about their salvation—enough so to have canvassed the state inventorying them and researching their hagiography, *Monuments above the Water: Montana's Historic Highway Bridges, 1860-1956.* Also speaking with bridgers like myself, acolytes to America's fresh obsession with its implements of traverse—be they covered, suspended, trussed, timbered, or roped.

We reach shore and Jon relaxes. "I'm afraid of heights," he confesses, "but I have absolutely no qualms about crossing this bridge. It's one of my favorites, and it pains me to know it's going to go."

Many of Montana's steel bridges are a century old, and a majority of its approximately 310 remaining are endangered. "They've been threatened for years. The counties own most of them and they want concrete bridges that better handle modern traffic."

But as one local has argued, "Old bridges slow people down. How often do you pull off a new bridge, see your neighbor across the other side, wave him to come on, wait as he goes across, *then* you go across? These bridges have soul."

There is an Adopt-a-Bridge program in Montana, by which the state will donate a condemned bridge and its demolition cost to any person who will take, then responsibly maintain it. Jon is that program's point man. "We had some interest in saving the Craig, including that of a Helena group that wanted to adopt it in place, but they couldn't raise the money."

Jon parks by a boat ramp and we amble toward the Craig's west span, hovering like an alabaster cloud above the water.

"What I think is important about this bridge," he says, "is that it opened up this side of the river to the railroad. And gave people better access to their county seats."

The earliest Montana bridges were log or timber

structures, with stone piers in wooden cribs that washed out during high water. Steel truss bridges (with their complex terminology) not only were durable, but meant progress to the small towns that acquired them.

"Every Montana town wanted a good bridge," Jon says. "They'd order one from a factory back east and the fabricating plant would build the bridge, then take it apart and load it onto railroad flatbeds and ship it out. A lot of bridges were built right around towns that had rail connections. Because the farmers and ranchers needed those connections to survive. And they were proud of these bridges. There are quite a few accounts of celebrations at their openings." He shrugs. "Unfortunately a lot of that pride hasn't hung around."

We appraise the Craig—which Jon has conceded will go to scrap. An Easterner, I pose the obvious: "Do people commit suicide off these bridges?"

"No," Jon says. "I've never heard of that. But there's a story about a labor organizer in Butte being hanged from one." He studies the Craig. "I don't think they're high enough to jump off. Unless you didn't know how to swim."

We are on a journey today that has taken us from Helena, where Jon's family settled in 1872, up old Highway 91, "my favorite in the state," he says, north to Wolf Creek and its 1933, "four-span, riveted Warren continuous through-truss," crouched like an erector set across the Missouri, to Hardy and its 1931, "*three*-span, riveted Warren through-truss, with a sloping upper cord," used in Sean Connery's *The Untouchables*, its silver trusses racked like martini glasses before the canyon walls, and Jon would have included the Dearborn River High Bridge, near Augusta, an 1897, "half-deck Pratt truss with the deck attached midway," if it hadn't been off its abutments for restoration. As I field his enthusiasms, I'm reminded of my own passion for bridges, one that blossomed in 1976 as I rode out a broken marriage and struggled for appreciation of that odd, bicentennial summer. The country had extricated itself from war, and concomitantly my wife—a nurse veteran—had extricated herself from wedlock. Let the fireworks begin. I stayed at Livingston's Murray Hotel, but found myself daily in Paradise Valley, driving, hiking, fishing, or boating near the Yellowstone River's steel bridges, lacy sculptures dropped onto banks or strung between bluffs, spiderwebs on the wind. There was impermanence to them, a fragility unlikely to endure. Yet it had, and I took comfort in that grace.

Pine Creek's 1910, "single-span, camelback, pin-connected through-truss," (*camelback* was a bridge's humped top, *trusses* were its triangular supports) was situated near friends' houses, and I crossed it regularly. Two more remote bridges in Paradise Valley, one at Tom Miner Basin, the other at Corwin Springs, spanned the Yellowstone. They were nearly identical to Pine Creek's; often I would take a book and sit beneath them. The Yellowstone ran clear, low, and eminently fishable there, and an ecosystem thrived beneath these bridge's planks: swallows, wasps, bats, small mammals, trout, and occasionally hoboes. It was peaceful. As vehicles crossed, a big city rattle-clack broke out, comparable to that heard from an elevated subway. Novelist William Hjortsberg, a New Yorker moved to Pine Creek, took pleasure on summer nights at "the sound of bridge planks rattling, a mile away." And Ianthe Brautigan—Richard's daughter—recalled in her memoir, *You Can't Catch Death*, that when she was a girl, her horses were afraid to walk across its open deck because they could see the river below. She would idle beneath the bridge, reading. One day a neighbor looked down, surprised, and said, "I thought you were a fairy."

Montanans are drawn to bridges. On September 11, 2001, photographer Barb Walker—whose family owns Livingston's H Street Bridge—left the televised carnage and walked to her pre-1915 camelback spanning the

Shields River. There she captured an image of sunlight on trusses that did much to convey the emotion of that day: "The sun spot was strikingly centered in some steel beams which formed a cross," Walker remembers. "I was down by the river seeking peace of mind. I turned around and saw the centered sun, snapped the pic, and when I processed it, saw the sunbeams coming off the sun and steel, sending pinpoint rays of light up to the sky and down to the river. It offered me a bit of solace." And beneath an I-90 bridge crossing the Yellowstone is a Tolkien-like mural of Judgment Day, sketched after 9/11 in *Magical Mystery Tour* kitsch by "Sara B." and Parks Reece, that is scarifying in its reassurance. "In the Midst of War We Shall Endure," it proclaims.

Not every tale is sanguine. On May 3, 1979, Johnny McGee, a Pine Creek resident, broke a twenty-two-foot hole in that bridge's deck by riding a dump truck full of gravel into the Yellowstone. "A guy named Dan Indendi, passing with his family," Hjortsberg says, "grabbed a lariat, rappelled from the superstructure, and helped break the truck's window to rescue Johnny from drowning."

"I was going over toward Pine Creek," McGee recalls. "I went about halfway and felt the planks get a little spongy. All of a sudden my rear end went down. The truck hit on the driver's side window, which was open, and all that muddy water blew in the cab. I tried to open the passenger window, but the handle came off. I tried to beat out that safety glass with my hand, but it wouldn't give. There was one little space of air, two to three inches in one corner of the cab. I went up and got that and knew the next time I came up it would be water. I kept thinking, 'oh man, this is it, I'm going to drown in here.'"

"It was very close," Indendi's mother confirms. "I'll never forget Johnny's hair and face underwater, pressed against that glass."

Of steel bridges today, McGee says: "I don't cross them. They're totally unsafe. I'm leery, you bet."

I too was afraid as a boy in Maryland, where our town's

1864, single-lane, Roman arch bridge extended from one side of Cabin John Creek to the other. The bridge was high (perhaps 200 feet) and the challenge was to walk its stone parapets the length of the 450-foot deck. Reckless kids rode their bikes across them. I couldn't. Once, I got a wheel up, went giddy, and did not try again.

We'd moved from Washington, D.C. where my physician father had taken me hiking in Rock Creek Park beneath the towering Connecticut Avenue and Calvert Street bridges. On those mornings he would glance upward and say, "Don't jump off the Connecticut Avenue Bridge, jump off the Calvert. Old Washingtonians use the Calvert." He'd say it jokingly, but I was six and the message stuck. Later in New York, I'd watch a man leap from a highway overpass to his death in speeding traffic; and, tipsy on my wedding night in 1974, I'd crawl from a sixth-floor window of a Washington hotel and inch several feet along its cornice before turning back.

"If bored with your life, risk it," James Dickey used to say. And, "He not busy being born is busy dying," Dylan sang. But that bicentennial summer I cocooned in the pleasure of inverse heights: the undersides of bridges with their mossy residue of fear. The crisis passed.

Then in 1996 both my parents died of cancer, my father ending his life with morphine when the pain grew intolerable, I ending my mother's by authorizing the relinquishment of life support. An only child, I sifted the wreckage. This summer was the seventh of that inventory. "Man," I'd read in *Collier's Encyclopedia*, "has expressed through bridges his will to overcome obstacles." I was besotted with bridges.

My interest was not unique. Perhaps it was Clinton's "Bridge to the twenty-first century," perhaps it was war abroad and terrorism at home (New Yorkers were never so anxious as when alerts closed their bridges), or perhaps it was *The Bridges of Madison County*, but America had gone dotty over bridges. Symbolically, they were old yet new, permanent yet impermanent, historic yet visionary.

"Books on them sell like hotcakes," Jon Axline assured. A Federal Highway Program, in conjunction with the National Historic Preservation Act, had been inaugurated to save and preserve historic bridges. Since 1966, Axline's department had been mandated to list all historic sites endangered by highway improvement, and to make good-faith efforts to "gauge that impact." Adopt-a-Bridge had been established in 1997. And by 2003 Google listed, internationally, over 51,350 references to historic bridges. Most states kept a website and adoption program, and in Pennsylvania or Vermont, all a village need do was hang the sign, "Covered Bridge," to insure tourism. Yet Montana jaycees seemed oblivious to the old bridges' draw.

In late May I began a bridge journal, a diary of bridges spotted, an industrial-age equivalent to the birder's life list. I started near Three Forks, at Willow Creek's 1898, two-span, pin-connected, Pratt through-truss, the Jefferson River murky with runoff and the bridge aswarm with kids diving from its deck and high back. That morning I'd interviewed Patrick Hemingway, son of Ernest, a literary suicide, then driven to Willow Creek, cooling out. A sign, "Williams Bridge Road," led three miles to the Jefferson. Teenagers from as far as Bozeman and Butte clustered on the bridge's planks, joking, playing boom boxes, and leaping in feats of bravado. The runoff made this dicey, as the water was strewn with cottonwood branches. A red-haired boy wearing balloon shorts and a prosthesis below one knee struggled to the bridge's top. The ravers went silent as he balanced, prosthesis discarded, stick-like tibia bared. He leapt, surfaced on the current to "Yeah!"s and "Awesome!"s, then dog-paddled toward shore.

The boy's courage startled me.

"Have you jumped yet?" a smirker demanded. "Jumping *is* the bridge."

I crossed the Williams to jeers, then drove three miles to Cemetery Bridge, a 1914 two-span Pratt through-truss on Meridian Road, where in 1864 a cowboy had frozen to death after swimming the Jefferson, and been buried where he fell. "Half the bridge is in Gallatin County, half in Broadwater," Kenny Williams of Willow Creek told me. "The half in Gallatin is painted, the half in Broadwater's not." I photographed its plaque—"Fred M. Brown, Engineer, 1914"—before heading west on Route 2 to Rockin' the Rivers park, where one span of the silver, 1930's Sappington Bridge rested in a pasture, with a dozen black Angus beneath it. Concert promoters had rescued it. "They were going to make it a stage," Williams said, "then put it on fifty-foot pylons and make it the only place in the country that had a bridge for a stage." That plan had foundered, but the cows were a nice touch. I drove on to the ghost town of Pony, where there is no bridge but a fine saloon, perfect for contemplating my quest.

The blue-ribbon poster child for Montana's Adopt-a-Bridge was its 1930 Wolf Point Bridge, crossing the Missouri below Fort Peck Reservation, in the northeast corner of the state. Jon had cited it as a "must see." I would check that and ancillary bridges, motoring east to a second "must," 1913's Snowden Bridge (and its cousin, the Fairview in North Dakota), the only vertical-lift bridge in Montana, a behemoth spanning the Missouri near the North Dakota border. Then zigzag home, casing one thousand miles of bridge country.

On June 22, I left Paradise Valley at Carter's Bridge and headed for I-90. The morning was cool and the fields spring-green as I tracked the Yellowstone east. Sprinklers snaked across them, and I thought, someday their silver might be all to complement this landscape. Nine steel-truss bridges survive on the Yellowstone; my first stop was Pompey's Pillar and its Bundy Bridge, a decommissioned 1915, three-span riveted Warren through-truss that has been adopted. The site, though Crow territory, was visited by William Clark on July 25, 1806: "This rock I ascended and from its top had a most extensive view in every direction," he wrote. I ascended it myself and photographed a most-reassuring view of Bundy—its 650 feet of steel, roseate in the sun.

The prairie flattened, widened. At Forsyth, one span of a multi-reach camelback, its mates discarded, jutted into the Yellowstone. And at Miles City, the 1897 Tongue River Bridge at Pacific Street endured as back door to the Bucking Horse Sale and "the oldest surviving vehicular steel-truss bridge in southeastern Montana," Jon had written. I asked a red-faced cowpoke in the Bison Bar what he knew of other bridges, and he said, "Go to Kinsey, got a whopper there." Heat building, I drove eighteen miles of gravel east to Kinsey—little more than a rail stop. At the Yellowstone, a cathedral-like four-spanner stood converted from loco to automotive traffic. I kibitzed with Sunday bridgers, then puckered across the narrow one-laner, channeling Johnny McGee—water sixty feet below glistening between the rail ties.

A 1930s three-spanner, at Powder River, preened theatrically in the clover. I hiked through a field where Clark had camped in 1806, and photographed it. At Terry, empty pylons by a concrete bridge pointed toward the badlands, and its Prairie Drive-in was for sale. This was mastodon and sabertooth country; each mile northeast was a step back in time.

Fallon's steel-trusser still bore traffic, and at Glendive I accidently discovered the 1926, six-span, Bell Street Bridge—at 1,352 feet, the longest in the state. Like Wolf Point's, it was closed to vehicles, but owned by the Montana Historical Society. Kids spun bike-donuts there in a steady rain. At Intake, a flock of pelicans rose. And as I dallied by the Yellowstone, watching a rainbow, a fat man in Bermuda shorts and basketball shoes, heaving at a surf rod, landed a sixty-five-pound paddlefish—its spade-like snout a prehistoric sex toy. He grinned then "reached for the tartar sauce," as Hjorstberg once wrote. The rain blistered through Savage, and near Crane (where I admired a perfectly petite, 1908 pony truss) a cop nailed me for speeding. Twenty bucks and I had both ticket and directions—to the Snowden and Fairview lift bridges—the trooper looking envious.

Pheasants strutted through hail and the wind blew unfettered off the grasslands. I was nerve-racked. In Sydney I refueled at its Cattle-ac Steak House, deliberated. It was 9:00 p.m. I had one hour's light, and with luck might locate the Fairview or possibly the Snowden. I crossed into North Dakota on Highway 200 and within five miles cut the Yellowstone. From its mist rose a 2,994-foot, 4 inch-span, decommissioned steel-truss rail and auto bridge, the Fairview, with its east section raisable by counterweights to permit barge passage beneath. I stared, dumbfounded. It dwarfed anything I'd seen, but was in North Dakota. I peeled back to the borderline.

The sky went eerily green. Highway 58 ran north past Fort Union, then dissipated to red gumbo and gravel on County 227 toward the pinprick town of Bainville. There were no houses, no traffic, just fifteen miles of ruts and high bluffs, thunder clapping and rain slicing in sheets. You could die out here. I made Bainville, bought gas, then limped toward Wolf Point where I slept poorly on the Fort Peck Rez, in nightmares of the white man's folly.

"The Indians had no bridges that we know of," Jon had told me. "They may have had ways to cross some of the smaller creeks, but I don't think they had bridges in the way that we think of them." What a distance between tipping up a log and raising a bridge like Fairview's. A log went with the flow, so to speak, the Fairview was industrialism run amok—a mannerist kink in the Neoclassical impulse to dominate nature, a rattle-clack finale to Jeffersonianism that poor Lewis and Clark, bivouacked nearby, could not have envisioned. The Fairview, and no doubt the Snowden, were vast aesthetic leaps from those spider web camelbacks in Paradise Valley. Fort Peck elders *did* bless the four-spanner at Wolf Point, but the jury was out on their wisdom.

I found Wolf Point's next morning, in a haze of

melancholy. Jon had dubbed it "the finest remaining example of a Pennsylvania through-truss in Montana." I crossed the Missouri on its adjacent concrete bridge and looked back. The Wolf Point's four spans appeared seedy, unmaintained. This was Adopt-a-Bridge's poster child. A cyclone fence blocked access to its deck, where yellow weeds grew. The trusses were rusted and, standing before a historical marker, it was difficult to envision either the Crow and Assiniboine, who'd forded the river here for generations, or the fifteen thousand celebrants in 1930 who'd gathered for the bridge's dedication, gleefully crowning "Miss Wolf Point Bridge" (part Anglo, part Native American) and applauding the speeches, bands, cowboy shenanigans, Indian dancing, and fireworks.

I retreated east in a major funk. This trip was a pipedream, a bust. What was I searching for, the perfect bridge? But the morning was bright, clear. I rallied at Culbertson's lost bridge site, fingering a rusted pulley, and supposed the Snowden worth a second try. I headed south and, twenty-six miles later, was in Fairview, getting better directions, then retracing my path up Highway 58 to "a beige house past the Christmas tree farm," and turning left on County 147 toward the Missouri. A quarter mile and the asphalt became dirt; a mile farther, past oil derricks and abandoned trailer houses, the Snowden hit me. I locked up my brakes, stared. Blackened with rust and 3,257 feet long, it rose from the prairie like a Victorian space station. Where Lewis and Clark had camped on April 27, 1805, there now stood four gothic spans, the nearest of which held a million pounds of steel that could be raised vertically by 350-ton, concrete counterweights, hanging like guillotine slabs at either remove. It was horrifying. Jon had called it "a superstar, an engineering marvel, the state's most massive steel bridge." Used for both rail and automotive traffic, the Snowden had been Montana's only toll bridge. It was the "failed dream" of Great Northern Railway president, James. J. Hill, and a monument to industrialism's pretense.

It stood abandoned, closed even to pedestrians. Yet a wrecked pilot's nest—its rusted levers visible—perched at the lift span's peak. I recalled my father's advice, and that of the Williams Bridge kids: "*Jumping is the bridge.*" I climbed aboard.

A ladder angled up at fifty degrees, then back toward the lift span's top. Its steps were steel-and-concrete, one gone here, another there, but negotiable. The deck ran thirty-five feet above the water, its top cord thirty-five feet farther. I gripped the handrail. A wooden catwalk, steps broken or missing, led toward the pilot's nest. One misstep and I'd drop. Bracing against the wind, I hopped, skipped, and made the nest. I hugged its controls.

Seventy feet below ran the Missouri, much as the Indians had seen it, certainly as Lewis and Clark had, plus whatever brainsick malcontent operated this bridge—one lever for counterweights, one for the rail gate, a call box for autos, a wheel for whatever. I crouched there, rattling them like some crazed master of the universe, and felt this knowledge: a bridge is for *crossing*, not jumping. For leaving things behind. I howled that at the wind. A bridge is for *crossing*. Then I let go. It was no more subtle an epiphany than Jack Kerouac had mountain climbing—that you can't fall *off* a mountain, if you just stop trying.

The drive south was blissful. Taking Highway 12 toward Ingomar, I wolfed cheeseburgers at the Jersey Lilly Saloon, then pushed toward Roundup. East of town I spied a delicate, single-span, 1890s camelback crossing the Musselshell. I stopped, and with amazement discovered it to be made of timbers. I could not believe my luck. "A timber truss bridge," Jon told me later, "perhaps the last in the state." I fingered its gray wood lovingly, then photographed it in the violet gloaming.

A rancher drove up. "You like that bridge?" he asked. "Well, it's for sale."

Big Sky Journal
2003

Outlaw Blues: Thomas McGuane, Jimmy Buffett, Hunter S. Thompson

Corinne and I split up the night I bought *Saloon* its final ticket on a Greyhound to New York. Galleys polished, drudgery completed, we had meant to share a vacation. Instead there'd been ugly confessions and threats of desertion. My reaction had been to finish the review I'd been writing for Sunday's *Washington Post*. I walked from bedroom to study and coldly, professionally, immersed myself in prose. No way to shift gears. I'd spent the greater expanse of our two years together locked in that room, hitting the keys. Though I'd married Corinne it was my book *Saloon* I'd consorted with. Both contracts had come through simultaneously. Without one I couldn't have tolerated the other. Nor could she have. *Saloon* neatly wrapped, review properly typed, I invited Corinne along to dump the mothers off. Outside the *Post* and again in a midnight Greyhound depot, each of us wept for something nearly inexpressible.

Saigon's fall had been rough. I'd watched Corinne waver toward evacuation; her nerves shot, her resolve as diminished as that of those American troops garrisoned in-country. She'd volunteered for Red Cross duty; had been refused. A vet, she was angry to help, hungry for an excuse to return. After the fall she'd toppled into a kind of reverse shellshock: working full-time, attending classes, studying—a schedule mated to mine, which left us two hours' daily companionship. As Vietnamese flooded the country and refugee camps popped up like A-sites or firebases, she grew more unsettled. I finished a first draft of *Saloon*. She begged to leave, hop a next plane anywhere. I wasn't able. I kept accepting assignments, decompressing, coming off the hard stuff with profiles and reviews. Refugees poured into the cities, old friends called, friends of friends; the war intruded as maliciously as my writing. Then Vietnam was finished. America's first draft, anyway. *Saloon* was in galleys. Without war or writing, life faced head-on seemed unendurable. Neither of us was primed for a peacetime resolve.

We headed west: She to Honolulu, then to a Vietnamese relocation center at San Jose. I to Montana. Where I'd been working to reach Tom McGuane by telephone these past two days.

My call was expected. I stood in the New Atlas saloon, Columbus, Montana, waiting to be put through. Last night Tom's line had stayed busy for hours, then strangely was vacant. I'd holed up in a trailer motel at Kaycee, Wyoming, drinking beer with locals and commiserating with a young woman who'd fixed me sandwiches and told when she'd radiophoned her husband in Vietnam every time she said "I love you" she'd had to add "over." Columbus was eighty miles from McGuane's. I'd researched New Atlas for *Saloon*. Sipping cold draft at its mahogany bar, I noted how much less romantic the spot was minus the imperatives of art. A frightening realism inked fixtures lately perceived as quaint. Its old bars were darkly grotesque; its stuffed animals sandbagged cadavers flecked with dusty hair. My call came through.

"Oh, God," McGuane moaned. "Well, you're here. I've just spent three days with no sleep behind a weekend of partying. Today's my day with the kids. But come ahead."

He offered directions. "Why do we do it?" he said, cataloguing his-weekend's indiscretions. I mumbled something about amalgamating the neuroses and rang off.

Art had not been kind to Thomas McGuane this past year. The film version of his novel *Ninety-Two in the Shade* had been panned by film critics, then buried by United Artists, its distributor. Wounding deeper because McGuane not only had written book and screenplay, but had directed. A contemporary Western, *Rancho Deluxe,* directed by Frank Perry from a McGuane screenplay, had fared poorly at the box office. The heavyweight *Missouri Breaks,* a ten million dollar extravaganza directed by Arthur Penn, which starred Marlon Brando and Jack Nicholson, was likewise climbing feebly up the charts. McGuane's original screenplay of *Breaks* had been partially rewritten by Robert Towne and metamorphosed by Brando's reinterpretation of a principal character. McGuane was being blamed for all this, and critics had not been kind, adding swipes at his personal life. Interviewers had proved most vitriolic. It was a wonder McGuane had consented to see me at all.

Perhaps because we were friends. In that tenuous manner in which writers maintain association, through shared work and the occasional postcard. I'd first met McGuane in January of 1974, at his house in Key West, Florida. I'd knocked on his door. Walked through a gate which stated: BEWARE OF DOG, ignored the snarling antiquarian, and rattled McGuane's screen. I'd read *Ninety-Two* and, being in Key West, thought: There is no way I'll not risk approaching this man. The book had simply changed my perception of things. Seductive as rhythm and blues, incisive as middle Dylan, mindwarped as Hunter S. Thompson, literate as who could say—the work was mind candy in a sour season. It isolated certain confusions of seventies apostasy precisely. And it was lonely. I held this mental picture of a man, its creator, lonely, slight, shy. McGuane answered the door and he was huge. His face was tan as saddle leather, roughed up but friendly. I fumbled through an introduction, said a complimentary word about *Ninety-Two* while we shuffled around the doorstep. McGuane wore a Hawaiian shirt, Levi's, and was barefoot. His sun-streaked hair hung in a ponytail below his shoulder blades.

"There's this book I wish you'd help me with," I said.

His face sagged.

"It's called *Saloon* and it's about my search for the Great American Bar."

A grin broke across McGuane's features. "You look like a man who could stand a drink," he said. And invited me in.

We shared dinner that night at a Cuban restaurant where McGuane was known. Complimentary sangria; cold beers to follow. Conversation revolved around fishing, music, writing, and movies. Both of us knew Key West, had fished the Keys. But McGuane had not been fishing much lately. He was embroiled in a screenplay, *Rancho Deluxe*. That corralled his energy. At one point, circa 1968, McGuane had worked toward being a fishing guide, figuring he could make seventy-five dollars a day, guide one day a week, write the remaining six. He lived higher in the Keys then, where one could survive on seventy-five a week. To that end he once fished sixty-eight consecutive days and boated 104 tarpon, each a hundred pounds. Beat to shit from gaffing these fish, skin blistered nearly cancerous from the sun, McGuane entertained second thoughts. Yet he'd seen wondrous things. McGuane sketched these adventure stories avidly. Irony crinkled his smile, but it was slight, obligatory. You could laugh all you wanted but the universe stymied. He'd written a book about it.

Ninety-Two in the Shade had received top reviews, remarkable praise, most notably in a front-page *New York Times* rave which compared its author to a gallery of greats. McGuane seemed unswerved by this attention.

He was eager to talk books, talk literature, talk the sort of whacked-out experimental journalism I'd been practicing. At evening's end he'd said, "Why don't you sort of consider my house your base of operations," and invited me for dinner the following night.

Becky Crockett McGuane was everyman's paradigm of the perfect writer's wife, that fact impressed itself up front. You could substitute "perfect wife" without shattering your demographics. She was small, blonde, cheerful, with an unthreatening sensuality and a steady diligence any man could work behind. She was charming; magically so. She had a way of listening to what you said which overstepped politeness. And she knew men, how to mother untamed herds of them. Descended from Davy Crockett, you'd never have guessed frontier lineage until you'd seen her defuse various Alamos of masculine unrest. She and Tom had been married since 1962. They had a son, Thomas IV, aged six. Everyone was in love with Becky McGuane.

She fried yellowtails caught that afternoon with Dink Bruce—son of Toby Bruce, Hemingway's good friend in Key West—the fish served prettily on attractive china, domestic wine poured into beveled crystal, five or six of us seated about an antique dining table in Victorian side chairs, Cuban artifacts around, paintings by friends, McGuane's house itself settled amid subtropical foliage in a yard cluttered with large-boy's toys: a sailboat, dinghy, ten-speed Peugeot, nautical miscellanea. In truth, the yard was immaculate. As was the house.

The evening unfolded not unlike half a dozen others I enjoyed over the next ten days: food, drink, conversation, joking, hilarity, jitterbugging to the stereo, and a warming to newcomers which approached the familial. That familiarity was peculiarly smalltown. Its warmth was the McGuane's near-perfect life together, one which hesitated to travel. "Let's stay here," it seemed to say. "We don't need outside. The party is us."

Tom was working hard on *Rancho Deluxe* and reveled in these hearthside gatherings. Becky ran the house, cooked meals, screened calls, took care of Thomas IV, entertained guests, to the benefit of McGuane. Who, up at dawn, wrote eight to twelve hours a day in a converted outbuilding behind the house. At supper his mood was even-tempered and sleepy. "When Tom's writing he's no problem," Becky said. "It's between things that the tension rises."

Even in the face of work, a mild tension percolated. It had been six months since the publication of *Ninety-Two,* a year and a half since its completion. Though McGuane had produced scattered journalism and two screenplays, he had no novel in the fire. Movies intrigued him—he had taken an MFA in drama at Yale, and saw his work with screenplays as an extension of that training—but the novel remained his métier. "I really need to get up to my elbows in prose," he'd say wistfully. Then head back for another stretch with *Rancho Deluxe.* "Writing screenplays is fun," he'd blurt, letting the thought drift. Movie rights had been sold to *Ninety-Two* and there was speculation as to who might direct. Robert Altman was first choice; apparently he'd bowed out. McGuane was not speaking of directing himself, yet his fascination with movie-making at every level intruded upon conversation. While he wrote, however, contradictions leveled themselves off.

It cannot be overemphasized the degree to which McGuane had captured what later would be maligned as "every English major's wettest dream." Prizes for his novels—a Rosenthal for *Bushwhacked Piano,* National Book Award nomination for *Ninety-Two*—contracts for screenplays which had downpaid a house in Key West and a ranch in Montana; time for fishing, hunting, sailing; a compact family, a broad circle of friends which included the most energetic of sport, screen, rock, and literary figures...he was soon to become the first novelist to direct a film of his own book. He'd expanded a seventies version of the prototypical writer's life to have eclipsed

Ernest Hemingway. He wintered in Key West, spent summer and fall in Montana. He had talent to back it up.

My last day in Key West, Becky invited me for lunch.
Tom looked distracted. He had stuck *Rancho Deluxe* in
the mail that morning. His screenplay was finished. "I
woke up at six without an idea in my head and slumped
out here to the typewriter," Tom said. "Nothing." With-
drawal had set in.

We ate at a little seafood restaurant beside the shrimp
docks. Tom stayed nervous, preoccupied. "I feel *awful,*"
he complained. "I can't think of *what* to do." Driving
home McGuane's Cortina ran out of gas. We shuffled idly
through verdant streets, along sidewalks contoured like
jungle paths, suffering writer's unease. A family dilemma.

McGuane's discomfort in the face of leisure did little
to dissuade me from emulating his perfect writer's life.
Single, I sought companionship and found a smallish
blonde, delicate, attractive—though substantially less tolerant than Becky. How much, consciously, I was imitat-
ing McGuane is difficult to gauge. I remember driving
north through the Keys, however, and thinking, Tom's
domestic situation seems an effective way to counteract
the loneliness of writing, the chaos of existence away
from one's typewriter. Corinne and I were married about
the time McGuane's marriage tore apart at the seams.

"Just checking in," a postcard read, April, 1974. "*We're
going to Montana this week to make the movie. Hope to
see you somewhere...along the way...—Tom.*" That film
was *Rancho Deluxe,* shot around McGuane's Livingston
and starring Elizabeth Ashley, Jeff Bridges, Harry Dean
Stanton, Sam Waterston, Slim Pickens, with a soundtrack
by Jimmy Buffett. The ruckus of partying could be heard
in Kansas City. Tom spent that spring studying movie-
making in his back yard, with a cantilevered eye toward
directing. By fall he had convinced Elliot Kastner, *Rancho's* producer, to pass him the throttle on *Ninety-Two.*
Tom would direct. A shooting schedule was set for Octo-
ber-November. That film would star Margot Kidder and

Peter Fonda, among others. Within a year Tom would be living with Kidder, Becky married to Fonda.

Articles came out in *People, New Times,* and *The Village Voice* exploiting these new relationships. *Rancho* appeared. "Don't know that I *like* that film," Tom admitted in a telephone conversation. *Ninety-Two* appeared and disappeared. A long silence from McGuane. Then, the following fall from Montana, on Beverly Hills Hotel notepaper *("Big Snazz. A Real Hot Spot."):*

"Dear Toby. Here's some stationery from when I was in movies. —Had a baby girl, hard at a novel; been hunting in the mountains off my house. Having a good old time. Yeah, that guy from the Voice. *I guess that's what they do there though. I sent off a letter enumerating the lies but I don't figure they'll print it. That stuff just makes me tired. Stay on that saloon book now 'til you get it. Hope to see you. —Tom."*

He'd see me, all right. But it would take a year, the dissolution of my marriage, and the intention to collate another book—some sort of guide to the pitfalls of the generation, concentrating on writers—before we got together.

"I want to be Writer-hyphenated," Tom had said. "I tend to transgress categories."

My plan, in that book, was to profile a novelist, poet, journalist, songwriter, scenarist, dramatist, and technical writer, with side trips into the world of writers' psychiatrists, grade school teachers, and parents. To try and establish why certain people were drawn toward language as art, why some people used it as offense, some defense, and why some hid behind it as if it were a mother's skirts. I wondered why in this age of TV and film anyone should want to *be* a writer. Endure the seclusion, rejection, endless wait. In short I wanted to learn about myself while studying others. McGuane was first on my list.

"No Hunting," a sign read at the edge of McGuane's property. "Children, Pets and Livestock. Thank you." That sign itself intimated a ducking behind language. I bumped my jeep across a cattle guard and swayed down the short drive. Another sign, RAW DEAL RANCH, hung from a log outbuilding. Three or four outbuildings crowded McGuane's ranchyard. A white clapboard house faced them contrastively. The effect was frontier and rugged.

A pale blue pickup sledded across the cattle guard, coughing to a halt before McGuane's front door. Tom stepped out. An exhausted grin. His hair was redneck short. He was dressed in boots, jeans, a James Dean jacket, and high-crowned summer straw; he carried a beer. He looked roughed-up as his ranchyard. We tossed arms about each other's shoulders and headed for the house.

That night I slept in Margot Kidder's studio. She was in L.A. filming a series. She'd return by week's end. Tom was sitting Thomas IV and Justin Fonda. But only for the night. Becky slept several hay fields away at the ranch house she shared with Peter Fonda. That was part of the McGuanes' agreement, to live close by so that Thomas could ramble. Still, hayfields were hayfields. With a marriage in between. Tom was more alone than had seemed possible a year and a half previous. His compact family had split, he'd halfway constructed another, his father and sister had died, and art was treating him most unkind.

That art was the art of the Western movie, I could not help thinking; a difficult taskmaster, one which had done its damnedest to rifle the consciousness of our generation; and which continued to shuffle archetypes through choreographed violence and bloodied romance. Redneck Chic had evolved in the 1970s from clodhoppers and bib overalls to stovepiped Tony Lamas and sateen cowboy shirts. One could not help but credit the movies. The cowpoke ethos to redneck culture was the ethos of hip—it actuated silence, reserve, physical grace, competence in the face of danger, primitive ardor, and above all an inimitable style. That style had encouraged our first emulations of art as children...through costume and an appreciation of Wild West as theater: horse opera. Thank Hollywood, thank Saturday TV, the fact was established as Roy Rogers, Hopalong Cassidy, the Lone Ranger, Lash LaRue, Matt Dillon, or Palladin; it was as current as *Missouri Breaks,* inescapable as the entire outlaw notion in seventies culture. From Richard Nixon to Waylon Jennings.

That Peter Fonda—who, with Dennis Hopper in 1969, had released a film, *Easy Rider,* which would do more to perpetuate divisionism in a mindless youth culture than any other work of sixties art—lived in rural Montana, hay ranched, drove a four-wheel-drive pickup and kept horses, surprised. That he had used rock 'n' roll, the western ethos (cowpokes on motorcycles) and sixties technology (endless jump cuts) in the orchestration of *Rider* made perfect sense. That was hip. *Rider* was an essay on hip for 1960s deviationists, perhaps the final word. It had made Fonda millions and established him as box office. Hollywood movies were as serviceable a conduit of hip as had been rhythm and blues, hot cars, fast sex, and an absurd war. That *Rider* exploited an ethos, capitalized upon deep-seated fears, is hardly worth mentioning. Somewhere, on Merv Griffin I believe, Fonda had said: "I worked hard during the sixties so that I could enjoy myself during the seventies." He was explaining an eighty-two-foot-long sailboat.

Fonda's character in *Rider* had represented the apotheosis of outlaw America...longhaired, dope-smoking, coke-pushing, hip-talking, motorcycle-riding freakdom...an antithesis to Redneck Chic. A pickup-load of Florida crackers had blown him away. In *Ninety-Two,* McGuane had cast Fonda as a Florida fishing guide and had put him on a bicycle. The opening scene of *Ninety-Two* showed Fonda riding in circles, round and round, on a totally unhip Schwinn. That was vision.

Tom's was mightily blurred when he roused from the sack at 1:00 p.m. next day. By three we'd piled into his pickup and were rattling along Deep Creek to Old Hoffman Route east of the Yellowstone River, heading for Livingston. Tom was frenetic, tensed up. He had a novel in progress but had not worked on it for five months. He'd been collaborating on a "redneck screenplay" with Jimmy Buffett about a gang of Florida low-lifers who take over an abandoned jet strip in the Everglades and run cocaine. He had another screenplay underway titled *Dry Run,* about a pair of Confederate blockade runners in Texas who never make it to the coast. But conversation tended to de-emphasize art: "This summer has been the happiest of my life," Tom said. "I broke two horses and planted a garden. My hay crop should pay off my hired man's wages. I don't care if I ever put another word on paper." Yet he did not cease ranting about movies, about New York critics, and that literary establishment which he felt certain would "shit all over" his next book for dalliance with the film industry. "Like I told that woman from *New Times,*" Tom said, "If I had spent the past two years shooting heroin rather than making movies, critics would have seen that as supportive of my art."

We had lunch at the Sandarosa Motel, Tom drinking margaritas and joking with the waitress. He rambled on about art, about writers such as Harry Crews, Larry Mc-Murtry, Ken Kesey, himself, who "never would be taken seriously" by the *New York Review of Books.* "Art's just no longer as important to me as living," Tom reiterated. Then we were on into Livingston for a round of chores. As if to show what he meant.

We stopped at a hardware store to buy nails for a corral Tom was building; at The Sport Saloon to pay a bill and to joke with its owner about dally roping—a craft Tom was learning; and at Colmey's Pet and Grooming to purchase deworming medicine for his horses, five of which had distemper. At each spot Tom had spoken with authority about ranching topics. He held each proprietor's interest, if not his respect. I marveled at how much tougher Tom's demeanor was in Montana; it showed through the roughness of his dress, but most notably in the shortness of his hair, so recently shoulder-length. "I don't want to look like Baba Ram Dass," Tom laughed. Once we'd climbed into the pickup, conversation ricocheted back toward art. "I'm dying to learn the secret of a film like *Texas Chainsaw Massacre*." Or, "There's this guitarist around town, Ron Taylor, who's played with the Rolling Stones—I'm hot to write rock lyrics with him." Back home, Tom's freneticism quickly eased to torpor. Retiring early, he would clock another twelve hours in the sack. A pattern which continued five days, until Margot's return from Hollywood.

During that time I did not come close to a formal interview but engaged myself in the diversions of Paradise Valley. I had my own psychic havoc to weather, a storm system I held in check with long hikes into the Absarokas, drinking at cowpoke saloons, dancing to hokey bands, and the ingestion of central nervous system depressants unobtrusively packaged in pharmaceutical vials. A community of artists had gathered outside Livingston, Montana—a band of refugees drawn by the charisma of McGuane and held in thrall by the awesomely beautiful countryside. There was William Hjortsberg, the experimental novelist, who had known Tom at Yale; Russell Chatham, a painter, writer, and fisherman who had met Tom in Key West; Dan Gerber, the writer, publisher, and Grand Prix aficionado; Peter Fonda, Warren Oates, both of whom had acted in *Ninety-Two;* Margot Kidder, whose credits, pre-*Superman* and besides *Ninety-Two,* included *Sisters, The Great Waldo Pepper,* and *The Reincarnation of Peter Proud;* and Richard Brautigan, world-famous as a poet, novelist and literary pied-piper to half a generation.

I saw Becky in town and at McGuane's. Where she'd appeared cute in Key West, if a trifle drawn, here she radiated a kind of frontier elegance—something fancy, a deeper, more relaxed physical beauty. I took Thomas IV and Justin Fonda fishing, letting them show me favorite spots, accepting hand-tied flies as gifts, remarkably well-wrought from the hands of eight-year-olds. They were bright, interested kids; if over an evening their natural restlessness got out of hand, McGuane would suggest: "Why don't you guys head back to the bedroom and read a little science?" I drove down near Emigrant Peak and met Warren Oates. Searching for a trail Tom had recommended, I startled Oates fishing the creek back of his house. "H'lo, I'm Warren Oates," he'd said. Then, "See this cutthroat I caught?" with childlike enthusiasm. Oates, an outlaw archetype of the Peckinpah genre, terrifying in his onscreen depravity, was here a mountain-struck Cub Scout.

The notion of a band of refugees dogged me as I hiked each day outside Livingston. If Vietnam represented the violent extreme of that journey to the East inaugurated by Columbus in 1492 and intensified through westward expansionism, a war with Japan, a war with Korea…then Cowboy Chic implied a step back to the frontier, physically and metaphysically. Since armistice, embarkation port San Francisco had received a thick stream of refugees, both Asian and American G.I. These people were filtering into the countryside, asserting their independence where practicable, more commonly settling in relocation camps. Livingston seemed a relocation camp of sorts. None of the McGuane clan had been born in Montana. Their migration to the Rockies was a seventies deal. And symptomatic of a shift in values collectively perceived by the public at large.

If the Green Beret had been an American hipster pushed to a nethermost extreme of America's hegira to the East, the American cowboy—or outlaw, more precisely—was his nineteenth-century counterpart. By meeting the Asian primitive on his turf and confronting certain ambiguities—that firepower would not douse shamanism, that technology could not suppress animism, that homeland was inviolate and inescapably spook-ridden—the Green Beret had conceded defeat. But his mission had been far from conventional, one could argue its design even as military. It had been the tail end of Columbus's search for the East, and in that sense may have proved successful. Both Lyndon Johnson's and Columbus's treks eastward were business ventures which had failed, but which, arguably, opened broader vistas. America knew the resignation of defeat from Vietnam; there was one lesson which could be catalogued as victory. That Cowboy Chic had surfaced during the seventies, that Rocky Mountain High had become a way of life, that McGuane's Livingston—an intentional community of sixties malcontents, albeit highly successful ones—existed, that both Corinne and I post-armistice had felt an irresistible pull toward the West, suggested paradoxes worth considering.

Outlaw Chic was a concept that had been toyed with by popular artists for nearly ten years. Bob Dylan had broken from the circularities of a limitless recording technology with the primitivist production of *John Wesley Harding* in 1968. Hardin had been a notorious western outlaw, and Dylan's album proved as much of a renegade, shifting rock toward its Country Western roots. Sam Peckinpah filed the notion sharper in *The Wild Bunch* (of which Oates was a member), but laid open the wound with *Pat Garrett and Billy the Kid,* a post-combat, Wild West swan song in which he cast rock stars as outlaws... Bob Dylan, Kris Kristofferson, Rita Coolidge...hiring Dylan to compose a score. *Billy* was an affirmation of the theatricality of all combat, ritual, hunting, and a railing against its imperatives. Discouraging, *Billy* nevertheless hinted America had instigated a retreat, and was winding its way home through a cast of psychic archetypes.

Street theater had worked as psychodrama for millions during the 1960s; street demonstrations, street riots, street collectivizations of rage inexpressible but for frenzies of rock, fast cars, easy sex, and technologies of approved warfare. Cowboy Chic was just another role; its dedication to the rigors of hip, even Western Hip, was no more serious than the pretentiousness of a hundred million hippies to alternative consciousness.

The irony of mass attraction to Cowpoke Chic was that, again, "rebels" were assimilating an ethos more conservative than their intellects were equipped to fathom. Just as hippies had embraced urban hip, with no bow to implied psychopathy, these new cowpokes adopted accoutrements of a lifestyle few had thought to assess. Dylan had turned away from the conformity of sixties culture with *John Wesley Harding,* all those hippies and communalized beatniks who'd been gumming up the life, and now things were coming full circle. Cowboys *hated* hippies, hated that concept of self-indulgence and dependence. Cowboys wore their hair long and smoked a little dope, but their ethos remained firm. You were your own man out here under a peopleless sky, taking gaff from no boss. An ironic bit of horse opera on its face, but never mind.

"The Cowboy was an instrument of the cattle industry," Peter Snell wrote in 1978, in *Preservation News.* "His job was to protect and move an investment in cattle for ranch owners and their backers." Eleanor Aveling, daughter of Karl Marx, had painted the cowboy as slave to economic forces in her book, *The Working-Class Movement in America.* The romantic era of the cowboy (1866 to 1890), such as it was, had been short-shrifted by the railroad to haul and, by the introduction of barbed wire, to fence what was left of the open range. During that time your average cowpoke was just another footling for a faceless corporation, moving the product from point A to point B. His concept of himself as romantic emerged from art: popular song, theater, the dime novel, penny journalism, Hollywood. When Buffalo Bill couldn't make it any longer on the tent show circuit, he packed the first Hollywood crew on location to Wounded Knee, South Dakota, for a "real-life re-enactment" of that massacre. He hired General Nelson A. Miles to play himself, plus real Indians, many of whom had lost real relatives at the battle. Nelson's shenanigans so enraged Indian actors that Wild Bill nearly had another massacre on his hands. *Cinéma vérité.* Indians had never felt much affection for horse opera, but like most Americans they'd face anything for a buck.

The West had suffered businessmen grudgingly, from its earliest trappers, who systematically depleted wildlife, to miners who created boomtowns while wrecking the countryside, to cattlemen who fenced with barbed wire or crisscrossed with railroads that land which had provided graze for migrational herbivores and hunting ground for nomadic tribes for eons. Tourism had been big business since Theodore Roosevelt opened Yellowstone Park as America's first western playground in 1903; but until recently one could not say the Northern Rockies had been threatened by art. McGuane, Fonda, et al., posed problems—particularly McGuane, who had set a book and two movies in the region. Yet location scouts for Hollywood film crews had advertised in neighborhood yellow pages some years now. The art which threatened Big Sky most thoroughly was the theatricality of style. Everyone, stepping back, sought a revamped ethos. For most, commitment skated the surface. But ice was thin. No one wanted Paradise Valley desecrated to another Aspen. Hip attracted unhip (the falsely committed), and unhip encouraged speculation. Business had done its best to unhinge the West, cowboys were both first and last perpetrators.

You could argue trappers; many had worked independently but most had been agents of the great fur companies, even legendary frontiersmen like Mike Fink, Jedediah Smith, and Jim Bridger. You trapped your pelts and traded to the corporation. A similar spiel could be coaxed for the miner. Many had toiled independently, but sooner or later most encountered corporation, government or national currency. True western primitives were its Indians. Model for black and white hipsters alike: the holy aborigine.

Like Cochise or Al Jolson? I'd speculated, while contemplating Green Berets painting up for night raids in Vietnam. *Like Billy the Kid or Burt Reynolds?* I conjectured, assaying their counterparts here in Fantasia land.

Hollywood had made the down payment on Tom's ranch, he freely admitted, and screenplays were the chores which kept it from the bank. Margot Kidder helped with the odd TV series, but care of her infant daughter, Maggie, had forced a sabbatical from films stretching toward a year and a half. Margot was the least *Hollywood* actress I'd met. Unkempt, loosely organized, beautiful. She was beginning to pick up her career. She returned home Friday after being stranded overnight in Salt Lake City with the baby; something about a lost wallet, missed connections. McGuane had hired a plane to fly her back. "What could I do?" he said. "Leave them forever at that airport?"

By then I'd moved into Livingston. I'd located a four-dollar-a-night room in an old railroad hotel, the Murray, which boasted saloon, restaurant and lobbyful of oldtimers who vied for impermanence with aged buffalo heads and stuffed trout encumbering the walls. Across from Burlington Northern's tracks and at the center of town, the Murray was a timeless caravansary of western disorder. I slept on the fourth floor, but I had mountains within view plus a scenic diorama of the town. I had three excellent saloons on my block. There were old-fashioned luncheonettes nearby, general stores, and a dusty pharmacy. There was a pint-sized movie theater. A railroad café open twenty-four hours where strangers broke off the Amtrak for coffee and homemade pie. There were softball games in Sacajawea Park, trout fishing at the center of town. Rows of quiet houses. There was roller skating at the in-town rink. An objectless circling of pickups on Saturday night, whooping, hooping, horseshit in the street, kids leaving bicycles unlocked, friendly teenagers and old men who would bend your ear. A sensible town.

One week passed, then two. I didn't mind. I was familiar with Montana and knew how to amuse myself.

I unwound. I made friends, kept McGuane's troupe to visit, but most often struck out on my own. With the poet Ken McCullough, I met three fellows living in tepees west of Emigrant. They were logging the summer season. Their tepees were kinetic art, sculptural folds of skeletalized canvas. White men, their shelter suggested a step back from cowpokes. But their work was current: Chainsaws promising early deafness, a stench of blue smoke, ravaged tree trunks. They offered summer elk hospitably and a sweat lodge banked with volcanic rock. Grouse browsed in the sage behind their tepees like Rhode Island Reds. Fridley Creek ran a constant forty degrees.

I'd set a date with McGuane and showed up on time at the ranch. He came busting out saying he had to get a blood test, why didn't I ride along. He and Margot were getting married. Our interview was postponed. Once again life had intruded upon art. We stopped at the Tastee Freeze, then drove straight to Livingston Memorial. Tom disappeared, reemerging with a bandage inside his elbow. The sole conversation revolved around why not just go ahead and do it. Tom had other errands. We walked into Sax and Fryer's, a combination sporting goods, stationery, artist's supply, photo, hardware, book, and souvenir store, where Tom greeted John Fryer, pulled back his sleeve and said: "This is how close I am to getting married." Fryer kept a collection of antique saddles in his basement; we admired them as if to celebrate. I was impressed again at the *convenience* of Livingston. Everything was right there. If the frontier represented Step Two back from Vietnam, a small town or neighborhood such as Livingston approached One.

Over lunch we discussed hay ranching, dally roping, quarter-horse breeding: crafts of the white man's West much on Tom's mind. "I'm just going to do it," he said of horse breeding. "It's very complicated. It has a tremendous amount to do with bloodlines and other stuff that has to be learned. People say: You don't know anything about it. Which is true. I know a lot about using horses but I don't know anything about breeding them, in terms of what bloodlines cross with other bloodlines and how to get results genetically. But I'm going to do it, that's all." He said the same for dally roping. Hay ranching he had a handle on. These were chores of the Old West which had a firmer hold on sanity than producing screenplays or jackpot journalism. They were crafts whose mastery paralleled the disciplines of art.

Driving home along East River Road, Tom talked about drugs as occasional escape from his Natty Bumppo existence. He'd toughed out a cocaine jag in the early seventies that lasted approximately a year. At one extreme he'd snorted a dime-sized hole in his throat doctors thought would have to be closed with sutures. "I'd get incredibly violent," Tom said of this period. "I had this huge capacity for drugs. I can take more drugs than most people ever dreamed of. Drinking with Marlon Brando one afternoon I downed two fifths of Jack Daniels while he sat nursing a beer. The adrenalin kept me sober. Concentrating on something I'm really interested in will do that."

We set a later date for our interview. That date was broken. Another week passed. I hardly minded. Livingston was balm. The simplicity of small-town life with a proximity to wilderness was healing me. I awoke each morning by ten, boiled water for coffee, and munched granola, studying rooftops and the crewcut ochre of Mount Baldy. I glassed mountains which encircled the town, for snow, game, or tractor-trailers which slid along I-90. I read. By eleven I was mobile. I kept forest service maps for a hundred-mile radius, depicting trails. I chose between Ramshorn Lake, Passage Falls, Emigrant Gulch, Palace Butte, Coffin Mountain, Snowbank Camp, Bear Creek Meadow, Fairy Lake, Flathead Pass, Battle Ridge, Soda Butte as objectives—their names were enough. I walked through the Crazy Mountains, hitting Big Timber for a rodeo. I drove up to Ringling, a semi-ghost applauded by Jimmy Buffett in song. I parked back of McGuane's ranch and hiked into wilderness which ran sixty miles to the Wyoming border. I saw a bear. I saw a moose. I saw innumerable wildflowers, birds, and small mammals. What's more, I communed. I fished spring creeks, glacial lakes. I soaked in hot springs. I ran seven, eight miles round the high school track daily. A track ringed by snow-tipped Absarokas where footballers trotted alongside wondering at my southern accent, trading regionalisms. I caroused with Richard Brautigan, supped at William Hjortsberg's, partied at McGuane's. I hung out at Peter Fonda's—his housekeeper ranch-sitting while he and Becky sailed off Maui—Fonda's mountain view unsurpassed, house simply western, primitively furnished, spooky in Fonda's absence, redolent of an archetype. I drank in Livingston's saloons, danced until closing. One evening a lady trucker said, "You ever ride in a semi?" and off we went circling town, before eighteen thousand pounds of plywood bound for Rapid City, South Dakota. Another midnight I stepped through the Wrangler's swinging doors in time to hear a hometown girl stand and sing "I Want to Be a Cowboy's Sweetheart," the yodeling of which brought Wrangler's eight stupefied patrons to their feet. By the time a week was done I had forgotten art, reassessed fear, worried only slightly over McGuane's interview.

Tom and Margot got married. That was Monday. We set an interview for Wednesday, two mornings later.

The phone rang. "I'll do it," Tom said wearily. "'Cause I've put you off. But I am exhausted."

I drove to the ranch astride a mood of confidence that approached exultation.

"Let's walk out to my study," Tom said.

This was one of the several log outbuildings in Tom's ranchyard; part of it comprised an implement shed, part of it a tack room. Tom slumped to a ragged couch with Hudson Bay and Indian blankets spread across its length. I had visited this study to pick up mail but never had taken a serious look. Tom's desk fronted a picture window, affording an unobstructed view of trees, outbuildings, a vegetable garden, corrals, stable, Deep Creek, a dirt road and mountains beyond. I touched his desk top—laminated butcher board—and his typewriter, a venerable Olympia upon which Tom said he'd produced all his major work. Tom observed my perusals tolerantly, answering questions, flipping out information. The room was indelibly McGuane. A pair of saddle bags with T.M. tooled into their leather dangled from its rafters. I'd owned such a pair when I was seven. A stuffed hawk adorned a wall; two identical five-pound trout ("caught on consecutive casts") hung to the left of Tom's desk, above several rifles: a Hawken's gun, a Bedford- style Kentucky flintlock, and a 1903 Springfield 30.06, with Lyman scope. Minus esoterica, this was like my bedroom as a child. Both flintlock and Springfield were custom made for Tom by Montanan Don King.

Bookshelves lined three walls and contained editions on hunting and fishing, a leather set of Dickens, editions of *The Bushwhacked Piano*—one leather, a gift of Simon and Schuster—other McGuane publications in other printings, some foreign; and a small stereo tape machine with assorted rock and Country Western tapes. There were books on film and film editing, a veterinary handbook, books about the Confederacy for his *Dry Run* film project, a leatherbound *Diary of Samuel Pepys,* and perhaps a hundred novels.

Crowding study walls were a needlepoint of the cover to *Ninety-Two*, a rattlesnake hide, drawings by Thomas IV, photos of daughter Maggie, of Margot, novelist Jim Harrison, and Elizabeth Ashley. On a far wall was the casting-call bulletin for *Missouri Breaks,* welcoming the "physically eccentric—those with permanent physical injuries such as scars, missing teeth, broken limbs, broken noses, missing limbs, etc."

To the right of Tom's desk was a cartridge loader for his 30.06. A tree-stump table faced the couch where Tom lay, the tack room off to its side containing saddles, bridles, pack gear, fishing equipment, waders, an Orvis

146

creel, rucksacks. A framed ad for *Ninety-Two,* novel, hung near the tack room door. To its left was a raised topographical map of the immediate countryside. Books on quarter horses and calf roping shared space on Tom's desk with several pages of his novel-in-progress. A Confederate cavalry pistol, used as a paperweight, rested at what would be Tom's right hand. A .22 rifle and Browning over-and-under leaned against one corner. An Estate wood-burning stove provided the room's heat. Gun-cleaning emollients soiled its shelves, one a homemade mixture resembling pea soup, which Tom insisted "did the job." I studied this junk like a kid at the Museum of Natural History. This was where the work got done; what a wonderful place to hide.

Tom looked shaky. He'd had scant sleep in the two days since his marriage. Propped up by pillows, he watched me with resignation. I'd not seen him so accessible since Key West. All the toughness had flown.

I began with remarks about sanity and art, their inter-relation, particularly concerning language. Tom shifted to his side.

"I have no theory of language essentially. But I have this—there's a thing that's fascinated me for years, a notion in Zen philosophy, which is that to name a thing is to kill it. And I've often used that as an excuse not to learn the names of plants and birds. But the Japanese—Chinese poets, too—felt often very relaxed about having no idea what the name of a thing was. And they would try to surround it with a kind of envelope of language rather than try to catalogue or tag it. But I do think the interesting thing about the use of words as a way of killing or holding reality in essentially a death grip, is that it is a key or an index to the way in which extreme language-oriented people like myself are people who are or have been fear-ridden."

What was this?

"I know that when I go back to the part of my life when I became fascinated with language—and this applies especially to comic language, and for a Catholic like myself, to the wonderful sonorities of Latinate language with the kind of comic echo that Joyce made a science of—within that kind of English language, it's a way of saving yourself. I mean, as a kid, I was afraid of absolutely everything, and now that I've grown up, I'm only afraid of most things."

"You want to elaborate on that?"

"Yeah. It's like breaking the butterfly on the wheel, though. I don't think there's a lot to be made of the point. Except that we know how you remove fear from things by getting some kind of grip on them. Say you're afraid of snakes, even garter snakes. If you can get to the point that you can pick up the snake, you're going to cancel the fear. Language is a handhold on things more universally applicable than, say, physical contact. If you can name things, ridicule, surround, or conceptualize them within language, you can detoxify them for yourself to a great extent."

Born in 1939 to Irish Catholic parents who'd raised him on Grosse Isle, Michigan, near Detroit, Tom said, he'd attended a "crappy little parochial grade school" with eight kids in his graduating class, where he'd first become intimate with fear.

"I never went on any of those playground things, for instance. I mean I never had the nerve to go on the monkey bars or a swing. I was just totally afraid of other children. As a young kid I was a terrible student. I remember that I was so uninterested in reading that my parents tried to bribe me to read books."

"When did language come in as defense or escape?"

"I think that I began to escape from this world of terror—of other children and everything else—by becoming known as sort of a wit, as being a funny person. People began to like me for that. It was an excoriating sort of humor that was actually a kind of humor based on hostility...but it was so carefully funny that there wasn't much recourse for the victim. It was sort of a black humor, but people liked it, and they valued me for it. You know how all young boys want to be tough guys. Well I was a tough guy because I said a lot of outrageous, unrepliable things."

The genesis of a hipster. "Can you remember when you started doing that? The actual point? Of using language as a club?"

Tom smiled. "It isn't anything much more profound than discovering the ability to talk your way out of things."

An artist conceived.

"My earliest memory is of being in some kind of terrible trouble in school. And the monsignor came over to deal with me. He took me off into this little room. Instead of just attacking me he decided to come in from an unusual angle. And his angle was: Exactly what is it you want to do with yourself, McGuane? We don't know what to do with you. You're a problem to everybody, and—what do you plan to do? Because we don't have any idea how to cope with you. So...I told him that I was in some distress at that time because my conduct, my sociopathic side, seemed to be at odds with my desire to become a Jesuit. Well, this was a complete lie. But what I knew was that he would say to himself: My God, here's my chance to reform a real stinker and turn him into a really energetic priest. I remember watching him swallow this whole thing hook, line, and sinker. And to me it was like cracking the atom."

Tom had spent childhood summers in Fall River, Massachusetts, at his grandmother's house, where crazy uncles pitchforked malarkey around the kitchen and a story of more than two lines was met with open derision. "My concept of paradise for a long time was to be in my grandmother's kitchen. I had one uncle who would come to the door, after not having seen me for ten months, look at me very solemnly and say: Tommy, remember, you're among friends and this is no clambake. Then he'd turn on his heel. He just knew how exciting the absolutely ludicrous or absurd was. You'd stand there dismayed, and by that time he'd be on the second floor. He might hang out the window and say: Remember that. Then he'd vanish and you might not see him for a day. That used to absolutely fascinate me. So language, playing around with it, became a happy place to live, almost. Just in the sense that now, when I'm writing a novel, however grim, I'm absolutely happy. For me there's no suffering associated with writing. Except touching pain centers, stuff like that."

Tom shifted.

"What's happening with your life now?"

"I haven't been writing for a while, and I just barely have a kind of grip on my existence, you know, from not having written for about five months. But I feel confident of kind of pulling it out of the fire. In fact, this week, for this first time in five months, I've written fiction. And it's just, it's absolutely, it's...it's...for me, writing is literally a matter of mental survival. If I were unable to write for two years, I'd definitely be a psychopath."

"What happens in your head when you're not writing?"

"I'm trying to write, very often. Or I must say, recently, like in the last couple of years, I've tried quite a lot *not* to write, because writing can become kind of an emotional panacea for me. Not necessarily directed toward good writing. It's a way of staying happy. So as I get into the middle of my life I find that one of the tough things about this era is that I now have to make real choices about that. I can't simply write because I need or want to write. I really have to constrain myself to writing when there's something to be said. The easiest, the laziest, most self-placating thing I could do would be to just hit the machine all day every day."

"What's the new novel like?"

"Well...it's in the first person...and about somebody really having trouble with his mind. This guy seems to be unable to get into specifics on anything. For instance, he has a dog who's dying of old age in this book, and he's not named it yet. And he has this relationship with this lady that's gone on for years and years, and he's had a period of taking too many drugs. He's talking to her, and she makes some sort of remark about their marriage. And it absolutely baffles him. He says: What marriage? And she says: Panama in 1967, and I can prove it. Then he goes on, the whole point's dropped. Sort of later in the novel, she brings the papers over, you know, and he looks and he puzzles over his signature, and he says: You're absolutely right. But he notices things on another level. And I associate mental health in myself with the noticing of all those things."

"Noticing what?"

"What people do. How birds move. What trees birds pick, around here, when the wind changes angles, so they can keep turned into the wind and keep feeding. Why they stand on one leg. I'll pick up that stuff all the time when I'm in a good mood and I'm working and my energy's going well. When I'm not, I don't notice anything. The car runs out of gas all the time. I forget to look at the gas gauge. And I guess I associate a kind of solidity with intense observation."

"Even when you're writing? If you get up from your desk and go out, do you still notice those things?"

"Well sometimes I carry that thing around all the time. But a typical observation in this novel, from this character's point of view, would be: Something shot by, a car—or something. Like he's at a place where he really wouldn't make that much of a distinction between a car and a pancake."

I mulled that over. "Right. That's where I am now."

"That's a tough place to be. I'm a little bit in that, because I've been just slopping around and not taking pains."

A knock on the study door. "Oh, here's Margot."

Kidder, the new bride, was lovely in a bright western blouse and snug Levi's. They talked a moment about horse shopping. "I want to buy a colt for you as your wedding present," Kidder said. "That horse that's for sale for $2,500, that seems to be the one to buy, doesn't it?"

"Well, I need like ten of them. But that's the best."

"Well, why don't we get the best for your wedding present, and then you can get the rest with your own money?" She chuckled.

"Okay—we'll get it figured out."

Kidder said she'd called a friend the previous night, looking for Tom.

"You did?"

"I called Morris wondering where you were. We had a nice jolly laugh. I was drunk as a skunk."

"Gee." Tom turned toward me. "Margot said, 'I'm going to bed at eight o'clock.' And I said, 'I'm sure not going to sit around here chewing my nails until I feel sleepy.' So I said, 'I'm going to go ride around in the truck and listen to tapes and watch the sun go down...then go up Mill Creek and drink in my old bar at Pray.' So anyway I got into trouble."

Kidder smirked. "I suddenly woke up and then sat there waiting for him to come back so we could go out drinking. And I was sitting there with my bottle of wine—one of those gallon jugs—by the fire listening to Waylon Jennings, first getting excited at the idea that I'd woken up and he was going to come right out of the woodwork..."

"And I would know this telepathically in my truck out on the American highway."

"...this after two-and-a-half days of no sleep at all, the two of us. By eleven-thirty I figured he was off being gang-banged by a bunch of women, and I got totally morbid and took some knock-me-out drug and put grease over my face and locked Tom out of the bedroom."

"I came walking in," McGuane said, "and I went to the upstairs door and it was locked. I said, 'What the hell's going on?'" They both laughed. "Anyway, that's what they call crashing."

They made plans to shop, and Kidder departed.

"Nothing like talking about yourself to liven things up," Tom said.

Again, about his new novel: "Do you have a working title?"

"Oh, my God, I've had a bunch. *Eleven Ways to Nigger Rig Your Life* is the present one. It was called *Fuck All That* for a while. It was called *Third Mourner from the Left*. "

It would be called *Panama*. "What's this character do?"

"This character—one of the things I'm going to do all the way through the novel is, you absolutely never really know what he does. What you know—the main thing— is that he has been some kind of stupendous success. I mean the kind of person who was literally almost killed by mobs in places like Tokyo and Ankara. You just don't have any idea why. And what's happened is he's in his home town, you know, where he was the creepiest person in town before this happened to him. I mean, there's a kind of life that can be led in our time because of our communications and the number of people on our planet, the kinds of lives in which you can essentially nova in your mid-twenties, and then you have this incredible task of reconstituting yourself. And that's kind of what it's about. Say Fitzgerald or Faulkner or Hemingway or Ford Madox Ford might open a novel, in the way in which they intended to exemplify the age, by having a man coming back from war. And World War I was apparently a war that had an enormous force for horrifying people at a very, very fundamental level. I have a feeling, with the perceptions that these people grew up with, and came to war with, that the horror was unbelievable—the first World War. I think it was probably much worse than Vietnam. Not because it was a worse war. Vietnam was a worse war. But I think the kind of Novocain factor in our era is such that you're just not set up to be really horrified the way they were."

"Right."

"But I think—we have another thing going on. We have this kind of ambient war of souls and spirits and minds that exists in a kind of zone, like the war zone that Mailer proposes be set up as a permanent part of planetary society. I think there's a war zone, and I don't really know very much about it. But I know that it's out there, and I know that I've been in and out of it, and I know to enough of an extent—that I want to write for a couple of years about it. I know that I've had a kind of shell shock, and received a kind of damage."

"You talking about movies and the success of your books?"

"No. I was never in a place where success was going to do anything except produce a check. I've never lived in a place where I got a lot of adulation. I remember walking into Elaine's and getting a lot one time. I remember how startled and shocked I was. Being buddied-up to by older novelists, things like that. And I remember thinking: Jesus, if you were living in New York and you had a successful book come out, you probably could get yourself all fucked around by this. Because you'd get into it if you were at all flatterable, or liked people and wanted to be liked. And then it's like coke or something. It's one of those things where you keep snorting it up—and you find that you can't get off."

"Say more about this war zone."

"The war zone I think is really this. I mean—war is kind of an effluent from a cultural uproar. And increasingly, we will manage to civilize ourselves to the place where we won't have wars anymore. But what we do have right now is cultural uproar. And we have another kind of effluent. We're living in a kind of regressive period right now. But I think in this strange kind of symmetrical way, turning twenty in 1960 and thirty in 1970 as I did, I can sort of see the grand scale running up through those ten years. And I know that the center did not hold in the sixties. And what happened is the culture went apart like a frag grenade. I mean it just literally did. And I think what happens is that you begin parceling yourself out, your spirit or whoever you are, into the gambles you are taking on what the cutting edge of the best life you could lead was. And you took terrible risks with yourself, and you paid terrible prices. I'm not—I mean, drugs is one of the least impactful aspects of that. I went into the sixties a fairly ordinary Midwesterner wanting to be an old-fashioned American novelist. I had an absolute model nuclear marriage and compact family, with no sense of missing anything. And by the time it was over, my wife, my family, my sense of myself, my belief in a set of standards in anything that anybody did in the world, et cetera, had all completely fallen apart."

"Due to—"

"I don't know. I'm trying to find out. That's really why I'm writing the book. And that's why I have to rewrite it and rewrite it and rewrite it. Because I'll only start to find out in that first draft. The reason I think I can write the book now is that I feel I'm on the other side. And the reconstruction is beginning. And it's going to be successful. What's peculiar is that I have the feeling I might just reconstruct what I was doing fifteen years ago."

"In terms of writing?"

"Writing and my life. And everything."

Twenty-five years ago Tom had been a radically skinny kid growing up in Michigan, where his father was a salesman. In the ten years or so before he decided to become a writer, he would suffer various metamorphoses. The most notable his slipping from a fear-ridden grade schooler toward a more aggressive, nearly sociopathic teenager.

"The house I lived in was 135 years old. A very beautiful place. Grosse Ile Jim Harrison defined perfectly as sort of the Midwest's equivalent of Tidewater. It was a resort before the Civil War, and an extremely Protestant kind of place. Not upper-middle-class Protestant, but Joe Midwest Protestant. And we were Catholics, and I think all us Catholic kids felt funny about being Catholic. We'd get a lot of riding, you know, and that kind of ridicule."

Tom had brothers and sisters, "but I didn't feel terribly close to them. Until I was in about the fourth or fifth grade, I lived in total terror. I mean I couldn't ask to go to the bathroom. So for like the first three or four years in school, I just wet my pants every single day in school, which made me sort of famous. And I had a collection of turtles which were my friends. I used to bring them to school in a box, and I had them all named. I had about five different kinds of turtles I brought everywhere, and the safety patrol—when I was in the third grade—the two safety patrol guys, the kids with the white bands, took my turtles away from me and at forty-five miles an hour splatted them one after another on the highway. Which is—and I'll never escape this—the beginning, middle, and end of my impression of authority. That's absolutely the way I feel about authority at all levels. And I'll never escape it, even if I reason my way around it."

He nearly flunked his first year of high school. He got into trouble; went to jail for being drunk and disorderly, concealed weapons. "I was hanging out with hoodlums, had a ducktail haircut, and you know, we used to get beer and go out in the swamps and spear pike at night. And break into boarded-up houses, steal copper tubing, and sell it to the junkyards and buy camshafts for our hotrods. And, I mean, something had changed by then." Tom's parents, alarmed, got it together to send him to an okay boarding school: Cranbrook, thirty miles from their house. "I arrived right in the middle of the Ivy League era. Everybody had crew-neck shirts, and they had J. Press and Brooks Brothers outfits, and I arrived in blue suede Flag Flyer shoes, you know—I had the kind you flipped open instead of laced. I had my ducktail haircut, a James Dean red nylon jacket, flyer's glasses, and believe me, was I ever out of place. I was in immediate trouble at the end of my first term. From then on I spent virtually half or three-quarters of the rest of my time on what they called probation. What that meant was that the few privileges you had as a boarding school student were cut by about two-thirds. I was also on what they called the Unsat List, 'unsatisfactory.' Which meant you sat in—year round—study hall on Saturday. Then Sunday, because I was Catholic, I had all these numbers I had to do with the Catholics. We had this priest who came to school; it was an Episcopal school, and he was very keen to make sure that the Catholics really stood up against these Protestant dogs. So I had a week of school, you know, classes. Saturday I sat in study hall for being an unsatisfactory student. And then I had this shit-heel priest who'd come around, and we'd go to mass, and have special meetings about what it meant to be a Catholic."

Nevertheless, Tom's interests were beginning to shift.

"All I had succeeded in doing before I went to boarding school was becoming a hoodlum. And getting into trouble. I mean, I wasn't even popular. I was an unpleasant kid, essentially. Somehow or other with that radical change of moving away to school, I got a kind of fresh start. On a *social* level, between me and my contemporaries. It was a boys' school. I had been quite unsuccessful as a young Lothario. I just wasn't good at that. I was essentially afraid of girls and didn't have the nerve for the dating game. Then suddenly I was thrown into a boys' boarding school. And that contact, that kind of male contesting in the presence of women in a public school, was something I was a failure at. That game was suddenly removed from the atmosphere. It was an all male world for the next three years and I was sort of successful in that world. I was considered funny, and as kind of a hood I quickly reformed and adopted some coloration. But people were fascinated by me, you know, because they hadn't stolen cars and stuff like that."

"You were still telling stories. Sort of leaning on language?"

"Yeah. My room was where everybody hung out and bullshitted about how much they'd get off chicks. Like: 'What'd you get off her?'—'Uh, I got a little covered tit, I dunno'—things like that. 'Well how'd you do last week?'—'Well, shit, that's what pissed me off. Last week I got covered box and covered titties, and fuck, this week I spent twice as much time and I only got covered tit.'—'Well could you French kiss her?'—'Yeah, she went for everything. It's just the whole thing about the snatch really put her off. I don't know what it was.'— 'Well I heard Al Smith was out with her Wednesday, and he finger fucked her, and it wasn't even *dark*.' And: 'Are you serious? He finger fucked her and it wasn't dark?' So anyway at that point I would get to say something like: 'Oh shit, I wouldn't fuck her with your dick.' And we'd talk dirty a lot. Also, I met two or three guys who wanted to be writers and who'd read a lot of books, and I got put onto kind of a reading list."

Boarding schools during the fifties were such stultifying places that anyone interested in language turned instinctively toward two immediate escapes: bullshitting and reading. Hip language as art derived from the bull session; in prep school those sessions were dormitory equivalent to street-corner jive, primers in expressing oneself with brevity and wit. Reading followed, for one could not bullshit forever, one would deplete energies, short-circuit any will to survive. Reading was the principal escape, nearly one's sole entertainment. There was no television at boarding school, there were few movies. One had the radio with its lifeblood of rock 'n' roll, one had reading, and one had bullshit. If one was hip one also had Style—a sense of presence which broached theatricality, presence itself an artistic mode of expression. What the budding hipster carried to boarding school, from years of home TV and access to movies, were role-models of mythic cowboys, silent, graceful, World War II soldiers barking a language closer to that our fathers spoke, and actors such as James Dean, Marlon Brando and Montgomery Clift, whose outrageous mumblings and defiant garb were tantalizingly contemporary. Throw in a Carl Perkins or an Elvis Presley, you had the stew. Prep school was prison, a limbo between infantilism and the adult gratification of infantile goals. The hipster could do little but fantasize. He could express himself through bullshit or he could lose himself in books. Mostly he groped through a fantasy-theater of unrealized opportunities, thwarted drives. That was prep school; that was the nineteen-fifties. Sixties culture (and college) would explode fantasized theatricality into the street. But this was 1955 and no clambake. McGuane sniffed around the books.

It's ironic that Tom's first exposure to "serious" reading was the decadent tradition in European literature: Huysmans, Oscar Wilde, Proust, Lautréamont. McGuane the hood. Tom had found a mentor, a bookish kid—now the author, Edmund White—who was "blatantly queer." He was impressed with Tom's bullshit and thought he possessed some kind of verbal brilliance. "This guy was absolutely, incredibly precocious, and he'd read everything. I mean, by ninth and tenth grade he'd read all of Dostoyevsky, Proust, Tolstoy, which was pretty remarkable for a sixteen-year-old." Tom at this time nursed a kind of secret life as a writer—he kept a notebook. "I wanted to be a writer by then. I think because it struck me as a very romantic life. It wasn't so much that I wanted to write. It was because I wanted to *be* a writer." Prep school theatricality. "I'd gradually begun to see the life of the writer as being the ultimate kind of free life. I had this thing about authority—which I am not jacking up for autobiographical interest. I am almost totally incapable of dealing with authority. Teachers, police officers, political figures, everything. It's been a huge force in my life. So I began at a very primordial level to try to figure out a way of never having to have a boss of any kind. Also, at that time, I was smoking dope. Now that was nineteen fifty-six, fifty-seven. I didn't know anybody else who was smoking dope, and therefore I concluded that I was a junkie."

Tom had become tremendously interested in jazz. When free, he would drive any distance to hear it. He was playing drums, taking lessons from a jazz drummer who would supply marijuana. "I used to go to Toledo. And in those days it was great, because you could go to, you know, very dense black neighborhoods and hang out in the bars and listen to bluesmen and stuff like that. I did that a lot. Also, all my sexual beginnings lie in that world. All the women I hung out with in any sexual sense, until I was maybe twenty, were black whores. I knew a lot of black whores, and they were like friends of mine. And—I look back on those years, the academic part was no fun, and I came away pretty unhappy about schooling—but I must say I had good friends in school, and I felt liked. I'd really started to come out of whatever my shadow had been before then. I felt kind of strong and ambitious about trying to do some of the things that I wanted to do and had kept secret."

"What sort of writing did you crank out in prep school?"

"Mostly melancholy stories about lost youth. They were just awful. I had two awful periods. My first was that, when I also wrote this lachrymose poetry about autumnal themes. Then when I went to college I became a beatnik."

Tom enrolled in the University of Michigan, where he flunked out with a 0.6 on the four-point system. He managed to con himself into Olivet, a country college which financially was so poor nearly anyone could get in, but academically was rather good. There Tom received his first adult encouragement to be a writer. He received certain privileges for spending time writing. He was experimenting with plays then. He transferred back to Michigan, flunked out again, and returned to Olivet. Then he attended Harvard summer school, taking a heavy load of courses centered about writing, and got spectacular grades. He took Harvard's advanced writing course: "I was young and scared, and all these other people were older and very sophisticated kind of East Coast people. And I got a lot of encouragement. At that time I was very much under the influence of beat writers, primarily Jack Kerouac. Which was a very unconstipating way of getting at writing. I probably wrote three hundred pages that summer. I mean I wrote continuously. I was also very heavily into southern lady writers: Carson McCullers, Katherine Anne Porter, Flannery O'Connor, Shirley Jackson, Eudora Welty. They were the best grotesque writers around, and I was very interested in grotesque writing in all forms. Nathanael West was a guy I liked a lot."

That was 1960. Tom had plans to be a writer. Planning to do anything was a scarifying notion, and even though Tom kept his writing self-consciously grotesque, hid behind a beat facade, he'd come to think being a writer "was the most splendid thing you could be in the world—it's still true—to me being a writer is the way some people feel about making the New York Yankees. I just wanted to be one so badly, it was a literal, absolute burning, consuming thing with me. At Harvard I explicitly asked my teacher with terrible fear: Do you think I could ever become a writer? And his reply was something to the effect that: Absolutely no question about it. If you can endure the waiting and keep writing. That literally blew my mind."

The University of Michigan, from which Tom had flunked out, then was considered the only Midwestern school with Ivy League standards. Its literary prize offered more than the Pulitzer. It had a large, self-conscious literary community, many poets, with a very stuffy literary scene. McGuane hadn't managed any cachet with that crowd. He went off to Michigan State, the cow college, and it had an okay English department. There he met other writers, so different from the pipe-smoking literati, that Tom sat back and took notice.

"They were these really *crude* sort of characters. Outrageous. And my impression was that they were much better writers than the ones at the University of Michigan. These characters were always shooting pool and getting thrown out of bars or throwing things through plate glass windows. I couldn't believe it, because we'd talk about writing and we'd get very excited, talk like maniacs about Apollinaire and we'd be gobbling these cheap steaks—we used to get these rotten steaks and marinate them in vinegar until you could get a knife through them, and we'd eat these things and shoot pool and buy Pfeiffer beer in what they called GIQs—Giant Imperial Quarts—and chug 'em, puke in our cars, and…it was the first time I was ever in a literary scene where I felt really happy with the kind of combination of the life and literature. We'd go to rallies of right-wing politicians and harass them by calling them fuckheads at the top of our lungs. It was pretty exhilarating. It was pretty exciting. It wasn't a bohemian literary scene. It was just characters."

Tom's ambition was some day to write a novel good enough to deserve that blurb he had observed on Dos Passos's *U.S.A.*: "An explosion in a cesspool." He was still being influenced by southern women writers and Nathanael West, he was slogging through his Jack Kerouac period, with a "phony Midwestern regional" period to follow, but the romance of simply being a writer had slipped toward the commitment of working a craft.

Tom's stages are worth repeating: Fear-ridden child discovering language as defense; hoodlum developing the patois of hip; beat dissolving into stream of consciousness, bop prosody of Kerouac, salted with Westian grotesque; convoluted hipster discovering pleasures of redneck unchic in agricultural literary milieu. By 1962, Tom had graduated from Michigan State and was accepted at the Yale School of Drama. Professionalism had set up shop.

"Somewhere along there the beginnings of the first really good influence on my particular needs as a writer came in—which were the classical European novelists. Those writers were Flaubert and Turgenev, mostly. They taught me that it was not enough simply to report that you had felt things. The conflict there was turning that line where you're trying to keep a kind of shapeliness in a novel and still keep that whole kind of kinetic energy driving into it at the same time, without one killing the other off. That seemed to be the important feat. It was the power- to-weight ratio in the novel that was its most important feature. That made me really concentrate on getting energy and strength into the most carefully made shape you could."

McGuane might have been speaking of building a race car. Or designing a rocket. Or otherwise delineating that early sixties fascination with mechanical construct which fell under the heading: Technology.

For subhead, read: Theater. Aristotle defined drama as "imitated human action," not a bad classification of that lull before the storm which affected American artists during the early sixties. For a young novelist, whose aesthetics were energy and compaction, playwriting was apt technical training. Tom's shift in interest from the self-consciously grotesque to the finer lines of classical European literature, paralleled, in painting, what would be the leap from abstract expressionism to pop art; in music, the leap from rhythm and blues to rock; in fashion, the leap from blue suede shoes to Pierre Cardin; and in cars, the leap from 1957 Chevies to Volkswagen Super Beetles. For the literary world, as with every layer of American culture, the early sixties provided a respite. Theater during the fifties had enjoyed a remarkable resurgence; off-Broadway boomed with success after success, the controversial writings of Williams, Genet, Weiss, Beckett, Ionesco, Pinter, Arrabal, Albee, Frisch and Duerrenmatt. During New York's 1961 to 1962 season, the *Times* counted one hundred off-Broadway productions, thirty-four more than on Broadway. A decline had begun by 1962 to 1963. Theater would remain the most powerful dramatic medium for exorcising cultural frustrations until those frustrations were primed to hit the street. But in between was that lull.

"I arrived at the Yale School of Drama just as the theater that interested me in America was dying. It was dying simultaneously with my education as a playwright. That was between 1962 and 1965. Plays—I still love them, I'd write them if there were a theater—to me, movies are plays. I consider my work in movies as the result of that part of me which wishes to be a playwright. By my second year at Yale, though, I had really lost interest in the theater. I was writing novels and just enough theater stuff to satisfy the academic requirements. The Yale School of Drama was really a dull place to be. It was that or the army."

Tom had simultaneously applied for fighter's school as he had applied to Yale. The power-to-weight ratio of the navy's monster Phantoms held that much fascination. But Yale came through and the technicalities of literature overrode those of bombadiering.

"The nature of things was that I stayed in school a long time. I used school in two ways. Once was to get a deferment from the draft, which was very important. There was no way I could have written novels in the army. Also, my father never gave me any money in a direct way, but he believed very strongly in education. He was a poor kid who went to Harvard on an athletic scholarship, and he saw education as being the panacea to everything. He had a deal with me, which was I think a very generous one. I could go to school anywhere I wanted, I could study anything I wanted, for as long as I wanted on a no-questions-asked basis, and he'd cover it. He'd open me a charge account at a bookstore, wherever I was in school, and provided I read everything that I bought, I could buy as many books as I wanted. Comparing that to going to Schenectady and writing the obituaries and doing your novel at night, it was ideal. There were a lot of kind of experiential things that beat novelists used to list on the backs of their books, you know; dishwasher, blocklayer, that kind of thing. Well, I didn't do any of that stuff. I worked on ranches, farted around a little bit. But mostly I was just an American idler. As soon as I got any kind of directed energy, it was toward preparing myself as a writer—and I would modestly say that I don't think I've met another novelist who knows as much about novels as I do. At one point I *technically knew* the novel métier. I knew it backwards and forwards. I had just read every bloody novel there was. It had become systematic. I was reading a novel a day, for I guess close to three years.

And in honing that technique, Tom found his life inverted. "I turned from a sociopath into a bookworm." He was exploiting the lull. Instead of laying back like most of the culture, he was laying into literature. "So my life as a writer was curiously reversed. Most writers would have, at twenty-six, suddenly decided to educate themselves, after having been oil-riggers or something. You know how that goes. What happened to me at twenty-six was I started to become a complete illiterate, and a barfly, and a junkie. I spent all my time fishing, getting drunk, hanging out, chasing women, just messing around. I've had periods in recent years where I literally can't even read a newspaper. Just absolute, almost pure illiteracy. Now things are starting to balance back."

Tom and Becky were married in 1962, the year he disappeared into literature at Yale. He quickly learned what a valuable tool was marriage in the technical kit of a writer.

"You know that line of Flaubert's: 'I live like a bourgeois so that I can write with passion.' That's very true. We didn't have any money, but I had a really good little bourgeois life, in the sense that I had three absolutely regular, well-cooked meals a day, and enough clothes, and enough room to get away from the noise to write. I'm in a very different situation right now. Margot has enormous ambitions of her own...she'll soon be going back to work. I'll kind of be cooking for myself. I no longer have the sense of that kind of perfect household for writing, and I have to find a little bit different way of doing it."

While at school—an extended foray which would lead Tom from Yale to the Scuola per Stranieri in Florence to Stanford, and which would not culminate until 1968 when *The Sporting Club* was sold—he exploited every technical aid accessible. He exploited his marriage, but most thoroughly, he exploited himself. His earlier "sociopathic" side, his hooliganism, hipsterism, his propensity toward the overtly theatrical, became sublimated in the systematic study of literature. By removing himself from "life" he believed he could master "art," and in doing so proved not much different from millions of white, middle-class males who had been suckered into the cure-all of formal education. And who were dodging the draft. The paradox here was wicked. They were being encouraged to remain in school because school was the ticket to perpetuation of that postwar wealth their parents enjoyed; simultaneously they were being denied the experience of war, thereby frustrating all horse-opera dreams of heroism. One might endure prep school if one played the hipster, college if one professed the beat, but grad school was a stymie. Especially during the mid-sixties. All one's psychic energy lay sublimated in technique. The mastery of "life" through technology, during those years, saturated the culture at large. Illicit passions lurked between the pages of typescript as surely as monster engines lay hidden beneath the hoods of family automobiles, blue jeans hung in closets behind three-piece suits, Richie Valens discs inserted themselves under insipid Ahmad Jamals, sex boiled, and legitimate theater sagged. Yet theater was impossible to kick. It was after all ritual, formalized expression of unspeakable practice. For the literary artist to abandon it would be to admit defeat. Or start dancing in the street.

The development of Tom's art throughout the sixties and early seventies was a case in point. Tom would write three novels before *The Sporting Club* was published in 1968, but parts of *Club* were written at Yale and theorizing on its construct was fomenting.

"I had been thinking back about plays. I was thinking about three-act plays, a form that really fascinated me. Because the proportions are something like sixty-forty-thirty in the acts, and there's a thing where you come out of the chaos of the original material with new information for the audience that culminates in this interesting way at the first-act curtain. Then there's a mysterious thing in the second act, which is this very strange zone in the play, and then a third act, which is the conclusion of the piece. And I was thinking in those terms. I was looking for a kind of novel, I mean a setup for a novel, in which you could isolate the usual inputs of the modem realistic novel. In other words I wanted an almost *theatrical* situation—to write a novel. I was going through my own experience, trying to think what I knew about in actuality that had that quality, and I suddenly thought of hunting and fishing clubs, which were these peculiar enclaves in the middle of forests, with people who don't belong there. And it's really theater. In life it's theater. It seemed to be absolutely perfect. Fundamentally there was something inescapably comic about it, and I didn't see how to write *The Sporting Club* except as a comedy, as a kind of savage comedy. It's the shapeliest of my novels, really."

The Sporting Club, though published in 1968, reflects sublimated conflicts of early to mid-sixties America precisely. The tone is a mixture of sixties jockishness and redneck vulgarity, cased in a Victorian preciosity which lends the drama shape. Two young men, one a conscientious businessman, the other an irascible idler, joust about a gossamer female character and, in their fumbling, manage to hurry the collapse of a one-hundred-year-old sporting club...the republic, symbolically...with assist from a bizarre outlaw hero: a post-cowpoke, pre-redneck, seller of bait. There are Harley-Davidson motorcycles and expensive fly rods all gone up in smoke. The scenery is quintessentially McGuane. As in most of his work, two principal characters represent the split in Tom's nature between pragmatist and sociopath. Or businessman and dreamer. Or realist and artist. In no later work, however, is the split so neat. And it fits sixties culture to a T.

"The kind of fiction I write is one in which the line

between autobiography and pure fiction is laminated. Those two panels are laminated in a way which is the secret of the author. One of the things people wonder about my books is whether or not they're autobiographical. And the answer is: yes and no. They're autobiographical where it suits my purposes, and they're not where it doesn't. Our best writers have always done that. We live in a fast-forming civilization, and artists are always going to be people who are telling you about their lives to some extent. We're not really situated to produce an art-for-art's-sake type of novel culturally."

Tom's life had begun to change by 1971 when *The Bushwhacked Piano* appeared. He had forsaken school, had been shuttling semi-annually between Livingston and Key West—and the road burn showed. *Bushwhacked* is nearly Rabelaisian in tone, if one can imagine that monk suited in Kerouac denims with a side order of sixties roiling in his gut. "One book for me is always a reaction to the previous. I got very interested in picaresque novels, all the way from Lazarillo de Tormes and *Don Quixote* to Gogol. And I got fascinated by the *idea* of picaresque novels. I was reading Fielding all the time, *Tom Jones*...I got interested in English sloppiness in fiction. *Tristram Shandy* was a book I liked very much at the time. And instead of trying to plan a novel—as I had done in *The Sporting Club*, on a three-act play—instead of trying to get a projectile shape for a novel, I began to be interested in a paste-up kind of book."

The late sixties was nothing if not paste-up, and by 1970 when Tom was adding final touches to *Bushwhacked* the culture was certainly picaresque. The long-sublimated drives toward sex, speed, violent sport, war and unfettered art had split America like an overripe melon. Everyone had his role. Theater had gushed into the street, either through formalized demonstrations, costumes, unshakable positions, or Dionysian revel. The tone of *Bushwhacked* is late sixties, but its themes and time frame are set back. *Bushwhacked*'s characters struggle against an impending chaos by hanging on to earlier conceptions of rebellion. Notably, sociopathic prep-school hipsterism and a dilettantish indulgence in art. Art is attacked most desperately in *Bushwhacked*. The piano symbolizes America, bushwhacked since Columbus with unfair assaults on its potential. Most contemptuously by business and art. The drygulchery of art here is vivisected by McGuane as thoroughly as that of business. One encounters the usual sociopathic protagonist, railing against these extremes. There is his artistic foil. But a curious amalgamation occurs in the form of a third character, a pest control magnate bent on "curing" America with a prophylactic chain of coast-to-coast bat towers. His target is mosquitoes but his intention is bloodsuckers. C. J. Clovis is an entrepreneur and something of a charlatan, but he is foremost a romantic, an American businessman with an artistic dreaminess about him which McGuane applauds. At *Bushwhacked's* conclusion, art, in its popular guise, remains an escape from reality, and experience for experience's sake remains unmoored sociopathy. There is no resolve. Clovis, the pest-control magnate, dies consummating a fraud, his heart "on the fritz."

About this time, Tom had started to make money. He had sold *Sporting Club* to the movies and was writing screenplays himself. For ten years he had stuck with fiction; he had stayed broke. A certain uneasiness was attendant to receiving those large checks.

"The vanity of literary poverty is pervasive," Tom said. "But making money's fun. Especially the first couple of times it happens. I'm a pretty good businessman, which is something that I guess until recently I felt fairly embarrassed about as a writer."

His father was a businessman, a tycoon in fact; in the larger sense all our fathers had been businessmen, bricking up the postwar economy to stifling heights—so far as we were concerned. To be an artist during the late fifties-early sixties and lust after Mammon was less than despicable. It was Eisenhoweresque. Yet those artists who

169

came to maturity in the mid-sixties toiled under a more complex imperative. Just as WWII had produced hip—a post-Holocaust aura of doom, war heroes to emulate and a war ethos to protest—so had it engendered in the sixties artist a powerful drive to pull in the cash. If our dads had proved heroic in their mission to save us from fascism, they had been equally heroic in their rescue of a prewar economy from postwar depression. But to make money was so *unhip* for the fifties artist. His sixties counterpart felt the same negative ions but was jostled in contradictory spheres.

To be a success at art, outside cultism, one had best have the business acumen of a Colonel Tom Parker and the presumption of an Elvis Presley to back it up. One had to sell one's product even as one need sell oneself, and this was the great lesson of Pop. Born of fifties adsmanship, Pop Art said, "See me, I'm simple, I'm ironic; buy me, I'm expensive but I'm hip—you're in on the joke." It's not insignificant that Bob Dylan's association with Andy Warhol led to his embracement of Pop, its aesthetics and munificence. Dylan's father, like McGuane's, had been a hard-driving businessman. Dylan's business sense during the sixties separated him from a dozen other talented songwriters, propelling him to the top of the heap. As Dylan, Warhol, and later McGuane lampooned the business ethos, they profited from it. It was hip to rip off a stooge. Take the money and run. It was all part of the carnival, sideshow atmosphere of the 1960s. That was it on the surface. But running deeper was that fiercer imperative: beat dad at his game by flinging it in his face. The outlaw notion in popular culture thereby was born, where artists like Dylan and Peckinpah were literally "knocking over the stage," then hightailing it to the badlands.

All this of course was contrary to any notion of serious literature. It smacked of bestsellerdom. Tom was not ready to compromise there, but he was willing to reevaluate theater, his notions thereof, and opportunities for recompense. Hollywood beckoned, as did Key

West and its more immediate avenue of street theater. Key West during the early seventies was a microcosm of American culture. At land's end, it attracted a special breed of zany...cloaking any style of specious behavior in a gauziness that decried pretension. Tom reverted to "sociopathy," became a "junkie" and a "barfly," fished the live-long day and consorted with loose women. This phantasmagoria he intensified with work in movies—a medium phantasmagorical itself, less real than theater, more fantastic, but closer somehow to the street. You made movies in the street and people walked in off the street to view them. "There are these great physical excitements about moviemaking," Tom said. "It's thrilling." You were taking theater to the streets, yet maintaining control, through a phantasmagorical medium. Movies' manufacture, direction, editing and photography were highly technical. To say nothing of their marketing. You needed the vision but you likewise needed the business sense. Making movies was like waging war, Tom would say. There was something Napoleonic about the adventure.

McGuane undertook that adventure in its totality only after *Ninety-Two in the Shade* had appeared as literature. Published in 1973, the novel (perhaps his best) proved an apex of Tom's technical approach to fiction—and it was hazy, jump-cut, like a movie. It was not unlike TV. Its passages were brief, as if to accommodate commercials— there were regular spaces in the narrative—and the prose shimmied with the opacity of television, colorful as Cousteau, caustic as Johnny Carson. Though that comparison is unfair: *confident* as Johnny Carson, with his chilled irony and technical expertise. Tom's drive into fiction had remained technical throughout the 1960s. As had other sixties technocrats, he'd applied technology to his work like a hot shot. The emphasis was on technical description, lyrical prose, little obvious emotion, everything technically funny and bright. Hemingway, of course, was the godfather in American letters of technical precision.

He showed how much could be hidden, emotionally, with a paucity of words. There was no paucity to McGuane's prose, it was flat out, full bore, technologically perfect overload. He was masking demons in his life: tensions of marriage, art, art's seclusion. His novels emerged as subliminally supercharged and as loaded for bear as sixties cars, sport, sex, rockets and Airborne Rangers. McGuane's technologizing would never approach that of more academic novelists—John Barth, say, whose *Lost in the Funhouse* he'd subtitled *Fiction for Print, Tape, Live Voice*—but it would remain aloof.

Ninety-Two in the Shade is simultaneously a monument to aloofness and precision, in life as well as art. It is about commitment. "What I tried out in *Ninety-Two* was the idea of commitment at an abstract level. Instead of taking the position that one's commitments will be a continually negotiated and continually supple approach to eventualities, what if one were to take one's commitments as being final and make that a basis for a kind of comfort and sanity, knowing that you were not always negotiating? This, I suppose, is not really all that far from Hemingway's idea of honor being that you would do what you said you would do, or something like that. But it's not the same thing."

For a novel set in Key West which concerns fishing and violence, an intentional piece of neglect is the omission of so much as Ernest Hemingway's name. Two fishing guides, one pragmatic, the other a dreamer, fumble to shape the destiny of a third younger guide, who looks to encroach upon their trade. This younger guide, Tom Skelton, seeks some mooring in his life above which he might anchor contradictory tendencies toward sociopathy and responsibility. Or dreaminess and precision, or imagination and conscious "reality." Or ocean and dry land. One of these guides, Nichol Dance, is a murderer and redneck sociopath, "an incessant addict of long shots," whose style of guiding Skelton favors. The other, Faron Carter, is a model of civic virtue, emblematic of

Key West's business world. Due to a complication in plot and the vile scheming of Carter, Skelton, and Dance are faced off—with the upshot that Dance forbids Skelton to guide. Skelton, whose family oddly mirrors conflicts of that business world he hopes to join, sticks by his guns. So does Nichol Dance. Skelton guides and Dance blows him away, is in turn blown away by Skelton's client. Both men die for "doing what they said they would do," and the business world profits. Skelton, the McGuane character if such can be named, is notably tragic. His maturity has been marked by a comprehension of extremes—between his father, the helpless dreamer, and his grandfather, the tyrannical tycoon, and between Carter and Dance. He is nearly a happy compromise, a harbinger of the seventies, yet he dies as the decade begins. His murderer should have been his pal.

"The novel was not so much pessimistic as it was critical," Tom said. "It was critical of a cultural situation in which we exist in this country, a cultural situation which puts people who should be friends on homicidal courses." Skelton, the prescient ex-freak, and Dance, the redneck dreamer, should have come together. In Tom's life, and perhaps the culture's, they had. That was the deeper meaning to Redneck Chic. Its layer of sincerity. It shadowboxed around commitment.

"I still believe—and I'm working this out in the novel I'm writing now—that you have to have some fundamental known things in your life that sometimes exist in the form of personal assertions that are the données of your going on, and that if you're always in the position of negotiating those things, then you'll never be sane.

"So if somebody says, 'How do you feel about killing people—you're about to go to war'—and you say, 'I'll figure that out when I get into that situation,' I consider that an absolutely insane position. I believe unless you bank that idea, or you bank that conviction, or you bank that commitment, you're continually in a kind of quicksand. I think it's better to be wrong, and then if necessary have circumstances demonstrate with their absolutely peculiar brutality that you are wrong—at which point you may have to make some kind of reassembly of your posture.

"As time goes by, I become more extremely interested in the idea of a *subject* in writing. I think the most interesting subject in fiction is the attempt to assert a code of life, a kind of personal metaphysic, that you can try out in the form of a novel. And one of the most dramatic things about a novel to me is very often watching that thing arise and succeed or fail. Right now, that's mainly what interests me in the idea of writing fiction. I mean that notion that Camus had that it takes a man ten years to develop a single idea with which he's comfortable. That's a very salubrious notion to me. I'm not looking for a complicated, systematic world view. I'm looking for some fairly simple tools of survival that can be demonstrated, not only to a reader who matters, but to oneself, in the forms of fiction—which is a real test track for that kind of thing, in terms of your own thinking."

In the film version of *Ninety-Two,* Tom changed his ending. Dance fails to kill Skelton and the two men emerge from their jousting as friends. It was 1974—the culture might have changed. Tom filmed his ending both ways, backing up the reconciliation with Skelton's and Dance's deaths. It would be 1975 and a winter of editing before Tom finally decided.

"*Ninety-Two in the Shade* is just a wonderful example of book-into-movie for me, because I wanted to try out a different set of conclusions with the same evidence and see if I could make them plausible. Whether or not I succeeded at that is another question."

His conclusions may have succeeded, but, it is generally agreed, his movie did not. Tom had the vision but he lacked the technical expertise. He technically could not pull off, on film, what he had on paper. He would spend a week in Livingston Memorial with a bleeding ulcer for his pains. Yet he learned.

"A movie, like a book, has its own gestalt, which in

some sense is immutable. It rolls forward and has a way of finding its own shape, as a book does, when you're writing it. Moviemaking is very much less intense, emotionally; when you're writing a novel the excitement of creation is much hotter and clearer. As for changing *Ninety-Two's* ending—my novels I consider as being very non-monumental. They're checkpoints on a kind of developmental curve. The conclusions are tentative, and because my life is changing at a very fast rate, I don't see why I should pretend to be speaking ex cathedra when I sit down and write a novel. It's very important for me to make it clear that I'm not sure about anything, but here's what I think. I have absolutely no fear or regret about contradicting myself."

The business of literature, combined with the business of running a ranch, seemed to have eclipsed the allure of film making. For McGuane the artist, fiction survived as the more attractive medium. He'd set certain aesthetics: his new novel would be in the first person, employ fewer technological ruses, and prove more heartfelt.

"I think the part of me that is sensible, the part that's most on the nose about making decisions about how and what to write, is the part which wants to continue working toward the Turgenev model in fiction. Which is simply based on the idea that novels have to be extremely efficient to survive. Also I think that one has no right to waste other people's time. That's really my main aesthetic conviction right now.

"I want to write a novel that contains important information which I can conceivably represent as *being* important. I want to write a novel that will represent whatever it is I've learned about living. And I want to write a novel which will be hyperspecific, and which will have some utility, you know. I'm not interested in writing a novel to dazzle or entertain right now. Reading Jim Harrison's novel *Farmer* was like a glass of ice water being thrown in my face. It had the pleasant quality of cleansing my eyes about literature at a time when it seemed like everything I picked up was sort of anticipatable or dull. Also, the fact that I had really not been getting anything done that I cared about for a while—to read something, a piece of work written straight from the heart, without any cheating, by my best friend, had not a little of the quality of reproach about it. There are books that remind me immediately of the extreme importance and dignity of the profession of writing. To me that novel improved the world. It's like if I go out here in a field where horses or deer are running around and I pull up a lot of rusty wire which will eventually catch the animal's leg and kill it, that *improves the world.* That's the way I feel about Harrison's novel. That's the way I feel about some things in some of my books that I've written. I feel that they've opened eyes, or they've opened perceptions. And that's kind of what I want to do. But I don't want to be Baba Ram Dass. I want to do it in those terms that I know."

Tom shifted on the couch, sat up, rubbed his eyes. "I have absolutely one major theme, which is: Why go on? It's been rephrased by lots of people. I almost think it's the master theme of literature. It's the thing that Camus said: There's only one serious philosophical question, and that's the question of suicide."

"Will what you've learned in these past years alter your life as an artist—how you go about getting things done—in any significant fashion?"

"The only thing is—here's one thing I know: that the perfect situation for a writer to work in is one that's tremendously diminishing to the people that he lives with. And I find it so hard to approve of any kind of a life situation in which there is a support team of two or three human beings for the prince." Tom laughed. "I mean I haven't got the conscience to do that anymore—especially now that I see it for what it is."

Fall descended upon Paradise Valley. Snow powdered the Absarokas, cottonwoods yellowed, cowboy hats molted from straw to felt, pillowy vests sprung from their vertebrae like winter fur, and fishing rods transmogrified to firearms as window dressing for pickup trucks. Tourists vacated Livingston's motels. Except for a few hunters and old men who lived at the Murray, I was alone there. Livingston's bars stayed lively, but the wind had frost in it and on hikes outside town you made certain you carried extra clothing. The high school football team played every Saturday, supplanting rodeo as Livingston's sporting concern. I shot grouse with Gatz Hjortsberg, fished mindlessly, and wondered why I didn't move along. In response to the season a slew of onetime Key Westers—McGuane's retinue—arrived, invading Brautigan's and McGuane's spare bedrooms like tide.

Tom brightened the moment Jimmy Buffett hit town. The two enjoyed a week of private frolicking before communalized festivities began. Tom and Jimmy had shared Key West in those years before they or the town came to symbolize excesses in seventies sharecropping. Key West had been a town where the sixties lingered through the early seventies, and where, unobtrusively and without camp, anything went. McGuane and Buffett had produced their best work there; in fiction and in song they had done more to mythologize the island than any artist since Ernest Hemingway.

I met Buffett one afternoon stooped beside a sawhorse near Tom's study, Lexoling an antique saddle. "You're the last decent reviewer I've got," Jimmy said, laughing over something I'd written for the Washington *Post*. Jimmy's recent album had not received favorable reviews, and though his career was progressing his creativity backpedalled. He looked healthy. He was tan, his blond hair was sun-bleached, and he affected a gold earring. He looked a trifle fancy for Montana. But I'd been away from the world awhile, certainly any world so fancy as Aspen.

Buffett was in Montana for a breather, to visit Tom, to shop for esoterica such as that forty-year-old saddle, a reliable Winchester, antique Indian rug for a house he was buying in Snowmass...but also for a conference on that screenplay envisioned, *Mangrove Opera*, about redneck smugglers in the Everglades. I did not hear them discuss that movie. They were saddling up for a ride when a hailstorm broke, spooking horses and dropping a curtain of translucent hailstones between ourselves and the setting sun. The spectrum was revealed; even a rainbow. "Spectacular," Tom said. I plucked iced beers from my cooler and we four, Margot included, hoofed it to the stable. Ankle deep in manure, seated on troughs and hay bales, we waited out the lightning—bullshitted about sailboats, pack equipment, and laughed about the significance of it all. The horses trembled.

There was familial small talk over supper that night. Jimmy seemed to relax Tom while simultaneously revitalizing him. Tom and Margot likewise had new saddles and the three spent hours after dinner oiling them, as I strummed a guitar. Next day there'd be a party at McGuane's with venison picadillo and jitterbugging to the stereo, everything innocent and non-excessive. Then some tendril would snap, and Saturday in Livingston would turn into all night at Gardiner, fifty miles south, with an overindulgence in chemicals above an old-fashioned sloshing of tangleleg. There would be nude swimming in hot pots along the Yellowstone, tagged by a fierce dawn illuminating Gardiner's Two Bit Saloon where we sat slackjawed and comatose. Somewhere during the night Buffett would pick up a guitar and sing a song whose lyrics were strikingly apropos: *Wastin' away again in Margaritaville....*

It was an unrecorded tune which, within a year, would escalate Buffett from the obscurity of crossover cultism to the heights of pop superstardom. It was a song about Key West.

Jimmy Buffett was the grandson of a sailing-ship captain and son of a naval architect who'd raised him in French-Catholic circumstances, with a smidgeon of ante-

bellum decadence tossed into that salad of gulf port extremes which was Mobile, Alabama. Musically, he was a
sixties folkie who had hopscotched rock for country, and
whose style was an amalgam of Latin rhythm, pop cliché,
and Texas sentimentality. He'd released one failed album
when he first saw Key West in November, 1970, and he
was running from a busted marriage. He and Jerry Jeff
Walker had driven down for the Hennessy Ocean Races,
they did that carnival right, but when it was over, Buffett
more or less stayed. He was working Key West bars for
$120 a week, it was warm, he'd found a place to stay,
he'd bought a little Boston Whaler, had excess time to explore Key West's day and night life...so when McGuane
wandered into Crazy Ophelia's one evening "it was like
no need for introductions, we were off on the streets going crazy."

Buffett and McGuane, career-wise, were in comparable straits. Tom had not settled yet into *Ninety-Two*, the
book which would secure his reputation, and his work
with movies had been limited to one screenplay. Buffett's
first album, *Down to Earth*, did not receive enough attention to raise an eyebrow, and he would not release
his second album, *A White Sport Coat and a Pink Crus-
tacean*—which would solidify the Key West sound—for
three years.

"We were both sort of on the edges there, still having a good time," Jimmy said. "And the town was right,
you know. It was pretty free. So we spent a lot of time
just raising a whole bunch of hell. That's the way I got
to know Tom. He started getting serious about his work
about the same time I did—I mean things started happening that took us out of the streets and into the studio and
back to the typewriter."

What inspired pause in this debauch was some sense,
in each man, of the passing of one era and the debut of
another. McGuane would explore the notion of commitment above reasonable excess as a seventies alternative,
while Buffett would vitiate the despair of post-sixties

tristesse with a total exploitation of physicality. His lyrics would become anthem to the seventies good life: sun, sailing, sex, righteous dope, and tropical libations in quantity.

The irony of Buffett as papa-san to this Key West version of Outlaw Chic was that he, like McGuane, had suffered a harsh Roman Catholic upbringing where any notion of physical pleasure induced nightmares of perdition. Buffett had attended McGill Institute, a Catholic boys' school in Mobile, where, like McGuane and prep school hipsters everywhere, he turned to bullshit as release. "It was the only way to let your imagination go. Because everything else was pretty well cut off. You were taught if you jerked off that you'd go blind, and if you died with mortal sin you'd go straight to Hell and be roasted like a goddamned piece of pork on a skewer. So any kind of physical pleasure was eliminated through religious training. Lying was the only outlet. I used to make incredible bullshit stories. I loved to do it and would risk punishment to see how far I could get. That's terrible to admit—"

But bullshit was excellent practice for the type of storytelling Buffett would incorporate into his music; songs which celebrated escape, fantasy gratification, and evocation of place; Key West, an island Xanadu which miniatured chaos and lent dreams focus.

Key West had remained a haven for writers since Ernest Hemingway stepped ashore there in 1928, taking the next ten years to inculcate in our parents that special brand of tough-guy hipsterism which was his forte. In a 1974 John Dorschner profile in *The Miami Herald*, McGuane responded to a comparison between his life and Hemingway's: "I can only agree that they appear to be very similar. What might be more pertinent is to think how my father was influenced by Hemingway. Places like the Keys and northern Michigan, those were places I was taken by my father." Romantic hipsters of every stripe invaded Key West during the seventies, seeking to weave loose threads of sixties illumination into the ancestral fabric of that Hemingway myth. Though few seventies Key Westers might have articulated it. They responded more to post-World War conditioning in another guise— the lure of small-town life with a tough guy, outlaw overlay, an attraction disconcerting to pinpoint. Of course no one could miss Ernest Hemingway. His face was pasted all over town.

Buffett rejoiced in the literariness of Key West. "I was writing a ton of stuff. Key West has always been a good place to write. But it took me out of the mainstream of music for a while. There were no other songwriters. They were all literary, you know, novelists. There was no music scene in Key West. There were local bands and I'd go in and jam with, but there was nobody on a contemporary level."

Removed from Nashville and L. A., Buffett allowed island music to launder his psyche; pulsating Latin rhythms adored since childhood underscore a Caribbean sense of *carpe diem,* above a down-home addiction to rock 'n' roll. Buffett's music developed in counterpoint to that late sixties cerebralism and obsession with technology which proved the bane of rock, as it lingered in most manifestations of sixties art throughout the early seventies. Buffett hid in Key West and let it all slip by. The music he produced was nearly prophetic in its concern for delicate ecologies of neighborhood and wilderness; or Key West and the sea. But he may have written too well. Key West would change more quickly for the precision of his art. Like Hemingway, Buffett was inculcating a fresh myth of salvation.

"You had to have the realization in the back of your mind that places like Key West were rapidly disappearing from terra firma. I feel no responsibility for hastening Key West's demise. To me, at the time, it was paradise."

Real estate people, greedy politicians, legions of the unhip capitalizing upon a once hip enclave—that is what befell Key West by the late seventies. Buffett had seen it happen before. He had lived in New Orleans (1966 to 1969) during its post-bohemian, pre-hippie phase, and had watched a beloved cityscape deteriorate. He had worked to capture that fragile period in song before it blew away. Much of his early composition struggled with Montana, its ghost towns; Livingston, the changing relationship of contemporaries to wilderness, and small towns which punctuated it. Buffett lived outside Aspen, Colorado now, a town which could not better typify the conflicts of hip and environment. Were mythographers such as Hemingway, Buffett, McGuane justifiable celebrants of magical landscape, or were they business speculators mining a product as guiltlessly as the most rapacious building contractors?

"Come on down to Colorado," Jimmy said, after we'd slurred goodbyes late Sunday morning. "I'm giving a concert Friday, then I'll take you on the road with Bonnie Raitt."

Buffett was off in a private plane he'd hired to fly himself plus acquired gear low over Yellowstone Park, back along the Rockies to home.

I took the next few days to say goodbye to Montana, so long to mountains, trails, saloons, backroads, cheap cafés, and good friends I'd consorted with for two and a half months. I saved heartiest goodbyes for Livingston. After a party Wednesday night at Hjortsberg's, I grabbed my gear at the Murray, slugged down a double dose of speed, and hit Yellowstone Park by dawn...not a camper in sight but a zoo's worth of deer, elk, antelope, and bear clumped together in herds as I brodied through cramped turns, mist clouding the valley, tape deck up high, the sadness of a chapter closed tugging as I powered through Wyoming, seventeen hours to Colorado and the prospect of something new.

I raised the Hotel Jerome, Aspen, at eight that night and before I had time to register, Buffett called, "Toby!" from the bar. He was drinking in a barroom which had the most glamorous women I'd seen—certainly in recent months. Expensive cars out front should have warned me; Jerome was an 1889 hotel left over from Aspen's silver mining days, a different boomtown era, one no less exploitive than Aspen's current incarnation as "Hollywood of the Rockies." I'd parked my Jeep out front and sauntered through Jerome's polished Victoriana attired in soiled Levis, Justin roughouts, and a leather flyer's jacket, Randall hunting knife at my belt. Everywhere people were in silk or tailored denim. I'd last visited Aspen in 1972, had thought it fancy. What I encountered now zapped me into culture shock more disorienting than coma. Within hours Buffett had ensconced me in a two-story condominium at Snowmass Village, fireplace warming each bedroom, fireplace downstairs, fireplace warming the fucking kitchen, costing God knows how many hundreds a day. I was to share it with Buffett's bus driver. Other Buffett functionaries inhabited condominiums about the Village. It became instantly clear that Buffett's and McGuane's turns on the road leaving Key West had charted startlingly divergent courses.

Buffett's bus was a 1976 Silver Eagle, Greyhound-size, customized to a cross between a psychedelic van and a sailing ship. It had six mag wheels, chromed, a mural on its flank of a sailboat with tropical sunset, portholes aft, and a mock-teak interior. It was parked before our condominium where vacationers in yellow jogging suits ogled it suspiciously. I took a look myself, then hiked through a forest of townhouses, past swimming pools, paddle tennis courts, callisthenic and outdoor ballet classes, hunting coffee and a bite to eat. I was fighting to regroup. The transition from a four-dollar-a-night room in a railroad hotel in Livingston, Montana to a condo in Snowmass Village I found precarious to bridge. Last evening had been long. Buffett had rehearsed with his band, then retired to Aspen's Holiday Inn lounge, where he jammed with Vassar Clements. It had gotten drunk out. I was exhausted. Artificial stimulants could not perk me up. All around was an army of functionaries—Buffett's band, sound men and road crew—which confused me further. I felt overexposed to the century. Suddenly I was back East, consorting with Easterners in an Eastern-style resort. Aspen seemed some Key West of the Rockies, stultifying in its pretensions toward chic, hopelessly opportunistic and dangerously bourgeois.

I'd first seen Aspen during the summer of 1969 and catalogued it, with Key West, as one of two small towns in the United States I could consider inhabiting. It was—simply beautiful. Like Key West, it was a nineteenth-century community with a hip overlay, offering easy access to wilderness with enough "urban" culture to keep one from flying back East every other month. Aspen had been founded on silver mining, but since the 1940s relied economically on sport and art. Specifically, skiing and music: the Aspen Skiing Corporation and Aspen Music Festival instituted concomitantly to attract athlete and aesthete. In recent years, sport and art about Aspen had spread to epidemic proportions. Backpacker and four-wheel-drive chic vied with skiing for top stakes in the tourist derby; rock and a stunted version of Outlaw Chic had supplanted "serious" music as cultural draw. On the tide of both swam speculators in real estate, housing, and art.

By 1970, enough sixties refugees and conservatives of unconventional bent had settled in Aspen to encourage Hunter S. Thompson to run for sheriff of Pitkin County—on an antigrowth ticket. Thompson, who then had one published book to his credit, *Hell's Angels,* campaigned with shaved head and the untempered promise to sod Aspen's streets, minimalizing vehicular traffic, and to more or less legitimize drugs. He wanted to change Aspen's name to Fat City, thereby discouraging commercial exploitation. Thompson lost, but not by much. He was ahead of his time. Between 1970 and 1973—when an antigrowth candidate was elected mayor—condominiumism hit its stride. Speculators did their damnedest to cash in. Pitkin County suffered. By 1976 the tide was said to have turned, but Aspen had become synonymous with Rocky Mountain High and legions of the hip unhip maintained influx. A Detroit automobile had lifted the town's name, as had a bestselling novel, plus countless fashion lines. Thompson himself, through his writing and lifestyle, had done much to celebrate Aspen. The fact that he *lived* nearby was enough. Superstars attracted by Aspen's microcosmic cultural life, plus its various chics, had transformed the town into a suburb of Los Angeles. Aspen threatened to supplant Palm Springs as Hollywood's favorite resort. Mercedes and lush four-wheel-drives jammed Aspen's streets at nearly any hour. The traffic was horrendous. To think, I had been attracted in 1969 to this small Rocky Mountain hideaway for its simplicity and quiet.

News that Cher had bequeathed herself "a condo in Aspen" as signification of her marriage to Greg Allman was, for me, the final word. I got on the phone to McGuane.

"Head back up here if you're freaked," Tom said. "We've got antelope chili for supper and I've just been firing my flintlock."

But I wanted the whole dose. Wanted specifically to ascertain Buffett's part in this cultural morass; how he might be exploiting Aspen through art, how he lived as an artist, and how he amalgamated business and art through the machinations of a seventies rock star.

The afternoon of Buffett's concert we met at the Jerome bar; Jimmy was intense but not tense. I tracked his borrowed Mercedes eighteen miles out Highway 82 to Snowmass proper, where he was living—in a friend's house, it should be noted, in a spare bedroom. We parked by a river where Buffett showed me property he had bought: a weathered ranch house connected to the road by a covered bridge. Eighteen miles was close enough to Aspen for Buffett. "I'd live in Montana except that I like to get a good meal—and a little excitement," he said. "I'm not ready to cash it all in for Friday night parties at the ranch." The house where Buffett stayed was less pretentious and, spacewise, less comfortable than the condominium I occupied. It was a suburban-style ranch house in a cluster of mates, no different for their mountain setting than a thousand others circumscribing Cleveland. The antique saddle Buffett had purchased jockied for space in a utility room with a matching washer-dryer. We settled onto a couch before the Indian rug with cans of beer.

"Artists are the most discriminated-against people," Buffett said, as if that idea had recently occurred to him. "Writers, musicians, painters...I'm buying this piece of property here and my business credentials are as clean and good...but like the realtor told me, he said: If this was anybody else's financial situation, any other occupation, there'd be no doubt at this moment we'd have the money. But for you, they want to check you out. So you learn to live with it. Because it's easier to play the game and beat them, than to try from the start to antagonize them. You just hope you'll reach the point where you won't have to pay more for a fucking phone deposit than a normal citizen does."

I thought about that. "There are so many artists in the world who are broke," I said. "You and I know a million of them. They feel guilty about making too little money. Have you felt guilty about making too much?"

"No," Buffett said.

"I guess that would be like, if you're a Catholic, getting to heaven and feeling guilty about that."

Buffett laughed. "It's—just the fact that I didn't sacrifice my integrity to become wealthy. The norm for a successful singer or songwriter, the way most people think, would be to live in L. A. or Nashville on a huge ranch, drive a Mercedes and hang out at the rock scene. You're supposed to be cast in these molds. I don't feel guilty about making that much money because I have worked hard for it. Long, hard hours. It's a fact that I'm generous with anybody who needs anything. I'm not sitting there trying to hoard it and spitting blue flames from my mouth to draw six bucks a head. It's obvious that people wouldn't come to the shows if they thought they were getting ripped off. We've had one commercial hit, *Come Monday,* and our albums sell a hundred to two hundred thousand copies. We don't have this huge following."

I had to admit, there seemed little of the rip-off in Buffett's attitude toward Aspen. Maybe he had learned from Key West. He'd written no hip Rocky Mountain Highs, sang no songs directly related to Aspen, and did no business there except for the occasional concert. He'd lived with the same woman for years. Buffett's business sense appeared slicker on its surface than, say, McGuane's— Jimmy wasn't breeding quarter horses. Perhaps that was the shiniest new tool of Outlaw Chic. Buffett consorted with musicians, accredited outlaws such as Hunter Thompson and politicos. He fit no precise mold.

Thanks to his background, I thought, which remained stolidly middle class. For all his frolicking, Buffett had taken a journalism-history degree from the University of Southern Mississippi, and had worked a year for *Billboard,* the music industry's principal trade sheet, as a staff editorial writer. There was something startlingly practical about having taken that job. Buffett quit the day his first album came out, but he'd packed in a year of learning Nashville's business side—a conservative move any post-WWII father would have applauded. Buffett's roots in sixties folk music, with its literary pretensions, plus the narrative focus of his songs in an era of technological overkill, likewise separated him from the norm. Buffett had been a reader from childhood; he'd disappeared into Mobile's public library, afternoons on end, with volumes of Coleridge, A. E. Housman, Rudyard Kipling. His push toward the theatricality of rock 'n' roll had been tempered by a real interest in literature. His songs were literary, some nearly Kiplingesque. Musically, he was original. Culturally (despite trappings of rock and pretensions toward Outlaw Chic) Buffett fit no category except middle class. He was like some disaffected grad student with a split major in Business and Art who'd decided to pursue both paths.

"You're trying from the start to be successful, and you're lying to yourself if you don't admit that. I don't go out for aesthetic value alone, you know. I want to live comfortably."

Buffett's secondary ambitions remained literary: to write screenplays, poetry, journalism, a novel about pre-seventies New Orleans, and nonfiction about rock stars—"a book which will probably tell the opposite of what everybody thinks. I mean, we don't get laid every night by beautiful women. Most of the time it's backgammon and getting stoned on the bus with people on the road."

I thought to ask what Buffett's earliest recollection of literary success might have been. Something far away as childhood.

"In Catholic school we had to write an autobiography. I don't remember what year. I was still an altar boy. Probably sixth grade. You were supposed to write it from the vantage point of when you were thirty. I was going to be a priest of course. So I wrote it from that viewpoint. It was entitled: *My Compass Points to Heaven*. I remember the cover. It was blue with a compass seal I'd designed showing north-south-east-west. It was one of the top five autobiographies and it got read in class."

Twenty years later that compass seal would reappear on the cover to *Changes in Latitudes, Changes in Attitudes*—an album which would top *Billboard's* charts and, with the popularity of "Margaritaville," establish Buffett as the most successful new product in rock: *Strummin' my six string / On my front porch swing...*

Wastin' away again in Margaritaville. Tonight, Snowmass Village chapter, where Buffett's music ricocheted about the interior of an overlarge circus tent, the tent itself rippling nautically in a valley of ski lifts, condominiums, chic brasseries, boutiques, hot therapy pools...in short, that barrier reef of monied excess which was Aspen in exurbia. Everywhere were battalions of the unhip costumed in predictable down vests, western shirts and leather Topsiders, hooting like frat kids at homecoming and stomping along to every favorite Buffett lyric. Jimmy onstage was energetic, vital, but reminiscent of something antediluvian in popular culture, something prewar, nearly surfer in its nonchalance.

Buffett wore T-shirt, jeans, and jogging shoes—physical embodiment of the relaxed life. His blond hair shimmered under the lights, perspiration dripped from the tip of his nose. His audience fell off their chairs, drunk, drugged and giving not a damn. Their unselfconscious enthusiasm was pre-seventies, but their inebriation was current. Not an unwarped brain in the bunch.

I'd been speaking with Hunter Thompson, himself cranked up with contradictions of this scene, enjoying Buffett's music but abashed at the surroundings, what had befallen his beloved Colorado. "This is as strange to me as it is to you," Hunter said, shuddering beneath the weight of Snowmass's condominiums. We stood on a wooden deck outside that circus tent where Buffett was well into his second show. The crowd had not ceased screaming. We were hard by the bar. The chic unchic pressed close. Hunter was dressed in a red-and-white golf cap, red windbreaker, and doubleknit slacks. He wore white basketball shoes. He looked like some Andy Warhol of Aspen's bohemia, dressed like what he most despised. His hair was professionally trimmed. In years past, when hip had been ethos rather than fashion, Hunter had flaunted black turtlenecks, Levis, and a shaved head. He had run with Hell's Angels and taken solace from a magical San Francisco underground. What transpired here, ten short years later, seemed beyond irony. Hunter had become culture hero to the sort of fraternity goons he regularly crucified in *Rolling Stone*. King Contradiction kept a drink in his hand, his right knee pumping.

The sixties had proved devastating to impractical romantics such as Hunter Thompson...to any artist who cringed at a capitalization upon his individuality, but who'd seen that first mass movement toward hip as the coming of a new order—one which might appease loneliness, particularly of the writer-hipster's life, by the wiring of community. Or communalization of the wired. Whenever fashion encountered business, however, compromises were effected which blunted the corners of hip. The ethos of hip was beyond compromise, it was too infantile, too grounded in individual gratification. Still, there had been a moment. The sixties were a time when anything had seemed possible, even the communalization of hip. Hunter and other fiction-oriented writers had turned from fantasy to street life as subject matter; now that street again was one way, and they were finding it difficult to reverse. Hunter was having real trouble producing contracted journalism for *Rolling Stone.* He was a novelist who'd been seduced toward journalism by the promise of the sixties. With that promise shattered, no wonder he and myriad artists were working poorly. How could one comfortably retreat to fantasy when the future fantasized was bleak?

We'd been discussing the writer's predicament when I hazarded this observation: "Everything you publish these days seethes with a contempt you bring to journalism."

Hunter stared at me. "There are not many people who get that," he said. "You're the first who's said it." I figured he was pulling my leg. But his expression was grave. What kind of sycophants had he been privy to these past years that such a comment could upset?

All I need do was glance around. They were everywhere, drunk as their fathers on aged bourbon, loaded on expensive dope, raucous, conformist, more rightist in their leftist posture than a hundred ad execs on Madison Avenue. Buffett riled them onstage, working the favorite Key West numbers, nostalgic canapés, the Montana hucklebucks, booze, dope and get-drunk- and-screw songs, like the Beach Boys in concert at a college weekend. There was innocence to the infectiousness of his music; half of that was comforting. But the nether half was dark. Distant from reality, lobotomized to lessons of the sixties—of war, race relations, corruption in government, exploitation of resources—to a point where it sounded like the sixties never happened. We had regressed to the morning of that decade suffering a lately-departed president, discord in the streets, and "Let's Go Surfin'" on the jukebox. I looked about this Snowmass audience and spotted not one black face, not one Indian. It was the American suburbs at Rocky Mountain High. That suburbia removed from Vietnam and Watergate as fish in the sea.

Thompson felt this, I thought, and it amused me to watch the old hipster fidget. Buffett in some aggravated posture epitomized the seventies unhipster in that he synthesized divergent tendencies toward business, art (the business of selling oneself), rock and theater, with its horse opera fantasies of Outlaw Chic. But something was terribly wrong. Aspen's return to theatricality was precise: If Vietnam had been the farthest reach of westward expansionism, tupping the Asian mind, a retreat to horse opera delusionisms which had promulgated Vietnam was, pathologically, a healthful step. But without some recollection of lessons learned there, some obeisance to that primitivism first engendered by rhythm and blues, later apotheosized by My Lai and countless slittings of countless Oriental throats—the culture seemed doomed. Most especially what survived of hip. The logical step back from theater was to street—not street theater of the late sixties with its middle-class solidarity in numbers—but to sidewalks of the inner city, a retreat to hipsterism, to urban life, and a reassessment of primitive beneath the scar tissue of the decade. These Aspenites were so far removed from street-corner hipsters who had godfathered their chic, they'd likely never make it home.

Aspen, once an end-of-the-road town sanctified as Key West, blew rank with their putrescence. Aspen appealed to the worst instincts of the white middle class, and was itself an environmental My Lai. What once had been primitive, the countryside, had been machine-gunned by speculators in real estate, sport, and art.

I looked around for Hunter, but he had fled. Buffett was slowing things down; he was singing softly now: *Feelings for movin' grow stronger / So you wonder why you ever go home.*

There was a despair at the center of Buffett's frivolity which rescued him as an artist. Speaking of Key West, and tangentially Aspen, Buffett had remarked:

"It's melodrama, you know. It's a lot of comedy heaped on a lot of tragedy. The despair comes from the fact that it's the end of the road. I mean you can't go any further without leaving your car, which would be too un-American for most people. Consequently you pile up this menagerie of people. Most of them have seen better times. They flipped out or they drank too much booze or their lady left them or they shot somebody. And they slid. If I couldn't get another date, another contract, it was done, I was broke, my car ran off the road, I didn't have a dime…what would I do? I'd go back to the islands. Because there'd be a terrible shock to my system. A terrible blow to my ego. But I know I'd survive, because I could go back there, and I could be living that life."

I wondered if it wasn't too late.

Postscript: In September of 1977, McGuane and Buffett's sister, Laurie, were married. Buffett had been married in August to Jane Slagsvol, his long-time companion. A daughter, Savannah Jane, was born to the Buffetts in June, 1979. *Changes in Latitudes, Changes in Attitudes* went platinum, selling 1,300,000 copies. By June, 1979, Buffett's subsequent album, *Son of a Son of a Sailor,* had sold 1,500,000. Buffett was composing sound tracks and had written an impressive cover story for *Outside* magazine, on Antigua Sailing Week. Hunter Thompson was holed up in Buffett's apartment in Key West, writing a screenplay. A movie was being made of his life. McGuane's novel *Panama* had appeared to mixed reviews, the New York press proving most vitriolic—a signed rave in *The New Yorker,* New York's most noteworthy exception. The following letter arrived from Tom in June:

"Dear Toby,

"Had a lariat break last night, nylon rope, came back and hit me right in the middle of my head and gave me a concussion. Percodan currently courses through my veins and consequently I'm a leetle goofy.... .

"A lot of the stuff I was saying came true, and some anyway didn't. My disenchantment with the word passed. Writing prose is again the ballast for everything. I'm at work on a long Montana book, hopefully a final outlaw volume, meant to take that disagreeable stance once and for all as far as I can. I want to: look deep into the eyes of Jesse James, try to figure out why democracy makes you trigger happy; and burn some churches.

"The ranch is a great passion with us. We are raising cutting horses, running yearling cattle and raising dry land hay on our place up the Boulder, on Poison Creek, where the eagle traps the Indians made are still in the rimrocks. I'm growing my own serrano peppers to dry and give my friends; and to make antelope chili when it gets cold again.

"It's grand to be able to report to you that I am absolutely happy, have one of those marriages twenty lifetimes might never produce. We're expecting a baby in December, a special thing because Laurie had major surgery last winter that left childbearing a little in doubt. Laurie's daughter Heather; Thomas and Maggie make this a frequently noisy madhouse but I think everyone knows where home is. The ranch is over 1000 acres now and I am sneakily pleased when people call me Big Daddy: I don't know whether it's Amin or Varner; or that I weigh 200 lbs: I just like it.

"I've been in this house longer than any house in my

life. I feel an inchoate devotion to the idea of 'Montana' as a society of government-hating nesters. As forty approaches, I want to write thirty indelible American novels, a shithouseload of original movies, have an unconscionable number of kids, train a world champion cutting horse, run a big cattle ranch that has no farmland on it, addict myself to opium at eighty and die five years later when increased tolerance makes it too tiresome for us to refill the pipes and fetch the scrapbook one more time.

Fond regards,
"Tom"

The '60s Report
1979

The Disappearance of Peter Fonda

The motorcycle Peter Fonda urges through its slalom course along the Yellowstone River is a café racer. A slate-gray BMW with trim fairing and clip-on handlebars, it's as culturally removed from the modified Harleys he rode in *The Wild Angels* and *Easy Rider* as Courvoisier is from Cold Duck. The bike is a gift from BMW, anxious to lure Fonda from his sponsorship of Honda in Japan, where he is huge, to a contract representing German two-wheelers. These motorcycle contracts are lucrative. And BMW's likely offer seems a step up, like the German art film *Peppermint Frieden,* in which currently he stars. Cheap bikes and low-budget films (twenty since *Easy Rider)* are potholes Fonda would like to think are behind him, but he knows that this is probably not the case.

These films are what I'm offered," Fonda said earlier. "And I'll do anything to keep working in front of the camera. It's my life flow, what I do."

The man who elevated the exploitation film to art, who introduced Hollywood to a hip, educated youth market, who paved the way for independent filmmakers of the seventies to make quality films within the studio system and who, as Captain America, counseled his generation that "we blew it," today has been confronting personal doubts. A good marriage, three bright children, and two sprawling ranches outside Livingston, Montana, with the finest views and over three-hundred acres of the most spectacular grounds in a region famed for its audacious homesteads, should weigh against his unhappiness. Yet despite two movies in release (the German film and *Dance of the Dwarfs,* an American horror quickie), a project with his sister Jane and Robert Towne under discussion, a miniseries about Thomas Jefferson on the hustle, and the chance that he might direct an adventure-doper flick called *Holy Smoke,* Fonda is restless, uneasy. Among other things, he has not appeared before the camera in over a year. Not since his father's death, in August 1982. And not since the death of his best friend, Warren Oates, earlier that spring.

"I sit around between films, and that's nothing," Fonda was saying. "I think, only if it leads toward motion pictures. I play my guitar upside down and backwards because I'm left-handed, and a lot of my friends think that's great. But I'll tell you, if it *were* great, I'd give up making movies, because they're breaking my heart."

Peter Fonda moves as a dark form against the brilliant landscape. His motorcycle jacket is blue and slashed with zippered pockets. His helmet swathes his head in black. Here and there stand yellowed aspens, but the grasslands are dun with sage to the river, and peaks of the Absaroka Range are snow-capped. Fonda swings the bike gracefully, dodging ruts and leaning through turns that snake down cirques and past glacial moraines as if his bike were a surfboard on this road, prehistorically an ocean. The light is exquisite, shifting by the second to paint the faces of mountains more eccentrically than extras in a Japanese movie.

We're rolling, the motorcycle throbs against its wind

chill, we're speed, machinery, the West, exotic light, everything that Fonda loves, but we're not twenty-four frames a second, so for him we're next to nothing.

It's been a strange trip for Peter Fonda—now patriarch of America's first theatrical family—from his birth as a kind of Prince William on "that insane cutting edge" between Hollywood royalty and the eastern, social aristocracy of his mother, Frances Seymour Brokaw, to his retreat here in the West. And it's been a strange career, one that has taken Fonda from his canonization in 1970 as "the decade's first authentic cult hero" ("Not since James Dean's *Rebel Without a Cause* or Marion Brando's *The Wild One*," said *Playboy*, "has a movie actor so captured the imagination and admiration of a generation.") to his livelihood as an independent actor and director in independent films, pulling crews together as if he were a guerrilla waging petty-wars.

Fonda did it backward: he started *within* the studio system ("they were grooming me as the next Dean Jones"), making films such as *Tammy and the Doctor* and *Lilith*. But by 1965, because of his inexperience and a reputation as, depending on who's talking, either a maverick or a brat, he was not landing jobs. He threw in with Roger Corman, master of the low-budget, fender-busting, tire-squalling epic, who taught Fonda about cutting costs and demonstrated how films could celebrate the poetry of the American Road. For Corman he starred in *The Trip*, written by Jack Nicholson, and *The Wild Angels*. "I wanted a man of some stature for *Angels*," Corman has said, "who could play the strength and the intensity of a Hell's Angel leader, but with maybe one percent more sensitivity—and who could ride a motorcycle." Fonda fit that profile, and the film became American International's biggest draw. When Fonda conceived *Easy Rider*, in 1968, Corman's company was to produce it. But the project went to Columbia, where in 1969 it accomplished for American movies what *On the Road* did for American literature—pinpointing a generation's restlessness, apotheosizing the long ride, and poeticizing the machinery necessary for that ride.

Fonda directed *The Hired Hand* in 1971, for about $1.25 million, and lost capital. "But it was the first feminist western," he has said enthusiastically, "and *The New York Times* called it masterful." He poured the last of his earnings from *Easy Rider* into "a film I believed in," *Idaho Transfer,* 1973, "about our irresponsibility with the environment—at the end, the characters use each other as fuel for their cars." That movie submerged without a bubble. He directed *Wanda Nevada* in 1979, starring Brooke Shields and with a cameo performance by his father, and that was also a commercial failure. Subsequently it's been B films to pay the mortgage and "to maintain the privilege of working in motion pictures."

The motorcycle groans, "This is us," Fonda shouts, "at the Old Saloon in Emigrant. Chug a few beers, fight a few cowboys, then slide on back to the ranch." He shuts down the BMW before the hitching post of this bar, a solitary false-front on a bluff facing the Yellowstone, where it's stood for a century like some dispossessed fixture from a John Ford western. His face, unmasked from his visor, is mischievous, even merry. It is a handsome face, lined now after forty-four years, yet touched with a youthful awkwardness that presses against the Hollywood bravado like a small boy into his father's side.

"Sometimes I sit on my porch and *study* this sky," he says. "The landscape is so much like the sea. It's constantly changing." Fonda leans against his motorcycle, facing the mountains. "People are concerned as to how our generation may have sold out. Well, I'm a Pisces and a tropical person. I feel like I sold out when I left the ocean, when I left that beautiful sailboat I bought with my earnings from *Easy Rider*. It's an elitist act, sailing and living on the Pacific—but on the boat my word is law, I pay no land taxes. I can enjoy *real* sovereignty."

Sovereignty is as much a preoccupation for Peter Fonda as it would be for any man who has been audited by the IRS so often (every year since 1972), is harassed at Customs by drug officials, and whose eighty-two-foot ketch has often been boarded by narcotics officers.

"I must have been on Nixon's shit list," reflects Fonda, whose adversaries do not appear limited to government. "We proved with *Easy Rider* that the suits, the studio heads making big movie deals, are irrelevant," he says. "And that a movie does not have to cost sixteen million dollars to be successful. That's hurt me, ironically. Executives don't *like* people who make movies. I mean—what am I to make of a career where my eighth film was *Easy Rider*, which has earned some one hundred million bucks to date, another was *Dirty Mary, Crazy Larry*, which may have made eighty-five million, and twenty-odd films later I haven't been offered a large-budget movie? Why aren't I offered the good scripts, like my sister? It's a male-chauvinist industry. If all the heads of studios and producers were women, maybe I could have fucked my way to the top."

Fonda stares into the diminishing light and pops his helmet.

"I'm a radical capitalist, and movies are the world's most expensive art form. You can pull a crew together for next to nothing, enlist your friends to act in and to write a picture, but Eastman Kodak wants cash. If I had been running drugs on my boat, as the government alleged, I could have directed a *lot* of movies. As it is, I'll have to sell that boat to make taxes."

Peter Fonda is doing business, two phones, a green and a white, scrunched against his shoulders.
"Sandy?" he says to an assistant in Los Angeles. "That Media Association Convention we were invited to—it's a *motorcycle* convention." Fonda deliberates. "I may be stuck with Captain America for the rest of my life, but I'll be damned if I'll play him for free." The white phone finds its cradle, as does the green, after he berates his other caller for a delayed check. "The *what?*" he says. "The

check is in the mail? I grew up in Hollywood and one law I know...."

Within Fonda's ranch house—a simple log structure—everywhere are weapons: a miniature automatic pistol used on Mrs. Tom Thumb in 1892; a Don King Ohio Vincent muzzle-loader; a tiger-striped maple tomahawk; skinning knives; shotguns and rifles; even an Uzi submachine gun. This ordnance surrounds paintings by neighbor Russell Chatham of Fonda's crowd: novelists Thomas McGuane, William Hjortsberg, Richard Brautigan, and Jim Harrison, singer Jimmy Buffett, actor Warren Oates, and others staring from their log perch off toward the mountains. It was on the set of *92 in the Shade*, McGuane's directorial paean to Key West (a film in which Fonda, Warren Oates, and Margot Kidder starred), that Fonda met Becky Crockett McGuane, his second wife and the great-great-great-great-granddaughter of Davy Crockett. In 1975, when Becky's marriage to McGuane dissolved and he married Kidder, Fonda followed Becky to Livingston, where they settled in a region that would come to shelter a remarkable artistic community: "a Bloomsbury," Fonda has quipped, including, in addition to those in Chatham's oils, at various times Jeff Bridges, Sam Peckinpah, Dennis Quaid, director Michael Butler, former *Rolling Stone* managing editor Terry McDonell, journalist Tim Cahill, poet Dan Gerber, and an assortment of others beating a fast retreat to some conservative, wholly American ethic of this contemporary West.

Beyond guns and portraits in Fonda's living-room museum of western history are wardrobe shots of his father as Wyatt Earp, as well as one of Henry's last paintings—of the hats he wore in *On Golden Pond*. "I learned so much about light from my father's paintings," Fonda says. "I remember a very simple painting Henry did of a wine glass on burgundy velvet that was beautiful. And he did it with pastels, with which it's so hard to do anything." A poem to Peter and Becky from Jim Harrison, on the occasion of their wedding, is framed. And Harrison's library card from Michigan State (where Becky and McGuane were classmates) is pasted, jokingly, to their refrigerator. The cats are Abyssinian and rare, the dog a black Lab, Bridget Jane Champagne—named for Peter's nineteen-year-old daughter, Bridget ("the most beautiful Fonda," says Becky), an acting student at New York University, who has already been approached by Francis Ford Coppola for a part in *Cotton Club;* and, of course, sister Jane, with her workout books, the most successful author in America. "I wonder how McGuane feels about *that?*" The group's work crowds several shelves. And the flag Fonda wore on his jacket as Captain America is enclosed in glass and hangs near his father's photograph.

"My father's photograph," Fonda sighs. "You know, he was never *there*. He would not notice me. Then there'd erupt these terrible rages...."

When Fonda speaks of his father, his voice becomes unsteady. Born in New York in 1940, Peter flew at fourteen weeks to California to launch a childhood that was like a career on some vile exploitation company's back lot. His and Jane's mother slit her throat in a mental institution when Peter was ten; Peter shot himself soon thereafter and nearly died; friends committed suicide; and his father married a total of five times, shuttling him from boarding school to relatives' houses to movie sets to spare bedrooms of stepmothers, until Peter quit Omaha University in 1960 to act in New York. There he won the Drama Critics Circle Award for most promising actor of 1961, for his performance on Broadway in *Blood, Sweat and Stanley Poole*.

"Movies for my father were what he did between plays," Fonda says. "All I've ever had were movies. I hated the East as a child, hated its bigotry and closeness, and have never felt much as an actor for Broadway. I didn't like anything about eastern life, compared to what I saw in the West."

We've moved to the porch of Fonda's ranch house and are slouching in perhaps the last hot patch of sun before winter.

"I have good friends," Fonda says, "and that's something. It was harder for me to accept Warren Oates's death than it was my father's, because I *knew* my father was dying. At the end, I looked into my father's eyes, kissed him on the forehead, and told him I loved him. Then I prayed for him to let go, he'd suffered so long. Warren was fifty-two. I know CPR and if I'd have been there when he had his heart attack, I might have saved him. But I was in the Philippines, making a movie. In his will,' Warren wrote, 'To Peter Fonda I leave nothing— but all of my love.' My father didn't even say that."

Fonda clears his throat. "I've steered away from close contact with at least people of the same sex because of the intensities of those relationships I'm able to have. And for fear that I would be hurt. It's been worse this past year. The friendship Warren and I had, as characters, in *The Hired Hand*, has such intensity. And it carried into real life."

We've spent two hours this morning viewing *Dance of the Dwarfs*, plucked from the sky by Fonda's satellite dish, and although Fonda has smiled during much of his performance, it is obvious the experience has depressed him.

"I felt responsible for that film, in that I pulled the crew together—got Michael and David Butler, my good friends, got them to take cuts in salary, as I did—because I thought we could bring in one crackerjack of a scary film. We did it for four hundred thousand dollars in four weeks. When we got to the Philippines, the director had no equipment for us, no generator, we had to build everything, but *we pulled it off*. Then they printed the film too red, they wouldn't let Michael Butler time it, he was furious, they screwed up with the monsters, made them unbelievable—I felt like I'd been sold out. And Warren died while we were there."

Jeff Bridges's pickup is a dusty speck on the horizon. He is coming to take Peter trapshooting. "I wonder what will happen for me next?" Fonda says. "I don't want to have to do a television series. The anxiety—I don't know an actor who doesn't share it. My father had it, he'd say, 'I'll never work again, no one will hire me,' and *he* was Henry Fonda."

Becky joins us on the porch. She is blond and small-boned, radiating an uptown frontier elegance. "Being the father of three kids," Peter has said, "that's hard—but loving her is so easy."

"Peter's always been Peter," she told me privately, "but he *is* Henry's son in the sense of his honor and justice and kindness to his fellow man. And like his father, *he's another crazy artist.*"

A long I-90 and the Crazy Mountains, the marksmen pour load after load into the leaden sky, tracing clay pigeons against the scoured landscape, shattering one, then two at a throw. Fonda and Bridges stand back to back—Fonda with a sawed-off piece a fraction longer than illegal, Bridges with "Grandpa Henry's shotgun," as Justin Fonda calls it, the boy himself pumping box after box through double barrels. As actors who are the sons of famous actors, one would think these three would have much to say. But today their purest eloquence is this show of firepower.

On the way home, Justin says of *Dwarfs:* "You were great in that, Dad." Fonda demurs, thanking his son, and soon is prating on about current projects. "Dennis Hopper and I are planning a book, Jeff, sixty percent photos, forty percent prose, that will address this *Big Chill* stuff— what happened to our ideals, how we blew it, why. Dennis and I will travel the country, as in *Easy Rider,* shooting the book and talking with people. Only he's been staying up at Larry Flynt's house in L. A. and I refuse to call there. Guess you go where the money is."

Bridges says nothing, but wrestles the four-wheel

through dips, and fiddles with his tape deck, blaring New Wave. Bridges has recently made a film with director Taylor Hackford *(An Officer and a Gentleman)* called *Against All Odds,* but he himself is at that edgy point between movies that Fonda has bemoaned. Long-haired and bearded. Bridges met his wife Susan, a Montana woman, in 1974 when he was in Livingston making *Rancho Deluxe,* the McGuane cult favorite. In a few weeks the couple will return to Los Angeles.

"I can't believe we didn't sell *Flashpoint,*" Fonda says to Bridges. Then to the others in the car: "It was a great script originally written for McQueen, that Jeff and I would have been perfect for—about these two border-patrol guys who discover a second rifle in the Kennedy assassination. I presented it to one studio and they suggested I get Larry Gatlin for the second lead. I mean, I wanted to work opposite an *actor.*"

Bridges is silent. He seems amused by Fonda's patter. And by his incessant talk of projects. "We'll play some music tonight," Fonda says. "All rock stars want to be actors, and all actors want to be rock stars. Jeff's good on keyboards, he plays guitar, wrote this amazing song about King Kong...."

As the pickup sways through Livingston it's evident that Fonda's mood has shifted. "It's gonna happen," Fonda whoops from the back seat. "It's fucking *got* to."

Tom and Becky spearheaded this intentionally non-intentional community of sixties malcontents with their move to Livingston in 1968. Tonight Tom and his wife, Laurie (sister to Jimmy Buffett), are entertaining. Warren Zevon has flown up for the weekend, there had been much celebrating the previous evening, and Tom, sober and witty, moves from a stuporous living room assemblage to a more lively kitchen crowd. "There are some people out there who're having trouble speaking English," he says. Then launches into a story about a horseman he's met, who last spring was attacked by a grizzly, lay still while the bear methodically sank teeth into every inch of his back and batted him around like a *foosball,* then got up and rode away. "The worst thing, this guy said, was the stench of the grizzly's fur. It had just come from its winter den…"

Bridges has perked up, and he chats amiably with Zevon in a far corner. He seems more at ease with the musician than he was with Fonda. Fonda himself has mysteriously disappeared into a downstairs bedroom to worry an old piano with McGuane's small daughter. Before long he's back, spelled by Zevon, who is beating out the familiar tunes to twenty people crowded about the tiny space. Zevon offers a song he has composed with McGuane and everybody hoots along. *"No one sleeps on the yellow line, no one's that alone,"* goes the roar, *"someone's in the window, so don't try to use the phone."*

The party breaks up early. There's been an air of hibernation to the festivities, perhaps the last such gathering before Montana's fierce winter. Above that is the sense that folks may be moving along. Richard Brautigan is selling his ranch and will winter in Japan. McGuane, who during summers of the early-to-mid seventies hosted a salon of nonstop berserkos, is sober and with Laurie travels six months a year on the cutting-horse circuit. He rarely entertains. Jim Harrison has not visited for two years. Terry McDonell's house has finally been sold and he is working for *Newsweek.* William Hjortsberg has moved to Billings. Sam Peckinpah is in L. A. Michael Butler is in L. A. Dennis Quaid is in New York, off-Broadway. Asked why he would sell his ranch, Brautigan shrugs and says, "Its time has passed."

"Maybe it's middle age," Fonda says on the ride home. "Patterns are shifting. We never were anything like a Montana Mafia. We were just people who happened to live together. The community goes through phases. People move in and people move out. But something *is* changing."

"Every time my father would remarry, my new step-mother would tell me, 'You'll always have a room here.' Well," Fonda says, "I'm still waiting for my room."

He is seated before the counter of the Livingston Bar & Grille, locked into his reflection in the back bar mirror. It was in a saloon like this, in Livingston, that Peckinpah once bought into a poker game, placed one thousand dollars on the table, quickly lost seven hundred, picked up the remaining three, said, "Boys, you'll never get this," and ate it.

This is a late lunch, and Fonda pokes uninterestedly at a cheeseburger.

"It's been better the last few times in Los Angeles," he says. "I've stayed in Shirlee [Fonda's] guest house, and there's been a bed for me at Jane's. The promise is no longer a thought, but an action. Jane and I are getting along. I played my guitar last time, and we sang old Everly Brothers songs. Singing always was one of our touch-stones. We have this movie at MGM/ UA right now that we want to do with Robert Towne. The Peter and Jane project—no, let me get the billing right, the *Jane* and Peter project. But the way we've presented it, I'll be executive producer, she'll produce, we're hoping Towne will write, and as the deal's for big bucks, we'll be able to hire a good director. It's about a brother and sister in their forties who come into an inheritance. There's never been a film about a brother and sister in their forties. It could be so great. I mean, I'll never be Tom Joad, I'll never be Julia, but I did make *Easy Rider* and *The Hired Hand*...."

The bartender nudges Fonda and hands him the phone. It is Becky. As if by telepathy, she has the news he's waited for. MGM/UA has said yes. Suddenly Fonda's face is twenty years younger and his voice is flooded with emotion.

"They bought it," he says, "they bought the whole package. And I'm producing the fucker." He drinks from his beer. "I can't believe my sister has done this for me. It's the *one wonderful thing*." He tosses his head.

"I never thought she took me *seriously*. But she must, if she's counting on me to produce this film."

A friend slaps Fonda on the back, pumping his hand. Peter gazes out toward the Livingston railyards and, as if hooking a highballer south, swings into some silent and cherished reverie.

"All life is possible if you learn to move and grow with it," he says, finally. "I've found I've had to be very still to feel life moving."

He is somber a minute, then cracks the slightest of grins.

"But if I *must* die in a rage, I shall."

Esquire
1984

West Boulder Runoff

The creek was milky with snowmelt and ash, and too fierce to cross. We eyed it, backpacks stooping us, and did not speak. The creek bisected a meadow brilliant with spring flowers, but a burned-over forest with blackened lodgepoles girdled it. "Water's too high," I said. Rick grunted. We were four miles from the trailhead, but wanted at least six between us and the campground. "Not worth the risk," I added. Rick nodded. The cliff above, with its protuberant outcroppings, its red and yellow shadings, looked like the face of an old man.

It was evening, so we retreated to the north meadow, perhaps one hundred yards wide and four hundred long, and made camp. The space was dotted with glacier-flicked boulders, and its grass was a foot high. Purple, red, yellow, and orange flowers rose in schizophrenic bouquet. I'd packed my rod but had small hope of fishing. The West Boulder was wilder than I'd seen it; runoff flooded the woods below our meadow and had transformed the burbling river into class-five whitewater.

Two years previous, a 29,000-acre blaze had

incinerated this forest. Wildfires had threatened to level Montana. Yet this was the spring of deluges. The Midwest was underwater, in Livingston a bridge across the Yellowstone had failed, and at this altitude we had driven through freshets to the trailhead. Still, I thought, tomorrow I might wade that flood and get to the river proper. There might be one confused fish circling the lodgepoles. And with foliage decimated, casting would be a snap. This was my first outing of the season.

We busied ourselves with tents and chattered nonsensically. The temperature had dropped. "A fire?" I said. Then scuffled toward the tree line for wood. I found little, and the forest felt spooky. Its trees were black-barked or copper-spotted wraiths. The understory was a paste of ash and soot, from which wildflowers grew in manic profusion. Tracks of large creatures were evident. I gathered six blackened limbs and retreated to camp.

I thought, twenty summers ago I soaked at Chico as smoke from Yellowstone's fires choked Paradise Valley. Twenty-nine Junes before that I stepped off a train at Livingston on the first day of my first Montana summer. Yellowstone Park had recovered nicely; I was not sure I had. I was sixty-three and feeling every minute of it.

Tents secured, we boiled water for supper and sat back to eat. I glanced around. We'd flushed a black bear walking in, and last week, in this meadow, a hiker surprised a grizzly sunning itself on a boulder. I jabbed at the wildflowers. A Yellowstone Park study I'd read noted that post-fire bears grazed more frequently at burned than unburned sites. Lupine, fireweed, and clover grew plentifully after a scorching. These were grizzly delicacies that choked our meadow and forest.

The river's metallic surface flashed through denuded trees, and an amber glow lighted the porcupine-quill lodgepoles of the snowy mountains. This was June 20, the summer solstice. At 9:00 p.m. our meadow held the brightness of afternoon. High on its northwest side hung a corrugated cliff, with caves and a psychedelic weir: a stone tower with serrated edges.

"We could shinny up there and drop acid," I said.

Rick smiled. "In the old days." He was eight years my junior, a guitarist by trade and a gear hound. I watched him sort his things with the light-fingered delicacy of a musician. Our conversation, while seated on a boulder by a spring-fed stream, covered the usual topics: life's me-anderings, nature, responsibility, craziness. Last winter Rick had left a thirteen-year-gig with an established band to make his own music and to start private practice as an alcohol-and-drug-abuse counselor. Even I was transition-ing. I'd republished a book I'd written in my twenties, to unanticipated acclaim.

Rick had brought that book.

"Do I seem different?" I asked.

"Not much. Reading it is like listening to you talk." We chatted further, but when a cold wind rose, headed for bed.

A volume I'd packed was *Fragments: The Collected Wisdom of Heraclitus*, and I settled in with it. Known as the weeping philosopher, Heraclitus (535-475 BC) had been a metaphysician and by birth an Ephesian. He'd wandered the mountains, was misanthropic and trouble-some. He believed that change was the only reality; all things carried within them their opposites, and any no-tion of constancy was mistaken. Of impermanence, he said famously, that one could not wade in the same riv-er twice: "The river where you set your foot just now is gone—those waters giving way to this, now this." He believed that fire, not water, was the fundamental sub-stance: "Fire of all things is the judge and ravisher." And: "All things change to fire, and fire exhausted falls back into things...air dies giving birth to fire. Fire dies giving birth to air. Water, thus, is born of dying earth, and earth of water."

Heraclitus would have liked our meadow.

It stayed light until eleven, and when I awakened at

two the moon held a corona that, with bright stars, lighted the meadow like a halogen lamp. I checked for bears, urinated, then slept. I dreamt of flame retardant pouring from the bellies of helicopters. At 4:15, I was awakened by a gaggle of birds that shrieked in the early dawn, then quieted. At 8:10, footsteps startled me and I peaked out to see a stunning blonde in halter top and hiking shorts leaning toward Rick's tent.

"Is this your water filter?" she asked.

"No," Rick said, groggily.

"Someone lost it," she said. And trotted up the trail.

Was she a forest sprite, a sylph? Too lovely not to follow, I yanked on pants, jacket and boots. But she'd vanished. Either she had crossed the raging creek or melted into the trees.

We weighed her appearance over breakfast.

"That filter," I said. "You could have said it was yours."

Rick studied me. "Two guys were with her. Backpackers. They were headed for the wilderness."

"But they couldn't have forded that creek."

"They're young," he said. "Get hold of yourself."

It was eleven before I uncased my rod and rigged up. I trailed our creek through flowers and blackened lodgepole toward the river. Tracks of moose, deer, elk, and small mammals pockmarked the duff. I chose as my fly a black wooly-bugger with emerald threading that evoked the green-against-soot of the forest floor, and waded through standing water to the river proper. It raged murkily, but a snag at the far bank made a pool, and I cast above it. The bugger raced past at the surface. I cast again, then reeled up and dug in my gear for split shot.

This time the bugger stayed deep and, on retrieve, a fish struck testily. It shook its head, dodged cross current, then headed north. I kept my rod high as I crashed to a downstream eddy and eased the fish to the bank. It was a handsome brown, fourteen inches by my rod grip, its ochre stomach and leopard-spotted back distinct against the loam. I palmed its weight then freed it to the current.

Upstream, I flung sinker and fly at the snag's head and came tight on another fish. It struggled against the current, but in forty-five seconds I had it at the eddy. Another brown, equally beautiful but, I could see, hooked deeply in its jaw. I'd forgotten to de-barb. The first trout had been lip hooked, but this one...I gripped its girth as I twisted the hook, shuddering to see it writhe. What an ass I was; this fish would die. And given that we had neither grill nor pan in which to cook it...I revived the creature, partially, and it slipped toward the flood.

I'd seen a film short once about a surfcaster landing striper after striper, tossing each in the sand to asphyxiate. A half hour of this and he needed a snack. He found a sandwich he did not remember packing and bit in. A hook went through his jaw. He was dragged belly flopping toward the surf.

I de-barbed my hook, cast again, felt a third strike, tangled my line in debris, and lost the fish. Relieved, I disassembled my rod and splashed toward camp.

Rick was eager to hike and, after a lunch of apricots and granola, we headed for West Boulder Falls. Our creek stopped us. It was deeper. The afternoon sun was hot, and an absinthe-green cocktail of ash and snowmelt clouded the runoff. "Shall we try?" Rick said. Flip-flops hung from a clip at his belt. "Sure," I said. "If that girl can do it...."

With hiker's poles and shower shoes, Rick crossed effortlessly. But I staggered as creek water pounded my thighs, my bare feet numbing in seconds. Then I was across, hopping toward warm grass and cursing. I pulled on socks and boots, uncasing my rod with trembling fingers. I thought, that run below the falls might hold fish. If I can reach it through the flooded timber.

We hiked past more wildflowers and glacial erratics, marveling at views of the West Boulder, invisible at this remove, pre-fire. I made ribald patter about our sylph, conjuring streamside dalliances with her campmates that left Rick chuckling. "You're obsessed," he said.

"We'll free her, then forgive her," I said. Enumerating acts of gratitude in forced-march cadence.

The falls were a mini-Niagara, twisting through boulders to a cauldron of resurgent water that howled. Our boot soles vibrated. Pools below were Maytags of debris, their churning hypnotic.

"I always want to jump," Rick said.

I snorted. "You'll be dead soon enough." We sat on a fire-scalped log and nibbled trail mix. We were deep in wilderness, near the heart of the conflagration.

During my first Montana summer, the ranch where I had worked felt the 1959 earthquake—the largest in Rocky Mountain history and 7.3 to 7.8 on the Richter scale. North of Yellowstone, tsunamis rocked Hebgen Lake, eighty-million-ton landslides buried canyon highways, and both flooding and fire destroyed property. Twenty-eight people died. The log structure where I had bunked shook like a wet dog, and the Madison's South Fork, which I had fished, ran murky and wild. Home, at fourteen, I wondered if the hormonal storm I'd known had caused this disaster. But nature killed by itself, it didn't need my help. As Heraclitus said, "How from a fire that never sinks or sets would you escape?"

We were quiet hiking back. I detoured intermittently, but mud had joined the river's ash, mixing snowmelt to a consistency of Frappuccino. Not worth a cast. In the trail near our creek was fresh bear scat, slick as stewed prunes. The creek tasted of sand and soot; it raged fiercely. I glanced at the red and yellow cliff face, in this light evoking the Indian-head ornament of my dad's '53 Pontiac.

"What do you think?" I said. But Rick, the whippersnapper, had plunged in. Slow steady steps, and he crossed easily.

"You want these poles?" he shouted.

"Maybe just one."

I tossed my boots and eased into the raging snowmelt. The pole improved my balance, but the cold was excruciating. Rocks bruised my feet and my ankles twisted on rocks. My Achilles tendons, already tight, felt snap-prone. Halfway across I staggered and slipped. I flashed on Japanese woodcuts I'd seen of monks crossing mountain streams. Leaning on staffs, they had laughed. To hell with that, I thought. Join your crippled fish. You're a young man in an old man's body. Forget your sylph. She's sweet clover, lupine, monkeyflowers, youth—she won't return. You're burned-out forest, and that's forever. I lunged sideways. My hands shook. Then I was at streamside, panting.

That night I slept like a baby. We ate breakfast, blessed the forest with our droppings, and broke camp. The picnickers' meadow, a mile from the trailhead, was flooded; the West Boulder's much-photographed oxbow was a lake. We panted up, then down the rise, and stopped at the river's footbridge. Water rose nearly to its deck.

"Makes the crossing easy," Rick said.

I'd been saving one: "*Just as the river where I step is not the same, and is, so I am as I am not,*'" I said.

Rick glared at me, prickling. "You're the same."

Big Sky Journal
2009

The Man from Mountain Misery: Gary Snyder

The landscape is otherworldly: acres of hosed-over diggings, jagged dunes of worked-out tailings, leached
gravel, and quicksand...detritus of a hydraulic gold-
mining operation that, between 1853 and 1884, was the
California mother lode's biggest. Gary Snyder peers from
beneath a camouflage cap to which he's affixed a silver
spade engraved with "a Tibetan Vajrahana," he explains,
making it "the magical shovel of Smokey the Bear." His
voice is deeply rural, his face—which Kerouac described
in *The Dharma Bums* as "a mask of woeful bone" with
pupils that "twinkled like the eyes of old giggling sages
of China"—is lined. He turned sixty-three last May. He's
not tall, perhaps five-seven. Yet his physique, beneath
filthy shorts and a *Saloon Pilot* T-shirt, is muscular as a
college wrestler's. A faded tattoo in Sanskrit—*Pranava*,
or "breath of the universe"—stains his left calf.

To hike with Gary Snyder is the wilderness equivalent
of having jammed with Charlie Parker. He's as influential in his way...a Pulitzer prize-winning poet (for 1974's
Turtle Island), proto-environmentalist (whom Earth First!

founder Dave Foreman calls "the legendary half-god, half-man who created the tribe"), professor of English at U.C. Davis, and American Academy and Institute of Arts and Letters fellow who, in 1958, served as fictionalized protagonist of "the book that turned on the psychedelic generation." *Dharma* Bums' jacket prates: "two rebels on a wild march for experience...the orgiastic sexual sprees, the cool jazz bouts...from Frisco's swinging bars to the top of the snow-capped Sierras." A Beat poet during the fifties, Zen monk and "Dharma revolutionary" throughout the sixties, counter-culture patriarch and radical environmentalist in the seventies, he's enough of a Zen elder that Alan Watts wrote, "Gary Snyder is what I've been trying to say."

At his side puffs Carole Koda, a slim Japanese-American in her forties who's Snyder's wife and cohort in overseeing these Sierra Nevada foothills. They were married in a 1991 ceremony she describes as "a rich funk ritual—a San Juan Ridge/Buddhist wedding," with guitars, trombone, and magical incantations. Snyder's hand-calligraphied announcement reported the couple had been married "in a ceremony with family and a few friends... yellow-rumpled warbler, flicker, nuthatch, acorn woodpecker, orange-crowned warbler, Anna's hummingbird, purple finches—rufous-sided towhee, varied thrush, many juncos, also there."

"These diggings," Koda tells me, "are two thousand acres surrounded by the Inimim Forest, which is Bureau of Land Management, state park and Forest Service land—an island. We see it as a keystone, almost, in terms of maintaining a corridor for various animals, but especially the deer herd."

Behind us stand hundred-foot-high ponderosa pines, fat incense cedars, Pacific madrones, black oaks, Douglas firs, and sugar pines, dense manzanita, and kitkitdizze of these northern Sierras. But ahead is moonscape. Snyder squints, his goatee as gray as the cropped hair it balances.

"You see the top where the big trees are?" He indicates

a bluff a quarter-mile across the ditch. "This level went from here to there. That's what has been removed by giant hoses. It all went washing there." He points southwestward. "There are gravels identified from this region that are on the floor of San Francisco Bay."

The diggings were stopped by a court order in 1884, Snyder continues. "It put an end to hydraulic mining in the Sierra. The decision was basically a demand that watersheds not carry any more sand and gravel."

"But Siskon Corporation wants to resume mining," Koda says. "Underground. My friends and I wrote a proposal for turning all of this into a land trust. We keep trying to emphasize what a great family place it is: 'the kids just love the petrified wood and the quicksand!'"

Snyder sweeps his palm over the destruction. "This was done with no bulldozers, no fresnos, no fossil fuels. The energy that moved that gravel was water under tremendous pressure."

Wonder at the mechanics of this catastrophe seeps into his voice; he might be describing a process for extricating poems. Indeed this moonscape, with its tan ridges and deep crevices, resembles a cerebral cortex. "The last several miles they ran that water into a giant canvas hose. The hose was two feet in diameter, laid along the grade of the ditch and the flues. That built up an extraordinary head. Then they mounted it on giant water cannon which were on swivels, and they could systematically bring that gravel down and it would be collected through rifflers. The gold would be collected through a system involving the use of mercury, to which gold flakes are attracted."

Suddenly he's crashing down the slope, leaping over then digging into the soft earth, as did his character, Japhy Ryder, in *Dharma Bums*: "I looked up," Kerouac wrote, "and saw Japhy *running down the mountain* in huge twenty-foot leaps..." Koda and I follow cautiously. Snyder does not pause at the first pile's foot but vaults from hillock to hillock, past dwarf pines and petrified stumps, "sometimes in a deliberate dance with his legs crossing from right to left, right to left...."

That from the mountain trek which taught Kerouac backpacking and impressed upon him Japhy's vision of "a great rucksack revolution, thousands or even millions of young Americans wandering around with rucksacks, going up to mountains to pray...all of 'em Zen lunatics."

Snyder catches his breath. "Jack had a great ear, a great memory. He'd sit down the next day and type up whole conversations from parties." *Dharma Bums* was the first book starring Snyder, but not the last. Eight critical appraisals of his poetry have been published. He's considered *the* postmodern successor to Pound and Williams, and "probably our best poet," Jim Harrison says. "Unequivocally grand." Two years ago, in celebration of his sixtieth birthday, *Gary Snyder: Dimensions of a Life* surfaced, with reminiscences by everyone from Michael McClure to Daniel Ellsberg. The freshest book—Martin Green's *Prophets of a New Age,* with its final chapter, "Gary Snyder's California," appeared in September.

Earlier I'd shown Snyder an *Archie* comic that featured Zen, an intergalactic, ninja eco-warrior. "The Secret Origin of Zen," its cover promised, and: "Rumble in the Rainforest." I ask if, when Kerouac, Ginsberg, and he were meditating in the mid-fifties, they ever dreamed Americans would take so to Buddhist notions. "I thought somebody might just be saying someday"—he heightens his rural twang—"'Yeah, I'm a Zen master in Kansas, got a little place just outside of Wichita.'" We laugh. "There's no doubt that Zen really touched something in the American psyche."

Though his new and selected poems—*No Nature,* five decades and four hundred pages worth, much of which concerns Zen—will be nominated for a National Book Award in October, at this moment Snyder's less taken with consciousness than cranberries. He tips back his cap. "*The Flora of California* describes this spot as the only place in California where cranberries grow." He hurries through the maze of diggings, past petrified logs and handsawn stumps from the forties, then stops. Directly above the bog.

"I'm impressed, Gary," Koda says. "You were so right on. And it's easy not to be." Below is a wetland of cranberries and carnivorous plants. "The mining cut into old water tables here," Koda says. The muck and gravel below had been Lonesome Lake, its bed punctured by mining. The neighboring wetland is a potential "Area of Critical Environmental Concern" for the Bureau of Land Management, whose protection may result in the Yuba Watershed Institute (a local research and information-gathering group) salvaging the site. Snyder serves on the Institute's board.

"This terrain further on," he says, "becomes a tangle of deep, steep-walled gravel canyons. You can't climb out of them, you can't get into them very easily, you can't walk up and down them. It's a wonderfully weird terrain."

Snyder steps toward the bog and sinks to his ankle.

"Cranberries are where you find them," he mutters, "right under your feet."

We pick the fruit, chewing it gingerly. It's green. "Good though," Snyder says. He surveys the ragged flora. "We look at that and think that's beautiful." His eyes narrow. "A thousand years from now that forest will have spread widely and there will be some sizable trees; to erase the presence of these gravels will take millions of years." He smiles. "But what you witness there is *the beginning of the recovery of the forest.*"

Recovery has been a first priority of Snyder since his Depression-era youth, on a hardscrabble farm ten miles north of Seattle, when his father dumpster-dived for food and Gary contracted rickets from malnutrition. His parents divorced when he was fifteen, having quarreled bitterly through his childhood. He has a younger sister, Thea (a sex therapist, radio talk-show host, and pilot who, on her fortieth birthday, wing-walked over San Francisco), but as he wrote in 1990's *The Practice of the Wild*, "The woods were more of a home than home." Despite the solace they provided, "I realized that I had grown up in the aftermath of a clearcut...the area had been home to some of the largest and finest trees the world has seen, an ancient forest...I was to some extent instructed by the ghosts of those ancient trees as they hovered near their stumps."

The ponderosa are ancient above Kikitdizze, Snyder's mountain retreat twenty miles north of Nevada City. And many reach one hundred feet. They remain Snyder's advisors; have assisted in his latest recovery—from the break-up in 1988 of his twenty-one-year marriage to Masa Uehara, and subsequent lung surgery to remove a benign tumor. Snyder and Uehara, a native Japanese, built a log house here in 1970 on one hundred acres which they owned jointly with Allen Ginsberg and Richard Baker, of the San Francisco Zen Center. They named the place Kitkitdizze after a local shrub (also called mountain misery), and raised two sons—Kai and Gen—under subsistence conditions: solar panels for electricity, CBs for communication, woodburning stoves for heat and cooking, spring water to drink, outhouse for relief with glass windows for light, black oak and incense cedar for company. Snyder bought out his partners and now lives with his new family—Koda and her two daughters—in a park-like wilderness that David Padwa's described as "the home palace of a forest king."

Despite Snyder's reverence for the wild, at this moment he's kneeling in an outdoor kitchen before a battered propane refrigerator he's delighted to have fixed. "That's an old gas-operated Servel," he says, affectionately. "They haven't made them for twenty-five years. But we who live in the back country without electricity cherish them. And pass them on from generation to generation as heirlooms."

Scott McLean, a colleague of Snyder's at U.C. Davis,

a longtime neighbor and editor of *The Real Work*, Snyder's collected interviews, breaks in. "Oh God, are you making up stories about that refrigerator?" McLean's a darkly-bearded fellow in his late forties. He's housesat Kitkitdizze.

Snyder ignores him. "That Servel came to us in the summer of 1970 from Celestial Valley," he says. "Clarence Butts sold it to me for twenty-five dollars. It was old then. Every year I clean it out, and this year I couldn't get it working again." He tests the flame. "I took the burner element apart twice, reassembled and cleaned it each time, and when I took it apart today I realized I had been reassembling it wrong. What amazes me is what a tiny quantum of error that was, and it was my own inattention. I can reach into the ice chamber and feel frost forming!"

McLean groans from a nearby ramada, where his wife Patricia, Koda, and Koda's nine-year-old Korean daughter, KJ, help serve dinner. Good weather means outside at Kitkitdizze—no screens, open doors, and windows. Bats sweep through the ramada, snakes rattle the understory, and insects dive bomb Patricia's sundried tomatoes and pickled okra. "Gary, why don't you get rid of the goddam old gas refrigerator?," McLean calls. "They have these very snazzy new ones you could get out here."

Snyder stirs the lamb curry he's prepared. "There's a general attitude that I've insisted on having, that machines are sad and pitiful creatures also, and deserve a lot of compassion and help. And that they too have the Buddha nature. An attitude of superiority and hostility toward machines is just going to be bad luck for human beings, and it isn't going to help machines achieve their fullest potential either."

One recalls Snyder's longtime opposition to monkeywrenching, his arguments about it with Earth First's Dave Foreman. "The secret of life in a mechanical world is that everything requires maintenance," Snyder says. "Instead of resenting that, and trying to overlook the fact that maintenance is also a part of what is necessary to our lives, we should see maintenance as creative in its own light. I refuse to be anti-machinery, as such."

An odd rap, given this setting. Yet Snyder worked as a logger, a wiper on oil tankers, and a laborer through his young manhood. "Gary understands," poet Greg Keeler told me, "that the soul of America is a Monster Truck."

Deer wander toward the adjacent pond and pass unflustered ten feet from us. A family of wild turkeys swagger to within fifteen yards of us, picking their way through immense pine cones which, like fallen Christmas-tree balls, dot the forest floor. Above us weave tall ponderosa and black oak in a woods producing so little undergrowth it's more a yard than a forest. The Japanese/California farmhouse, with its tiled roof and pine logs, was built by Snyder and a dozen friends—part of a late-sixties, back-to-Mother-Earth movement inspired by Snyder's writings: notably *Earth House Hold*, *Riprap*, and *The Back Country*.

"A lot of us are here because of Gary," McLean admits. "The people in the Watershed Institute are all part of a circle of original friends."

Ridge dwellers include carpenters and engineers, furniture and cabinetmakers, biologists and ex-marijuana-farmers, teachers and poets. What residents seem to share is a heightened verbal acuity and a proclivity to write. The Yuba Institute's journal, *Tree Rings*—composed in part on Macintoshes powered by solar batteries—is disarmingly well-produced.

As far back as *The Dharma Bums*, Snyder envisioned this community, "a fine free-wheeling tribe in these California hills," Japhy said, living "like Indians in hogans," eating "berries and buds...we'll write poems, we'll get a printing press and print our own poems, the Dharma Press—"

Snyder's nothing if not deliberate. "I know," he says, "it's embarrassing. Well, we never did get a printing press."

"Place" is the bedrock to this San Juan community's ethic. If Snyder's described his place, Kitkitdizze, as "on the western slope of the Sierra Nevada, in the Yuba River watershed, north of the south fork at the three-thousand-foot elevation, in the Shasta Biogregion, Turtle Island" once, he's done so a hundred times. "It strikes me as protesting too much," novelist Tom McGuane's quipped, "which is to say, 'God, I know I'm as rootless as all the rest of you.'" But such deliberateness is the essence of bioregionalism, "the entry of place into the dialectic of history," Snyder's written, including the hope that regional boundaries might be redrawn along natural rather than political lines.

"The watershed is a good organizing unit," he explains. "When we say 'place,' the push is to ask, 'what do you mean by place exactly?' That leads into a reconsideration. The one that we find most useful is the watershed as a spacial unit within which the people and the biological system have a lot of intrinsic connection. And so we are proposing that watershed organizations be an alternative model for a revitalized mosaic of regional entities that can become, to whatever degree they can, self-determining and self-governing. Bioregionalism's a kind of populism. It's a new and infinitely more biologically-refined populism in which the populism includes the non-human population. Ecological populism."

I ask him how that might effect, for example, Chesapeake Bay.

Snyder pours himself a cognac. "I know, for example, it was an extraordinarily rich fishery. There are sixteenth and seventeenth century accounts of waterfowl in the Chesapeake Bay that are almost unimaginable. The bioregional principal is, 'we will bring as much of it back as we can.' The condition of the place as it was on white contact should be the standard."

Conversation drifts as KJ's kitten, Coolette ("his father was Mr. Cool"), stalks a doe. Wild turkeys withdraw, *"Little calls as they pass...."*

We sit beneath the lighted ramada as if on stage.

Snyder's theorizing about drama: "My conclusion," he says merrily, "is that trees and animals like theater. And human beings are entertainment. I came down the hill at dusk one night, and there was a cougar only twenty-five or thirty feet under the window of the house, where our fourteen-year-old-daughter Mika was playing classical piano pieces. And he was sitting there. Then he saw me and moved on up the trail and up the hill. I like to think the cougar was there to listen to the music. I would prefer to think he wasn't hunting her. She was in the house and he was by the open window, but he couldn't see in because it was way up high. So I can only think that the music somehow was interesting!"

KJ's chasing Coolette who's chasing a buck. Someone asks Koda how she feels about raising a small daughter where puma hunt. "I feel fine. I think KJ's lucky. How many kids get to be raised where there are puma? When the first snow falls she just wants to go out and track."

The question of how adequately his tribe has realized its vision came up on an earlier trek round Kitkit-dizze. Snyder, a clothes horse in his way, affected a pink COYOTE T-shirt, gold earring, khaki shorts, and a bone-handled Randall hunting knife at his hip.

"It's the best designed blade for cutting up a bunch of meat. I've completely butchered, from the skinning to the last division of the meat, several deer—entirely with this one knife." He has a proclivity for gathering road kills. As a Zen student in Kyoto, he asked a roshi if eating meat and drinking sake were impolitic. "A Zen man should be able to eat dog shit and drink kerosene," the roshi advised.

"I'm still learning," Snyder chuckled. We scattered dry leaves across the pine needle floor. Two-hundred yards south he stopped before a log structure in a spotless meadow. His voice softened. "This is our local Buddhist temple, our zendo. We got together and built this in 1981."

It's the Ring of Bone Zendo, named for a line in a Lew Welch poem: "I saw myself / a ring of bone / in the clear stream / of all of it / and vowed, / always to be open to it..." Welch, a college pal of Snyder's, disappeared in the adjoining wilderness—presumably a suicide.

Snyder removed his backpacker's sandals. He bowed and we entered. A large bell stood by the door, black pillows sat on a hardwood floor before white walls. A fly droned. He walked to the altar, bowed and lit incense.

"This Buddha's a seventeenth or eighteenth century Thai image that was given to us by a wealthy friend from New York." The Buddha smiled enigmatically. "This Fudo," he said, turning to a one-eyed, horribly-fanged statue—"comes from Komkura, Japan and was a gift from Jerry Brown." The California governor has visited Kitkitdizze numerous times, having enticed Snyder to head the California Arts Council during Brown's administration. He still considers the poet an advisor; they've spoken twice this week. Snyder picked a long, slender board from the altar. The Jikijitsu's stick, a kyosaku. "That's to wake people up with," he said "if they're drowsing too much. They tap you on each shoulder." He raised it in both hands like a sledgehammer. I winced: he's written that shoulder taps are followed by "four blows on each side of the back. These are not particularly painful—though the loud whack of them can be terrifying to a newcomer—" He smiled, lowering the kyosaku. Its blade read, "Painful Stakes." I mentioned that one Ring of Bone sitter claims a planed-down Louisville Slugger makes the best kyosaku.

"Oh, God," Snyder moaned. And continued his tour. "This building has a lot of details that were brought from traditional Japanese zendos. But the construction reflects the California barn." It was startlingly peaceful, yet Snyder looked distracted. "I have taken a sabbatical from any teaching duties here. Several years now."

There's a division within Ring of Bone, a rift between Snyder-and-cohorts, and those loyal to Robert Aitken Roshi, brought to teach during the 1970s. Adding tension,

Aitken's successor, Nelson Foster, became involved with Masa Uehara in 1988. "It was while I was up in Alaska one summer," Snyder acknowledged. "I came back, and here was this affair going on." Aitken now lives in Hawaii, and Foster serves as Ring of Bone's roshi.

Because of Uehara's presence, "it became uncomfortable for me to even be there," Snyder muttered. But divorce is not a primary cause of the zendo rift. "It's a point of divergence" between Snyder's personality—informally rural and more open to eclectic forms of consciousness exploration, including peyote and LSD use—and that of Aitken, who's "a white protestant beneath it all."

"I invited Bob," Snyder explained, "to come and visit us as a koan teacher. It worked quite well at first. Then what I witnessed was that he was changing rapidly in the direction of a hierarchical and more traditional and more conservative approach to practice. And becoming more and more ecclesiastical and elite. Very distrustful of uneducated people. Very ill at ease with rough or ragged people."

"Aitken wanted everybody to wear black robes," Scott McLean told me. "My friend Chuck Dawkem, a plumber, said, 'Hell I'm going there and sit in my plaid shirts the way I always have.' I thought, 'that is the spirit of our zendo. We want to sit and do the practice, but it's got to be in some way San Juan Ridge practice.'"

Snyder chatted while showing me first Ginsberg's old house, where Kai and Gen live as bachelors working with radical environmental concerns—their house is named Bedrock Mortar, for Indian mortars in its bouldered foundation—then a Zen temple shipped from Japan and reassembled here by Richard Baker. The temple's dedication ceremony, as Snyder wrote in *Practice*, "was in the Shinto style and included offerings of flowers and plants." But they were plants from Japan, not San Juan Ridge.

"The ritualists had the forms right but clearly didn't grasp the substance." A twentyish couple (she batiked, he lank-haired and blue-jeaned) emerged from the building. They camp there while working with the Yuba Watershed Institute. Snyder kibitzed and we moved along. They were a vision of love in the forest.

Uehara and Foster (also a poet) are married and live a short walk from Koda and Snyder. But as one practioner made clear, Ring "is 'The Zendo That Gary Built.' It would have never been built if it hadn't been for him. And I think that for Gary that's hard, that there's somebody there who ended up marrying his wife who's teaching in the zendo. And Gary's not."

"It's not a big deal for me," Snyder countered. We trudged noisily through thick stands of purple-trunked manzanita. "When Nelson moved in and I pulled back, a few of the other people who remembered it the other way dropped out. Some still sit there, but the composition of it has changed, and some of the people who used to be involved with it have turned their attention to wilderness affairs. Doing their practice in the mountains."

Which is where he learned his meditation, first in the woods near his house outside Seattle, later as a fire lookout and trail worker. "When I was young," he said in *The Real Work*, "I had an immediate, intuitive, deep sympathy with the natural world which was not taught me by anyone…That sense of the authenticity, completeness, and reality of the natural world itself made me aware even as a child of the contradictions that I could see going on around me.…" Some of those contradictions were environmental—"I lived on the edge of logging country, and the trees were rolling by on the tops of trucks, just as they are still"—others were domestic. His father, Harold Snyder, was a handyman who could not handily support his children, an outdoorsman who spent few hours in the woods; his mother, Lois, was a published poet and journalist who attended the family's small dairy farm and had scant time to write.

"She still tells me," Snyder said, "'if you hadn't been

born, I'd have been a much greater writer than you.' She felt stultified and frustrated by the life on the farm. She cast blame out, mostly at my father and at the world." More distressingly, "she had hours of deep depression and hysteria" that drove Snyder farther into the woods.

Their farm "was only a couple of acres of fenced pasture," he recalled, "and in back of that going back for a long distance was recovering second-growth forest. Recovering from the clear cut. That was just home to me. There was one old cedar tree I describe as having been my advisor. When I had to make up my mind about something that I wasn't certain what to do, I would climb the tree and sit in the tree until I got an answer."

Lois Wilkie Snyder Hennessy, now eighty-six, lives twenty miles from Snyder and Koda in Grass Valley. "We encouraged her to move here so she'd have a place nearer to us. But she's alienated everyone. She was so hard on my sister Thea, who's two years younger than me, that my sister won't talk to her, won't write her."

"She's a rageaholic," Thea Lowry told me, "whose business is minding other people's business. She is incredibly intrusive. She's a person who would inspect her children's bm's before letting them go to school in the morning. So bossy and controlling. *Mommy Dearest* is a valentine compared to Lois."

According to Thea, her mother beat her with a belt, placed her on a drainboard, and scrubbed her vagina with soap until "my urethra stung and stung and stung," had an incision made in her clitoral hood when she was five, "to expose the clitoris so you'd enjoy sex more," had her pose nude for art photographers when she was twelve, wrecking "my self-esteem and my feelings about myself for almost twenty years," accused her of sexual behavior "when I was still a trembling virgin," and "had me jailed for being out of parental control four times before I was made a ward of the court" at sixteen.

"Lois didn't want to have any children after Gary," Thea said. "She's truly a son-besotted woman."

In *The Real Work*, Snyder spoke of a male poet and his relationship to the "tooth-mother." He noted, "the son relationship to the complex tooth-mother ecstatic-mother type is apt to produce environmentally, psychologically, genetically, by whatever means, the line of magic that produces poetry....To be a poet you have to be tuned into some of the darkest and scariest sides of your own nature. And for a male, the darkest and scariest is the destructive side of the female...to a male child the negative side of the mother is the darkest, scariest thing he can perceive."

Snyder added, as we hiked, "I try not to carry anger or resentment around for all kinds of emotional things that went on [with my mother] when I was younger: hysteria, depression and some really strange little sadisms and cruelties. It's a very complex, almost multiple personality."

Did she abuse him physically? "I think probably by modern definitions, yes. She would a few times whip me with a belt...but I would say psychologically she really put everybody through the ringer. She has a sadistic streak, there's no question of it. But it takes more the form of psychological stuff. When I was a little kid what I remember most clearly was her, when she was mad, telling me that there was something really bad in me and that I would probably go insane. Every once in a while she still says to me, 'I can't believe you seem to be all right.'" Which is a way of saying, "Why aren't you crazy like me?" He sighed. "Trying to figure out how to be with my mother has been a lifelong koan for me."

And one that required distance. He noted in *The Real Work*, "As early as I was allowed, at age nine or ten, I went off and slept in the woods at night alone. I had a secret camp back in the woods that nobody knew about; I had hidden the trail to it...from the time I was thirteen, I went into the Cascade Mountains, the high country, and got into real wilderness. At that age I found very little in the civilized human realm that interested me."

We'd been walking through the woods for some time, through pygmy manzanita, sticky curl, and yanda.

Snyder stopped. Ahead was a small house with tiled roof, gray/green walls and porch facing a gorge.

"This is my study." He quieted as we approached. "The Ditch Hut." It looked like a doll's house—or a child's secret camp. "This is where I work when I really want to work," he said. He unlocked door. A dead mouse lay near a lizard skin on the floor. An ocelot pelt hung above the window. Wood rats scuttled about the foundation. "Sometimes I stay here for two or three days," he murmured. "I've written a lot of *Mountains and Rivers Without End* (his long promised magnum-opus) down here. And the early drafts of essays in *The Practice of the Wild*. In fact *Axe Handles* and all my books written in the seventies and the early eighties were written here." The space was cozy. "Ten foot by eleven foot," he said, with "a four-and-a-half-foot plate, which means the ceiling is really low and the walls are really low. It's designed to sit on the floor in, not to stand up in, and not to use tables and chairs in. So if you sit in it Japanese style with this little low Japanese table, which is a Japanese student's table from the nineteenth century that I picked up second hand in Kyoto and took home on my bicycle, and a little tiny chest there that I also bought in Japan to keep papers in, and then a couple of modern letter file drawers and a bunch of bookshelves and a kerosene Aladdin lamp for light and a little stone fireplace for heat and for cooking meals if I stay overnight down here. And a few shelves for a few groceries. And a sitting cushion, a zafu. And a little altar for the Buddha!"

In former days he'd written on a manual typewriter, but today used a portable Mac. There were card files near the low desk, shelves of typing paper and a bunk bed. A ponderosa cone lay in the miniature hearth.

I asked who built this hut. "I did," he said. "All the materials were brought down this trail by wheelbarrow. There's no road."

What are its walls made from? "Cedar."

Of course: his boyhood advisor.

L ois Snyder Hennessy sits in her living room wearing a pink house coat. Her face is round and vaguely Indian. A sheepdog, Angus, scratches by her side. "He says, 'it's flea season and I'm getting a few fleas, and Mommy's spraying me and I don't like it.'" She sniffs. "I wrote poems to dogs and cats. I don't know why I don't send my stuff out, but I don't need any publicity anymore...."

The room's inundated with books, record albums, medicine vials, disorder. It's a writer's space. Hennessy offers a poem: "So many things a dog is good for, for working, sniffing, poking / For pleasing kids, for guarding homes, for playing fetching joking..." Then one less meditative: "Wives are barracudas / They devour mothers' sons / Leaving only the skeletons / For the mothers to love." She recites it wearily. "I have *never* had a friendly daughter-in-law. Gary has either warned them against me, or for some reason they didn't like me."

Over the next hour, Hennessy itemizes her brother's and "Uncle Joe's" sexual molestation of her, her mother's rape by a family doctor, resulting in her illegitimate birth, her mother's manic depression, her husbands' marital inefficacies, her two abortions, her harassment in the workplace, men's hypocrisy (her second husband was a bigamist), her daughter-in-laws' alienation of affection, and her children's inattention. She has encyclopedic recall.

Finally I ask about Gary's poetry. "One of his favorite poems was from *Mother Goose*, 'Heigh-Ho, The Carrion Crow.' He'd go around the house singing its refrain, 'Hi ding do, hi ding do.' Then one day, when he was about four, he came to me and said, 'Mommy'—and this is long before he could read—'gimme paper and pencil, I'm gonna write a poem.' So I handed him a sheet of paper and a pencil. And he curled up on the floor and went 'hmm, hmm, hmm.' And pretty soon he came to me and he had, in a little boy's hand, three blocks of straight lines. So he hands that to me and says, 'here Mommy, read my poem.' And my throat choked up, you know. And I said, 'Honey, I'm sorry but I can't read your poem. You have to go to school and learn to write and read, and then your letters will look like in that book. And then I can read your poetry.' And the little guy wept bitterly."

Thereafter, Snyder's sister told me, Hennessy "was very much like a stage mother. A real publicity hound. She shaped Gary and coached him and pushed him and charged him and tantalized him. Lois coopted Gary. She said, 'sit down, memorize poetry, do as I say.' And Harold would say, 'this is my son, he's supposed to learn boy things.' Lois would say, 'shuddup, you don't know nothing.' And I would go to my father and learn how to saw wood."

When she had tucked in daughter Thea, Hennessy says, "and done the laundry and washed dishes and everything, tired as I was, I had to give Gary, I felt, half an hour all his own." She read poetry to him nightly. As Snyder recalled, "My mother always expressed the highest regard for writing and writers and poets. There was a really strong validation of the work of writing." Both it and reading became linked in his experience with discomfort. He burned his foot severely during second grade. Recovering, "he lay on a quilt out on the front porch," Hennessy remembers, "and I brought him this pile of *Childlife* magazines. After four or five or six days, I heard a squeal of joy: 'Oh Mommy, I can read!' When he went back to school the teacher said, 'train him a little bit more on his languages, and he can be skipped a full year.' And he was."

Thea remembered, "Lois insisted Gary take Latin in high school, leaned on him to take French, bellowed at him to do his homework, pushed him into Boy Scouts, and very much managed him." Thea's and Gary's IQs were tested. "One was 135 and the other was 137," Hennessy says. "I don't remember which is which."

Despite her attention, there had been serious deficiencies. Gary had contracted rickets before he was two. "Of course his diet wasn't very extensive at that time," Hennessy reflects. "I was an inexperienced cook, so I probably didn't do too well by him."

During WWII, The family moved to Portland where Harold Snyder found steady work ("He couldn't even make a living as a bootlegger") and Gary won financial support, in 1947, to attend Reed College. Hennessy got him in, she says, by showing its admissions director a poem of his called "This Is My Youth." It was about climbing Mount Hood. "The white-haired fellow read it and began to cry," she remembers. "He said, 'yes, we can make room for this boy.'"

Reed was the proper school for Snyder, it was a highly intellectual, egalitarian hotbed of radical thought. And postwar bohemianism. He shared a house—with poets Lew Welch, Philip Whalen, and half a dozen others—which Hennessy describes as "a crash pad before the word was invented." His housemates became family. Carole Baker, in *Dimensions*, writes that "I suppose we were the first hippies." Snyder taught them Goodwill scouring, cooked bottomless pots of soup, shared CARE packages from Hennessy, helped support them as a copy boy at the *Oregonian* ("his editor had an odd thing," Hennessy says, "he longed to see women urinate") and as an office boy at radio-station KEX, working for its male, music librarian ("who'd been run out of Bend, Oregon for making up to high school boys"), took peyote with pal Michael Mahar ("Mike," he said, "I think it has a great future"), and transformed his leaky basement sleeping-corner, between furnace and laundry tub, into a boudoir. "Women of all persuasions found him attractive," Mahar remembers.

"Robin Collins was the poet's first love," Hennessy tells me. She was an honors student, beautiful and "the essence of myth and legend," Mahar contends. "She came very close to Gary but then she withdrew...it was a very long time before Gary could accept what had happened."

In *No Nature* are "Four Poems for Robin": *I remembered when we were in school / Sleeping together in a big warm bed....*"

During their affair, Hennessy tells me, "Gary began to change. He became very sharp-tongued and very caustic. And very critical of others, very difficult for me. Gary came and reported to me, 'Robin and I are breaking up. She's gone to,' I think he said, 'a counselor, psychiatrist, and he says she has to break up with me because I'm destroying her sense of herself.'"

In adolescence Hennessy had observed oddities in Snyder, ones she claims, drove her and him apart. "Gary and I have a love-hate relationship," she says matter-of-factly. "He was mean to his sister, from the time she was walking, or slightly thereafter. For instance, she'd give a shriek and I'd say, 'what's the matter?'" Hennessy's voice changes eerily. "'*Gago hoot me!*' Gary hurt me. Now if I'd had my way about it I'd have grabbed a comb or a brush or anything and hit him plenty. No, couldn't do it. His father didn't believe in corporal punishment. 'Children are made of love, they should never be punished,' he said. 'Oh shit,' I felt like saying."

"But," Thea told me, "one time she forced Harold to beat us both and he was sick about it. None of us can remember what it was about."

Snyder admitted, "I have parts of Lois, it's true. I think I'd have a lot more of it if I hadn't released a lot of what I did [through Zen]." In "For a Far-out Friend," published in 1959's *Riprap*, the poet addresses a woman: *Because I once beat you up / Drunk, stung with weeks of torment....*

Thea confided, "Gary has kind of a selfish, cruel side. He said one time, 'I enjoy hurting people.' There's a side of him that rebels against women. He has a lot of anger."

"In my own life and times, I enjoy roughness," Snyder admitted, but denied harboring anger at anything but the world. He observed, "there's a principle in Buddhist psychology that everything has a parallel. For the faculty of intelligence, its parallel is anger. The *drawback* to intelligence is anger. And imagination...across from it is lust."

Snyder married fellow-student Alison Gass to spite Robin Collins; he was with Gass only five months. "She had the most beautiful boobs I ever saw in my life," Hennessy remembers. "But Alison could not support herself, and Gary couldn't support both of them and finish school."

In 1946 Harold had left Hennessy, surfeited with her rage. "I had temper tantrums that you wouldn't believe," she says. He took a job in Oakland. Another son might have felt obligated to fill his father's shoes. Gary withdrew. He became obsessed with climbing mountains, tackling sixteen major peaks while a teenager. "I started writing poetry," he recalled in his introduction to 1991's *Beneath A Single Moon*, "to give voice to some powerful experiences that I had while doing snowpeak mountaineering in the Pacific Northwest." He'd read a poem by Hopkins with its lines, "Oh the mind has mountains; cliffs of fall / Frightful, sheer, no-man-fathomed...." And realized "literal mountains were not the only place to climb."

He'd worked summers—in a tanker's engine room ("I got a firsthand sense of what fossil fuel means to the world"), as a Forest Service laborer and a construction stiff—supporting himself and exteriorizing demons. If nature was Mother, it was tough not hurting her. He worked as a chokesetter on a logging crew, "looping cables on logs and hooking them to D8 Caterpillars—dragging and rumbling through the brush," he wrote. "Such work is terribly dangerous," Hennessy exclaims, "it takes a young man that's very spry. Many are killed."

Snyder loved it—"for the same qualities," he said, "that makes Melville write enthusiastically about whaling in *Moby Dick*: the energy, the use of appropriate tools; the good spirit that men have while working together. While at the same time being aware that this is the paradox of the working class in the world. That although there's a conviviality and a pride in the work, the ultimate result of the work is not to be admired." Nevertheless, he told me, "I wouldn't mind being a small-scale logger myself."

"When Gary was little," Hennessy says, "he asked, 'Well, where did all things get started?' And I said, 'I just call it Mother Nature.'" Which leant a certain ambivalence. "I remember once" Hennessy adds, "I heard a shriek from Thea and she was saying, 'Gago you killed it, you killed it, you killed it!' He had been given a BB gun. I went out and she was cradling a little bird in her hand. And he said, 'I was going to shoot that bird and I didn't think I could or would. But I shot it and it fell.' And oh, he was heartsick."

He grew obsessed with nature. As early as age eleven he saw Chinese mountains-and-rivers paintings in the Seattle art museum; he felt instinctive kinship, sighing, "It looks just like the Cascades." He was as of yet unaware of a paradox: that mountains "have mythic associations of verticality, spirituality, height, transcendence, hardness, resistance, and masculinity," he'd write in *Practice*. And waters "are feminine: wet, soft, dark 'yin' with associations of fluid-but-strong. "He told me, "one is thought of as relentless and uncompromising, the other as flowing, forgiving, negotiating." That paradox was captured in Buddhist sculptures of the demon Fudo, portrayed as "comically ferocious" in opposition to Kannon, cast as "a figure of compassion." To Snyder they seemed two sides of the natural world (he may then have envisioned *Mountains and Rivers without End*) and he'd juxtapose a lifelong dedication to mountaineering against a love affair with watersheds.

Mountains and rivers—ferocity and compassion—represented two sides of a complex personality structure: "We operate with a number of 'personality-selves' or 'selves' if you like. And it amounts to 'no self.' No one substantial, fundamental, permanent self. We become liberated not by formulating some kind of substantial and permanent true self, but by giving up the idea of any kind of self at all. Buddhists will say, 'no self is your true self.'" Or, as he commented on the title, *No Nature*: "Self nature is no nature."

Psychiatric theory was in the air at Reed, as was Far Eastern thought. Snyder studied Freud and Jung; calligraphy, Taoism and Zen. He was anti-psychotherapy ("we've had a hundred years and it hasn't worked") but by 1949 he'd embrace Buddhism. Its view of chaos as "a kind of order, more rich and complex than we're intellectually able to grasp" and the practitioner's acceptance of many selves, were congenial.

He'd note that "Zen is the crispest example of the 'self-help' (*jiriki*) branch of Mahayana Buddhism." And though Snyder's style was Samurai, the practice he chose was deliberately non-violent. Meditation and poetry would be the testing ground of violence. In "What You Should Know To Be A Poet," he suggested learning, *"all you can about animals as persons / the names of trees and flowers and weeds... / Then, / kiss the ass of the devil and eat shit; / fuck his horny barbed cock, / fuck the hag...."*

"That's a shift in psychology [in the poem]," Snyder told me. "What I was saying at that time was 'in the deepest sense to be a poet, you should be open to all those territories.'" He acted out his personal demonism "on a psychological level...in terms of certain kinds of investigations and explorations, some of which came to me with peyote, and some in my meditations." But also through scholarship. His senior thesis at Reed—published as *He Who Hunted Birds in His Father's Village: The Dimensions of a Haida Myth*, examines a Native American tale from the perspective of "bringing contemporary literary and psychological theory to bear on traditional Native American oral literature," he told me. "It's a story of lost love. I took a Freudian interpretation to it, a Jungian interpretation to it, and simply an ethnographic interpretation to it. I got impassioned by the case...."

237

Snyder's passion was Robin's departure, but much of his thesis deals with the true poet's relationship to an Earth Mother/lover, to whom he must be sacrificed. Snyder quotes Robert Graves's *The White Goddess*: "no poet can hope to understand the nature of poetry unless he has had a vision of the Naked King [himself or a double] crucified to the lopped oak, and watched the dancers, red-eyed from the acrid smoke of the sacrificial fires, stamping out the measure of the dance, their bodies bent uncouthly forward, with a monotonous chant of: 'Kill! kill! kill!' and 'Blood! blood! blood!'"

The telephone jingles beside Hennessy's chair; it's Snyder. She asks him, "Have you got a copy of the poem, 'This Is My Youth'? Gary! Where is it! Oh, I'm *killed*, Gary. That's my favorite poem—" She nearly swoons. Then: "Juvenilia *hell*, it's the best poem you ever wrote *and it got you into Reed*!"

Hennessy rings off, segueing to an elaborate description of Snyder's graduation: "He was broke, so I rented his cap and gown for him. And attended. I guess he was still very much in love with Robin. She was there and got her honors. Gary missed his by a hair—he was working fulltime—and was very depressed. I rose to my feet and focused my camera, a Speed Graphic, and got a picture of her. All over the building the parents were raising their cameras whenever their kids came to the platforms. When Gary came to the platform, E.B. McNaughton who was the pro tem president of Reed at the time, and also editor/publisher of *The Oregonian*, gave him his diploma. Gary was a copy boy there. I snapped the picture—which ran next day in the paper three columns wide. I told Gary, 'Oh Gary, I got that!' His face distorted in a terrible snarl, and he said, 'You bitch. You took those pictures and I didn't give you permission to take them.' I said, 'Gary, the parents all over were taking these pictures.' He said, 'But your camera was the biggest!'"

Hennessy shrugs. "He claimed he was embarrassed."

At Kitkitdizze, I brush my teeth in a water glass and wander outside to pee. The morning sky is California blue. I step back through sliding-glass doors of the barn where I've camped and notice Snyder's office corner is remarkably well-organized. A sleeping bat hangs pasted above file shelves of correspondence, there are small Buddhist altars, and wall space is crammed with topo maps that include Geographical Information System charts made by Kai. Gary told me, "That's a new digital computer mapping system being used by people in the conservation movement to locate old growth stands [through satellite photography] and map them." To, among other things, guard against clearcuts.

By Snyder's desk are catalogue files with decades of notes and addresses, there are Environmental Impact and Vegetation Management for Restoration reports, there's Giles Gunn's *The Culture of Criticism and The Criticism of Culture* and Emily Post's *Etiquette* beside C. M. Doughty's *Arabia Deserta*. Nearby are a handheld CB, various western saddles, an antique wooden pitchfork, a .44 magnum Smith & Wesson he carries backpacking in Alaska, and sundry notes pinned to a door:

"I.VI.92. Leaving the house at two, mileage 62562, wrote a note to Jack about the dope pipe. Get Bruce a copy of *This Incomparable Land*. Doobie's commandments: Stomp out greed, wipe out envy, never assume, leave only what can be proved, keep smiling, fake health, drink milk, I say drink tea, sex a lot, exercise your heart, never lose touch, make the whole world smile...." And: "Grasshoppers eating all the shrubs in the Great Basin this summer. *No Nature* gift list. Send *Practice of the Wild* to—"

Friends have commented on what a pack rat Snyder is. "He has typed-out, bound journals from when he was in high school," McLean said. "His archive at Davis is massive, one of the richest personal archives you could imagine." Everything in Snyder's life is ordered. "Which goes back to Zen practice," McLean added. "'Discipline' for Gary is merely putting the shoes in order outside the dojo. Then you have all that time inside to be wild...to be free...."

I meander up the trail, sixty yards to the log house. Snyder's slouched beneath the ramada, scanning newspapers and ingesting NPR's *Morning Edition*. "Coffee?" he asks. Then offers a cup that reads: EXPLORE YOUR INNER STRENGTH AND KARMIC ENERGY THROUGH CAFFEINE. He pours from a Nissan thermos, smiling wickedly. Koda's seated on her zafu in the open bedroom, not meditating but trapped by the phone. She and Snyder do meditate, a half hour each morning. Then caffeine.

KJ appears, rubbing her eyes. "Gary, there's a bat in the outhouse."

"A bat, huh."

"*Asleep* I think." Koda approaches and Snyder rises to hug her. "The lovebirds," KJ says. "They're always hugging."

KJ has dried seaweed and rice for breakfast. "Us Asians love our rice." It's Koda Rice, from the family farm near Livingston, California. KJ's a Korean orphan who, at one-and-a-half, was adopted by Koda. Koda is third generation Japanese-American, a status insufficient to have kept her parents from internment-camps during the war. "I feel as if I had a wonderful childhood, though," Koda says. "I had a lot of what some people would consider problems with my father—he died when I was thirteen—but he and I worked that out when I was twenty-three, through a series of dreams. He was essentially a workaholic. If I hadn't come to terms with my own father, I wouldn't have been able to be with Gary. He's not obsessive..."

"But I'm close," Snyder says.

"He's close. But there's that *little bit right there* that saves it." She laughs.

Today they've a potluck-dinner scheduled with a tribe from the adjacent ridge. "It's just another little community—in Forest City—we haven't been much in touch with," Snyder explains. Before white contact, he adds, it was common for native tribes on nearby ridges never to mingle. "But our groups could be of use to each other in expanding our observation of the territory."

Snyder's tribe is nothing if not cosmopolitan. Among those I've met, Scott McLean has a Ph.D. in German literature, Patricia McLean teaches high school in Nevada City, and Koda has a graduate degree in psychology and was trained as a physician's assistant. Last evening, they, Scott, Gary and I discussed literary politics, county politics, California and national politics. "I didn't vote for Jerry Brown in the Democratic primary," Snyder said, "because, as a member of the Green Party, I couldn't. But I'm not sure he'd serve us best as president. His role may be that of a maverick."

He worked with Brown from 1974 to 1978. "That was before we had telephones," McLean interjected. Brown would show up, more often than not, with Linda Ronstadt. They'd just sit around the fire at night."

"We'd leave guitars out," Snyder said, "but she never got the hint."

"When Brown couldn't get hold of Gary," McLean said, "he'd literally have this highway patrolman drive up from Sacramento. And there were some people seriously growing dope at the time. Down the fire access road this highway patrol car would come...'The governor wants to see you.'"

Breakfast drunk, we head for the barn office—past the pond's rowboat and kayak "for practicing Eskimo rolls," and numerous mountain bikes. I think, what a distance Snyder's traveled from Oregon—where he lit out for San Francisco in a beatup car, "The Wanderer," he abandoned on Highway 101 when it expired. Hennessy told me, "He left Reed for California that same day he called me 'You bitch.' I remember going to his vacant apartment and going through the cupboard...there was one lone sock. I cried my eyes out over that sock."

Except for one semester in 1952, studying linguistics and anthropology at Indiana University...plus his Kyoto years...Snyder would remain Californian. His was the endpoint of a migration begun 150 years previous by German and Irish ancestors, some of whom followed the railroad south to Texas, others of whom pressed northwest to Washington. Though Snyder claims "my father was not a significant figure in my life," Harold acquainted Gary with his tool chest. "He'd say, 'use any tool you like, but put it back.' He was a very handy person, with brothers who were all active in the logging industry. Or worked in ships. One of them owned a small tramp freighter, and was captain of it." Gary "never had economic career anxiety" thanks to his father's teachings. "I could always pick up work as a carpenter or work with the forest service, or work in the woods."

Yet Hennessy told me, "The absent father concept absolutely fits Harold." He built and sold houses around San Francisco during the fifties, and Gary occasionally worked with him, sharing the odd drink or dinner afterward. It was the only time they were close. Kerouac describes Harold at a party in *Dharma Bums*: "he was a tight-built little tough guy just like Japhy...completely energetic and crazy...He immediately began dancing wild mambos with the girls while I beat madly on a can... he was almost falling over, moving his loins at the girl, sweating, eager, grinning, glad, the maddest father I ever saw."

Snyder was studying Asian languages at U.C. Berkeley, translating Chinese poetry and writing a bit of his own. He worked summers outdoors. He still purchased clothes from the Salvation Army and scrounged food where he might. "Gary told me," Hennessy said, "that when he was at his hungriest, in going to Berkeley for graduate study and really needing any help he could get, his father was giving him none. But his father said, 'Oh, I've met the most interesting young man and I'm subsidizing him a little while he goes to school.' Gary told me this with some bitterness."

He appeased father-hunger through manual labor. "I went to a men's gathering just a year ago," Snyder says from his barn desk. "As one of the resource people. I enjoyed it enormously. But it was kind of just like what working men do when they get together. They get rowdy, they tell outrageous jokes, they act up. And I said, 'Oh god, is this what these guys need?' They just didn't have a chance to be in the working class."

He reaches for a book—Bus Griffith's comic, *Now You're Logging*. "You can't *buy* this book," he says, "it's out of print. What I love about it is the layout of rigging: it shows how you rig different poles, actually *describes* it in the comic book." He fingered a panel. "This pulls the main line up through the bull-block and down to the block on the log in front of the spar tree...shows all the rigging steps here, see." He patted its cover. "This is a valuable book!"

Snyder brazed his love of work outdoors to solitude, by spending summers as a fire lookout. On mountain tops, alone. "I'm one of the few people I know who at the end of a season on lookouts really didn't want to come down." Solitude was therapeutic. In 1952's *Lookout's Journal*, composed at Crater Lake National Park, he noted "the pressing need to look within and adjust the mechanism of perception." He began sitting hours at a stretch. "Almost had it last night," he wrote, "*no identity.*" Working on trails and camping outside, he wrote poems that would constitute *Riprap*, his first book.

Half of that volume consists of eighth-century poet Han-shan's "Cold Mountain" poems, translated by Snyder to hip vernacular. "Han-shan is a mountain madman in an old Chinese line of ragged hermits," he noted. "When he talks about Cold Mountain he means himself, his home, his state of mind": "*I wanted a good place to settle / Cold Mountain would be safe....*"

Ginsberg had met Snyder, "a bearded interesting

Berkeley cat," he wrote to John Allen Ryan, "a head, peyoteist, laconist, but warmhearted," when Jack Kerouac appeared in 1955. Kerouac had been on the road, cleansing himself of that Ivy League education he felt was in part responsible for the conventionality of 1950's *The Town and the City*. Snyder was deflating from Reed. He'd say, in *The Real Work*: "An education is only valuable if you're willing to give as much time to de-educating yourself as you gave to educating yourself...Get away from books and from the elite sense of being bearers of Western culture....But also, ultimately, into your mind, into *original mind* before any books were put into it...."

Snyder, Ginsberg, and Kerouac all had hysterically intrusive mothers. (It would be seven years before Ken Kesey's *One Flew over the Cuckoo's Nest* pigeonholed American men as castrati living in state-run nuthouses overseen by Big Nurse Ratcheds.) Each poet calmed the mindstorm of maternal interference through meditation. Part of Snyder's practice included challenging her by *quitting poetry*: "I finished off the trail crew season [in 1955]," he said in *Work*, "and went on a long mountain meditation walk for ten days across some wilderness. During that process—thinking about things and my life—I just dropped poetry." To his amazement, "From that time forward I always looked on the poems I wrote as gifts that were not essential to my life...."

That year Ginsberg organized a historic reading—Six Poets at the Six Gallery, in San Francisco—that launched the San Francisco Renaissance and married East Coast bohemianism to West as the Beat Generation. Snyder, Ginsberg, Michael McClure, Philip Whalen, Kenneth Rexroth and Philip Lamantia presided. Most were Buddhists. Kerouac passed jugs of wine as Snyder, dressed in jeans and work shirt, read his Indian/coyote poem, "A Berry Feast." Ginsberg, in charcoal suit, white shirt and tie, read "Howl": "I saw the best minds of my generation destroyed by madness...." The evening's verse, in harmony with Kerouac's shouted "Go!"s, was a poetic jam session. Snyder advised friend Will Petersen, "Save the invitation, some day it will be worth something." Mc-Clure recalled, in *Scratching the Beat Surface*, that each of the 150 people present knew "at the deepest level that a barrier had been broken, that a human voice and body had been hurled against the harsh wall of America...."

It was the age of McCarthyism; indeed Snyder had sacrificed his Forest Service eligibility to anarchist politics. McClure wrote, "We were locked in the Cold War and the first Asian debacle—the Korean War....We hated the war and the inhumanity and the coldness. The country had a feeling of martial law....As artists we were oppressed and indeed the people of the nation were oppressed...the art of poetry was essentially dead—killed by war, by academies, by neglect, by lack of love, and by disinterest."

Norman Mailer argued in *The White Negro* that "the psychic havoc of the concentration camps and the atom bomb" had created "the American existentialist—the hipster, the man who knows that if our collective condition is to live with instant death...why then the only life-giving answer is to...divorce oneself from society, to exist without roots, to set out on that uncharted journey into the rebellious imperatives of the self." Ginsberg's work was obsessed with the atomic age and radiation fallout; Snyder acknowledges that "the detonation of the nuclear bomb in Japan had a deep effect on me, and it was a deeply alienating effect instantly." Hiroshima proved the ultimate clearcut.

Nuclear anxiety cemented the Beats' existentialism. But it did not eliminate fun. Snyder and Ginsberg (costumed by Goodwill now) hitchhiked round the Pacific Rim, reading poetry in night clubs and college auditoriums, reveling in Beat excitement. Will Baker recalls that, at one Seattle performance, "Mr. Ginsberg looked like an undernourished deckhand. Pale, wearing spectacles thick as bottle-glass, he hunched into a pea jacket even indoors. The other, Mr. Snyder, I recognized instantly from his boots, his mackinaw, and a beard several weeks along...."

Toby Thompson

Each of them needed a bath." Baker's and his academic peers' reaction upon hearing their poetry was standard. They sat "nailed into [their] chairs. There were gasps, or course, and inadvertent moans," while Ginsberg read "Howl," then Snyder's work, "Like a "big, fresh, cold wind...carried us out of poetry, out of school, out of all the particular madnesses of our time and deep into pine trees, ice-scoured granite, and the elusive brains of birds, frogs, deer, coyotes. And also into the laconic, lewd brain of a working man..." Snyder had a "guitar of a voice...I remember thinking to myself: *This is tremendous. They can say anything they want to. This is like jazz, it really is.*" There were groupies. "A faculty wife broke down and cried over Mister Ginsberg's aloof, Byronic manner; a longhaired blonde sat so close to Mister Snyder that he was in danger of inhaling her."

Nothing like it had appeared in performance art (unless one counts Elvis or Chuck Berry). Rexroth suggested Ginsberg record "Howl" with a jazz group, and back East, Kerouac would declaim to Steve Allen's piano riffs—on TV, LP, and at the Village Vanguard—then cut sides with Al Cohn and Zoot Sims. Ann Charters noted, in her *Portable Beat Reader*, that the Beats' secret heroes were "bop musicians Charlie Parker and Dizzy Gillespie...the word 'beat' was primarily in use after WWII by jazz musicians and hustlers as a slang term meaning down and out, or poor and exhausted...." Kerouac insisted it also meant beatific or beatitude, and by 1961 Bob Dylan would be growling his Wobbly/Beat lyrics in Greenwich Village dives, to Guthriesque guitar accompaniment. The riotous lunge toward folk-rock had started.

"We first did folk singing during the Henry Wallace campaign," Snyder reminds, herding Kai, KJ, and me toward his truck. "I met Pete Seeger then, in 1947, at a rally in Portland. I was already singing folk songs and playing the guitar. Very soon, [following] Pete Seeger's vein, we were rewriting folk songs with current political language. And that led to the early Bob Dylan...he sang political folk songs in Minnesota coffee houses, just like a Beatnik."

Kerouac observed in 1958 that, after Korea, the "postwar youth emerged cool and beat, had picked up the gestures and the style; soon it was everywhere, the new look...the bop visions became common property...the ingestion of drugs became official (tranquilizers and the rest); and even the clothes style of the beat hipsters carried over to the new rock 'n' roll youth...."

The sixties had begun.

Snyder's Toyota 4-Runner weaves through tight mountain curves, past hydraulic diggings and broad stands of pine that comprise this stretch of Tahoe National Forest. "We're on Pliocene Ridge," he says. "That name was probably given by mining geologists who identified some of its history." He glances aside. "We're gaining quite a bit of elevation."

Kai and KJ sit quietly, looking, listening. "First this ridge was logged," Snyder continues, "then it was seriously burned. It was also settled very early in the gold rush; there have been settlements up here for a long long time, over a century. But never a real large population. There just isn't quite enough you can do." The 4-Runner shudders north. "Up until recently, most people were into mining or logging. Today they're sawmill workers, loggers, or log truck drivers." He pauses. "Keep your eyes peeled, you can see clearcuts along here. There's one."

Below lies a mange-bare patch of forest. We drive a bit farther. Snyder mutters, "This is a big territory. It basically has all the same botany as San Juan Ridge. Although this is more-disturbed feeling. Its inhabitants are just little peckerwoods people living up and down all these dirt roads. It's our own little sort of Appalachia, these foothills are, with a lot of poverty, especially with the mill and logging shut down. A lot of kids never get past the eighth grade; it's just too much trouble to try to get to high school."

Kai and Gen attended such schools (before Berkeley and College of the Redwoods), riding motorcycles three miles on dirt fire lanes in below-freezing weather to catch schoolbuses. They're quiet kids, Gen more than Kai his father's gadfly. He complained once at a community pot-luck that Snyder'd never taught them what they really wanted to know. "Such as?" Gary barked. "Such as," Gen said, "how do you figure sixteen-point-nine percent APR financing on a new Camaro?"

"Look at this," Snyder exclaims, pulling over. "We're way up in the sky now." Vast expanses of blue float below us. "It's just a great place here. A big checkerboard of forest service holdings and some private land, very complicated. You can see clear cuts out there." His voice softens. "I'd forgotten how beautiful this ridge is...there's Sierra Buttes ahead. Some nice rocky mountains." He taps the wheel. "There's going to be *good forest* up here in a hundred years."

Kai nods. Both he and Gen contributed essays to *Dimensions of a Life*. They're adulatory, except for noting Snyder's explosive anger. "He is one of those people who can get very angry quickly, and have totally forgotten about it twenty minutes later," Kai wrote. Gen added, "What is important to me as a son is the amount of confidence and patience he has shown my brother and me...."

I've asked Snyder how his kids, given their politically correct father, might rebel against him. "Let's not assume," he countered, "it's necessary to rebel against the older generation. I know of cases of societies which go for a thousand years at a time without ever rebelling."

Snyder's sister is not convinced. "My son Richard asked his cousins, 'how come you haven't rebelled?' They kind of shrugged and said, 'well Gary is really right about most things.' But on the other hand," Thea told me, "they may be identifying with a captor. My *mother* takes hostages. In some ways she's this prophet figure that you can't rebel against."

We hang left at the Forest City crossing. "More

goddamn dirt roads," Snyder says. "Every once in a while, when spring comes, we find a car down at the end of those roads with a couple of dead bodies." He looks over, grins. "Just kidding."

A few buildings emerge behind a sign reading, "Forest City, elevation 4,500 feet, population 40." He gears down. "Here we are."

The buildings are unpainted clapboard; ramshackle brown. "These houses were built in the century before," Snyder says. "That's an old mine." A black nanny-goat poses in the road, near a dubious-looking pay phone. Six or seven cars sit by a clearing. Someone tells Snyder to turn around and park on the opposite side of the road. "I'm glad to do that," he replies.

A blond woman in wire-frame glasses addresses a dozen people by the Main Street's shoulder. Her name is Birdsong. Foresters, some of whom wear the red dirt of Sierra County like a badge, make no fuss to greet Gary. Many appear not to recognize him, standing in grimy shorts and leather boots, arms crossed, listening. Six or seven wait in the picnic area. Several are old enough to have followed Snyder here in the seventies. Birdsong is thirty-eight. She details the history of this 1852 mining community, its challenges then and now against the Forest Service and local rednecks. "There's one person here, a white supremacist, who's so negative it's very hard to get anything done."

The government is nearly as difficult, insisting Foresters hold Special Use permits. "Our contention," Birdsong says, "is that people living in a [ghost] town protect it better. Our town was here long before there was a Forest Service."

The answer, Snyder insists, is dialogue. Such as that he's encouraged between Yuba Watershed and BLM, private landowners, loggers, and mining companies, which helped salvage his ridge. He has a watershed strategy that makes sense even for Forest City: "A sensible redrawing of lines here would put eastern Sierra, eastern Nevada, and eastern Placer counties together in a new 'Truckee River County,'" he's written. "Western Sierra County [where Forest City lies] plus a bit of Yuba County and northern Nevada County would fit into the watershed of the three forks of the Yuba. I would call it 'Nisenan County' after the native people who lived here."

Birdsong leads a brief tour, past a vintage fire truck, 1920s swimming pool, and various repainted houses. Trailing her are members of Yuba Watershed, including Bob Erickson, a board member and craftsman who carves chairs and tables remarkably vibrant— "the chair *is* the forest," he says—plus a friend of Snyder's from Berkeley who's helping supervise sixteen interns working to inventory plants and wildlife in the 1,500-acre Inimin Forest. Snyder blends anonymously into the group.

He pauses at a battered store serving as Forest City's community hall. Inside are tins of nineteenth-century foodstuffs, beans, coffee, and a ledger from the 1890s. He and Kai study a crosscut saw of the type Harold Snyder used. Then grow fascinated by photographs of Forest City during the early logging. "They cut everything to build the mine shafts," Snyder says. "Probably they sold some trees for timber, and kept a few for houses." He and Kai step outside to compare landscapes. Main Street is verdant; Bald Mountain capped in green. Snyder sighs. "That's encouraging."

Foresters may not recognize him, but most know his work and that Beat legacy of *Dharma Bums* trickling through the decades. Kerouac hadn't started *Bums* when Snyder left for Kyoto in 1956, but he was taking notes. "Jack was always writing novels," Snyder says, over potluck lasagna. "He would write a novel, go from place to place, friend's to friend's, party to party, and write in detail what was happening. He had a sense of living out a time; that 'everything I'm witnessing now has some significance, I'm recording something critical that's happening.' He'd write it down, and after he'd done that for a year and a half or two, he'd hole up in his mother's and retype it all. And at the last minute change the names...he saw Neal [Cassady] as one form of the American character, he saw Allen as another, and he saw me as another."

Cassady, Ginsberg, and Kerouac were captivated by Snyder. *Bums* is a love song to him. Sister Thea, who dated Kerouac, says, "I think Jack saw Gary had the discipline and focus and sense of purpose that he couldn't have with his alcoholism and substance abuse." He and Snyder lived together in Locke McCorckle's shack near Sausalito, during a period of writing, conversation, and orgiastic sex that Kerouac chronicles in *Bums*. A favorite Snyder pastime was yabyum, the Tantric rite in which a nude woman sits immobile astride her nude male partner. Snyder performed it at parties, prior to orgies that included Kerouac and Ginsberg. "There was a fair amount of experimentation," Thea says. "The emergence of marijuana made them more relaxed and mellow. And open to things that were theretofore unthinkable." Snyder's mother recalls, "Gary once told me what semen tastes like. Then watched me closely to see how I'd react. I *didn't* react."

Though treated comically in *Bums*, yabyum had its sober element. The practice symbolized, to Tibetan Buddhists, a union of mother and father. That union, for Snyder's parents, was impossible; for his combative sides, perhaps feasible. He'd unearthed a new mother-figure, Ruth Fuller Sasaki, who'd started the First Zen Institute of America in Japan. "She was a wealthy Chicago woman," he tells me, "who became one of the very first non-Asians to spend a little time in a Japanese Zen monastery, back in the thirties. She fought her way in, as a woman; she insisted, and she was stubborn. She started a little Zen study and research center in Kyoto in the back of one of the big temples, after the war. Alan Watts was her son-in-law. Looking around for some young person to help with the translation work, she came across me as a graduate student at Berkeley. And paid my way over. It turned out we were made for each other."

Kyoto, at first glance, seemed made for Snyder. It was a Zen mecca as well as a sophisticated postwar city of jazz coffee shops and bars—hospitable to Americans, despite the occupation. Snyder was among the first Westerners to study Rinzai Zen, and was undoubtedly the first American writer to become a Zen monk. As Hisao Kaneseki notes in *Dimensions*, "Since Emerson and Thoreau, there have been a good number of influential men of letters who have been interested in Oriental religions, including Buddhism—notably Aldous Huxley, T. S. Eliot, Kenneth Rexroth, and J. D. Salinger." But Snyder did more than intellectualize, he took vows at the Daitoku-ji monastery, studying hard for nearly twelve years. It was a grueling ordeal.

"His first assignment," Hennessy says, "was emptying the honey buckets before breakfast—they were taking the ego out of the young American." Thereafter followed hours of meditation—tantamount to psychic excavation—during which blows were administered with a Jikijitsku's stick between koan interviews...that "fierce face-to-face moment where you spit forth truth or perish." Meals were slight, sleep was short and great energy was spent to confront one's nature. "Which," Snyder reminds, slugging beer, "is no nature."

The mountain vs. river (or ferocity vs. compassion) facets to his personality stood out. Enough so that he'd spend decades writing of them. He'd told Kerouac in 1956 that, "I'll do a new long poem called 'Rivers and Mountains Without End' and just write it on and on on a scroll and unfold on and on with new surprises and always what went before forgotten, see, like a river...I'll spend three thousand years writing it, it'll be packed full of information on soil conservation, the Tennessee Valley Authority, astronomy, geology, Hsuan Tsung's travels, Chinese painting theory, reforestation, Oceanic ecology, and food chains." It would "play with right brain versus left brain." By 1958 he saw it as "one central long interconnected work...it will be self-informing to a degree that the individual sections are not now...they will reinforce each other."

Clearly he wished such reinforcement for his own disparate selves.

Between tantrums of Ruth Sasaki—nearly as difficult a matriarch as Lois—blows of his Jikijitsu, and the Harold-like reserve of Oda Sesso Roshi, Gary's selves felt nurtured. His roshi did the most to help integrate them. Oda Sesso was "very subtle," Snyder recalls, "a very soft-spoken, very gentle man, a good scholar, and he didn't fit the mold of the intense warrior roshi." We're eating chocolate cake in the clearing, and the nanny goats are pesky; Snyder butts one away. "He was very gracious and very kind to me, always." I ask about the process of koan interviews. "You go in and see your roshi, person-to-person, face-to-face, on a daily basis. As you pull forward your various mistaken views, and your various abstract intellectual ideas that you can't help bringing forth, even though you know better, the roshi from day-to-day keeps brushing the cobwebs away. And comes to know better than *you* do where all your cobwebs are."

Snyder's thickest surrounded Hennessy. She told me, "On one occasion, Gary said that his roshi had urged him to come home and straighten out his differences with his mother."

"Part of what you do in zazen," Snyder says, "and I'm sure therapy would do the same for some people—is understand what has been done to you and forgive it. And in forgiving it, release yourself from the necessity of repeating it. I couldn't even do what I do with my mother on a *weekly basis* if I hadn't forgiven her." He laughs. "And forgiving her is an ongoing process."

Despite his Samurai profile, Snyder did not wholly fit Kyoto. He wrote Will Petersen, "*Z bonzes here are all (mostly all) obsessed with snobbish aristocratic & insular self-esteem, & no sense of art except as 'traditional Japanese art' & no sensibilities for the wide world of people & nature as it is now...Anyhow I got faith in me own*

Buddha-nature so. & have come to realize that I am first-most a poet, doomed to be shamelessly silly, undignified, curious, & cuntstruck, & considering (in the words of Rimbaud) the disorder of my own mind sacred. So I don't think I'll ever commit myself to the roll of Zen monk, as free as that role seems to be."

And "I was lonesome for the mountains," he says now. "*These* mountains." He'd left Japan on merchant marine tours and for intermittent visits to the States. But his longest sabbatical was a six-month trip through India, in 1962, with his second wife, poet Joanne Kyger, and Ginsberg. It was a strained period; the Snyders' marriage would last only four years. Kyger was uncomfortable in Japan. Ruth Sasaki had insisted the couple, rather than live together, marry. As Phillip Yampolsky remembers, "Judging from the diary Joanne kept and later published, she had great trepidation about the proposed union... Gary was not the most tolerant of persons when judging the behavior of others. He was far too demanding, too insistent on requiring conformity to Japanese customs, too much away during his Zen practice."

From the first, acrimony had saturated his shipboard journals. He worked as a wiper with the engine room's black gang, "Tending seven red-eyed fires—roar and heat and sweat...." One poem called "The Six Hells of the Engine Room, cited, "The oily cramp Hell of the bilges/ painting underside pipes—saltwater and oil / ankledeep slosh in the shoe. / Inside-the-boiler Hell, you go in through a / hot brick hole where it's black / and radiates heat...." Violence was pandemic. "The worst fights I ever saw were on ships," he says. Hennessy pointed out, "He's got a wretched scar on his arm. Either he got it in a fight, or in some way backed up against the hot steam pipes." Like other seamen, he dissipated anger in whoring and boozing, to deaden "the pain / of the work / of wrecking the world"; his 1957 "Tanker Notes" were Chaucerian with misogynous fury: "Then the cook says that women are no good after twenty-nine, they start getting female troubles, you can't fuck them the way you want, and they start going to preachers...."

Shipboard was a vastly different world than Daitoku-ji. But like that of his mother and the monastery, he was in part its captive. He brooded upon that "Rape of the world" his oil tanker advanced, and puzzled over, "What curious forms love takes. Here in the belly of a whale."

Joanne Kyger left him in 1964. She explained, "I was looking for something of a looser relationship. Gary had set out a path for himself that was very demanding." Snyder offers, "The main thing was that Joanne didn't *like* Japan. We came back for a visit to the States, and she didn't want to go back. She also got involved with another guy. Which was partly, I think, to keep herself from going back."

Robin, Alison, Joanne, Masa—I ask Snyder if there's a type of woman he finds himself recurrently drawn to. He nods. "Intelligent, physically active, politically aware, independent, outspoken, difficult women." He smiles. "What I've done in zazen is go back and apologize to a lot of women. In my inner mind."

Joanne Kyger assured me that "Gary has his playful side." Eventually that would emerge in his involvement with Nanao Sakaki and his "Tribe"—a group of Japanese cultural radicals living communally on Suwanose Island. "Nanao's society was more relaxed, and Gary was into that by then," Kyger said. And it was nonhierarchial. Japan's class-conscious society grated upon Snyder, who "didn't know how to tie a tie" until he was in college. Nanao was a poet. One to whom Snyder—who "had not been comfortable with poets for three, four years"— could relate.

Nanao had been a Japanese Air Force pilot during WWII, who afterward lived in Tokyo "under the bridges with the beggars and the prostitutes for a few years," and wandered Japan, attracting followers. "That was an amazing part of Japanese cultural history," Snyder tells me. "They had their own kind of post-war existential angst, and it became a very interesting group of people, very strong." They were Zen Buddhists, informally; many were postmodern artists and revolutionary thinkers. Nanao's motto—which became that of Japanese hippies—was, "There is a dream dreaming us."

Snyder lived in the ashram at Suwanose Island, on a subsistence basis, for two summers. Photos remain of him grinning on the beach, naked but for a loin cloth, holding a spear. He and Nanao took long walks, discussing "Linguistics, Bushman ethnology, Sanskrit studies, Japanese archaeology, Marx, Jung, Nagarjuna—and above all, Revolution." The Tribe, with Nanao as leading teacher, became a model for San Juan Ridge. Snyder and Masa Uehara were married on Suwanose Island in 1967, in a ceremony not dissimilar from what would be his and Carole Koda's.

In Japan he'd gone through what he describes as "the process of tearing yourself out of your personality and your culture and putting yourself back in it again," and had begun to see Buddhism as a possible component for the growing revolution in America. "Buddhism offers the most humane, the most compassionate, and the most intelligent model for a cosmopolitan, diverse world," he says, "in its fundamental assertion of the authenticity and the inherent and intrinsic value to be found in all phenomena; its non-hierarchical vision of a complex universe, its willingness to see and to read complexity and interrelationship on all levels, and not to judge one part of the system superior to another, but to see every part of the system as in the ecology, playing a unique and valuable role. In that sense, Buddhism is a *spiritual* ecology that appreciates and values all of the working units."

In 1967 Ginsberg visited Kyoto. The two writers talked long about America's cultural revolution. "We said, 'the Vietnam war is going to wind down, and all of the antiwar energy will still be out there. What can be done with it?' We said, 'the environment.'" Snyder had been living mostly in cities. Now he vowed to live "somewhere in the country," for "the country is the revolutionary territory."

The deaths of Oda Sesso Roshi in 1966 and Harold Snyder (during exploratory surgery) in 1968 hastened Snyder's departure. His mother, whom he'd forgiven but not forgotten, lived alone in California. "All those years," she told me, "Gary never failed to send me some gift on my birthday, without my ever having reminded him." The death of his father seemed to intensify protectiveness. He'd write, of the environment, "Now we must become warrior-lovers in the service of the Great Goddess Gaia, Mother of the Buddha. The stakes are all of organic evolution." And: "My political position is to be a spokesman for wild nature."

Chocolate cake's been devoured and Snyder's speaking with a heavyset, middle-aged woman who grew up in Forest City. "I used to hunt cranberries on your ridge when I was little," she mutters. "Daddy took me to that pit there and we picked buckets of 'em."

Snyder crinkles his Asian grin. "You knew where they were, huh?"

"We knew where they were."

The tavern at Peterson's Corner is quiet, a few workers at its 1937 bar, TV flashing; no redhots to slam eight ball or jangle the video games. Snyder takes a booth, glances round. The barroom's dimpled with antiquity; from some parallel dimension, hovering within meditative reach—like skidrow bars of his childhood. A woman takes our order, scolds us for not sitting closer, flirts, then moves along. "*I went into the Maverick Bar... / My long hair was tucked under a cap / I'd left the earring in the car....*"

We've been touring, Snyder showing me first the Ridge's fire house and cultural center, then Mother Trucker's, a hip produce store...and introducing me to, among other natives, Doc Dachtler, a huge, good-natured fellow, a carpenter in leather tool belt and coveralls, who helped Snyder build Kitkitdizze's farmhouse. "When I ran out of money in seventy-two, building my house," Doc quippped, "Gary heard about it and gave me five hundred dollars to put the roof on. Someday when I'm rich I'll pay him back."

Everyone applauds Snyder's generosity, here in post-yuppie California, not without its anachronistic timbre. What of the gentrification of San Juan Ridge? "It's definitely coming," Snyder says. "And it's a mixed blessing. On the one side we know what gentrification portends. And on the other side, it means also a more 'liberal' voting block. It means more environmentalists, more people who join the Green Party, but it doesn't necessarily mean they know nature or the back country any better. And they definitely don't have a sympathy or an appreciation for the plight of the small scale miner or logger, which I certainly do."

In 1970, when Snyder moved here, a minuscule hip community existed; he was by no means its chief. Perceived as a culture hero in San Francisco, he'd emerged as a leader within that underground tribe spreading coast to coast. He'd helped organize Golden Gate Park's Human Be-In, addressed the first Earth Day gathering in Fort Collins, Colorado, put together the environmentalist "Four Changes" manifesto, and published his "Smokey the Bear Sutra" broadside, which *may be reproduced free forever*—advising that "if anyone is threatened by advertising, air pollution, television, or the police, they should chant "SMOKEY THE BEAR'S WAR SPELL: DROWN THEIR BUTTS / CRUSH THEIR BUTTS..." His poems had grown more prosaic, more polemical ("the real excitement may be with the essay"), testing that netherworld between poetry and prose which instinctively was home base. As Koda observed, this ran contrary to Mother's advice: "'Gary,' she says, 'don't write essays...nobody's ever going to remember you for that. Write love poems.'"
He'd worked through much of his captor identification,

but still conversed with Hennessy several times a week. Soon she would move nearby.

Those United States Snyder found post-Kyoto were in troubled multiplicity. Men walked the moon, Kennedys were murdered or self-destructed, Manson prowled Death Valley, thousands tripped at Woodstock, and the military was devastating Vietnam. Snyder's own states were stable: ferocity and compassion, mountains and rivers, stood in balance. He, Uehara, and the boys lived first in Marin County, then San Francisco. But news came of a unique acreage for sale in the Sierra foothills. "Allen Ginsberg and Dick Baker and I came up here and looked at it," Snyder says. "I ran some lines out real quick with my handheld compass, checked it out and said, 'this is a nice community of plants, I know what the climate here is going to be from the plant community. I'd like to go in on this, if possible.' We bought it all for a couple of hundred bucks an acre. It was a very smart move. I had no idea at the time how it would genuinely become my home."

"Place" had a calming effect on Snyder—whether his boyhood camp outside Seattle, his basement at 1414 SE Lambert, or the hardwood floor of a zendo. "My sense of the universe is that it's chaotic, impermanent, and uncontrollable," he says, "which is fine...[but] human beings cannot think without an environment. Thinking is a function of our environment."

Place anchored his disparate states, and Kitkitdizze—situated between mountains and rivers—held their skirmishes in check. He'd not hibernate, in coming years, but hit the road harder than Kerouac ever did, reading poetry, lecturing on environmental issues and spinning the dharma. It was pinballing round a hip network that salved his ego, paid bills, and fueled tendencies toward "permissive monogamy." Thea told me, "Gary is pursued constantly on the road. For years women were hitting on him, while Masa was home with the kids." Theirs was an open relationship, but "I don't think it started that way," Thea added, "it evolved in the era of popularity."

Snyder had won adulation when *Dharma Bums* was published, but that popularity was nothing compared to what he enjoyed post-*Turtle Island*. The nation was catching up with him. "I have seen Gary adored so when he reads his poetry that I was nauseated," Hennessy said. The Beats were grand old men of the counterculture. Ginsberg—who won a National Book Award in 1974—hopped the Rock Express and toured with Dylan's Rolling Thunder Revue (they improvised blues lyrics at Kerouac's grave), and recorded rags, blues, and ballads, accompanied by harmonium. Even Snyder recorded *Turtle Island* with the Paul Winter Consort. Poetic lyrics in pop music, weird dress, hallucinogenic drugs, Eastern religions, hip communality, ceaseless wandering—all were foot soldiers in that rucksack revolution he'd long envisioned.

Though an endless party of cultural radicals delighted Snyder, the seventies, by most accounts, were prickly for Uehara and the boys—who "spent their whole lives watching their father being lionized," Thea observed. Snyder wrote of his family with surprising intimacy: "*Washing Kai in the sauna... / the soapy hand feeling / through and around the globes and curves...*" Such poems were as intrusive, in their way, as stories Lois Hennessy spun of Gary's childhood. Yet their honesty proved instructive. And their homeliness helped elevate the Snyders to a kind of Ozzie and Harriet of the counterculture, their escapades chronicled dutifully in poem after poem.

But all was not compassion. "Gary has a lot of Lois in him," Thea said. "Which is, 'Do this!' He's very controlling of the boys. One of things that is sad about Gary, because of Lois, who's such a powerful, controlling, judgmental, bullying person, is that he incorporated a great deal of ego investment, in the same way that she has, of needing to be right. I'm surprised that his kids haven't kicked over the traces and left. He's so strong, powerful. And he's very hard, he doesn't cut anybody any slack. Who was it who said, 'The test of a sage is how he treats his family'?"

Lois told me, "I suppose you could sum it up by saying Gary believes he's top dog and you should recognize it. A poet gets this affirmed, you see."

This dimly-lit tavern seems a likely spot to speak of poetic demons. "I don't have *time* for demons," Snyder snaps. "I think demons are things you get to know, play with, entertain yourself with. Maybe fight with, maybe wrestle with." He pauses. "I don't need demons *inside*, there are plenty out there. My commitment to biodiversity and native peoples is deep. It's a warrior's work."

Is he angry? "I'm *not* such an angry person," he says, bristling. "I have certain strong senses of alienation and despair and all of that. But it had never occurred to me that it would do a whole lot of good to be angry about it. I don't have any personal sense of victimization. I don't have any personal anger. I've had a very lucky life. If I *had* anger it would be that larger, more abstract anger about the world, but the world is not that bad a place either."

But Thea argued, "Gary's internalized his mother's judgmentalism," and Scott Mclean admitted, "Gary's one of the few people in my life who can reduce me to a quivering mass of jello with just a few words, if he's going to cut hard at something I've done or said or not done or not lived up to. The times I've seen Gary get angry have been times when he feels people have been careless and wasteful. Somebody taking a big plate of dirty, skungy old dishwater and throwing it on the gravel. He'll say, 'What are you doing with that water? Don't you realize we're in the middle of a goddam drought? Take it over there and put it on that madrone.' When they built the house, the toilet paper was old telephone books and you could only use so many sheets."

Masa Uehara's departure from Kitkitdizze was not a surprise; nor was it particularly spiteful. "Gary was already involved with Carole," next-door-neighbor Will Staple told me, "and Masa would not have left him without his being involved with someone. Because she was a loyal Japanese wife. I was invited to speak with the four of them. Nobody was lied to, there was no deception, the kids were not an issue. Divorce happens, but it was difficult for both of them. Marriage is your history book."

Snyder was an *eminence grise* by then, and socially more integrated. "This last decade of zazen has mellowed him considerably," Staple observed. Impatient with his culture's lack of progress, Snyder as early as 1974 had tested establishment waters—heading the California Arts Council and learning as much as possible about budget policies of each university he visited. "In a certain sense, you have to actively go out there and plant ideas, and do that with poems, do that with prose. So I cut my hair and started wearing a suit. When I went on tour, I started deliberately breaking people's expectations in turning up at poetry readings wearing a suit and tie instead of my hippie clothes...I think my work became some tiny percent a bit more effective. And that might be reflected in some very subtle points. *The Practice of the Wild* (nine wilderness essays) is an interesting attempt to take really alien ideas and keep carrying them as close as you can to the center. So people who are *at* the center look at it....Rather than take a flauntingly adversarial stance, as I might have done ten years earlier."

Even his poetry—with a longer line and less abstract imagery—was more readable. *Turtle Island* and the *Mountains and Rivers* poems combined prose with poetry. Politically, he was accused of selling out. "But not so much from around here. Some people might have thought it; they didn't say so. But elsewhere people *said* that to me, including Kenneth Rexroth. Rexroth said, 'Jerry Brown is a closet fascist.' In fact he refused to speak to me after that."

Snyder orders another beer; the television blinks mutely as our waitress fetches it. "There are people on the Ridge who still really don't want to come into the eighties, let alone the nineties. They have long hair and they ride around on horses bareback, and hardly ever go to town—and it's wonderful. I know what their life is like and I love it. But I don't know if they're helping prepare their children for survival in the rough and tumble. It is to some extent often living in a dream world."

The new accessibility paid: *Turtle Island* sold one hundred thousand copies, and took its Pulitzer; Snyder was named a member of the American Academy of Arts and Letters, and given an honorary Ph.D.—from Reed.

"I've only seen Gary put up two certificates," Mclean told me. "One is the certificate he got for completing the reading program at the Seattle Public Library when he was six years old, and right next to it is his appointment to the Academy of Arts and Letters. But I think what pleased him most, recently, was the honorary doctorate that Reed gave him. I think he was deeply moved and honored by that. He asked me afterwards, 'Is this something you can put after your name in the catalogue at school?' I said, 'Absolutely.'"

Dr. Japhy, no longer worried that, "*I'm getting old. at least enough to be / a First Mate or an Engineer / now I know I'll never be a Ph.D....*"

"You know," Snyder says, "I just noticed *The Dharma Bums* in a bookstore with a new cover. It keeps being reincarnated. It's had a lot of stupid covers." Yes, but as Tom McGuane said, "For the generation [of writers] slightly older than me, *The Sun Also Rises* was it, in terms of conveying the romance of the literary life. And [*Bums*] was really *that* for us."

Snyder had grumbled against the Beat label for years. "I try not to allow that to be the only identification given," he says, shrugging. "It's simplistic for any of us who have lived through about thirty years of writing since then. Especially since Beat evokes pretty simpleminded ideas in the minds of most people."

But its Buddhist imperative served him well, poetically and familially. "Although Zen as such wouldn't take that as its purpose," he counters. "But rather Zen practice is to bring us to the point of dealing with the actualities of our own life and our own psyche, whatever they are. It could be to deal with *not* having a relationship, just as well. It could be to deal with what it is that you should be into. Whether that's on the mainstream or on the margins. How to be a good marginal person is as important in Zen as how to be a good normal person. There's no *normal* in this. It would be false to suggest that Zen practice is to make one able to fit into some preconceived model of what a good social person is."

But hasn't he always desired to be part of a family and community? "Yes and no. Actually that's what has transpired in my life. In a certain sense I've been able to live out something of a family life and something of a more stable family life than some of my friends. But not as much as others."

He pushes his glass aside. "But that's not really the question. The question is to do what your life brings you. To take it on, whatever the karma is, and to do what you can do with it. I'm also a person who's very comfortable being alone! And I don't have a great need for other human beings. So if that's your situation, deal with it and enjoy it! But if your situation is that you find yourself with children and family, enjoy that too! Of course we're all social and cultural beings, so as I'm all too well aware, transformation of social and political life takes place on a cultural level. And building community is very important. Building community is fundamentally a normal way to be; a normal kind of world to be in. And part of my understanding of a true community style is that it includes the space for solitude. And that people are able to step out of it as well as be in it."

What has he brought to this new family that's different? He sighs. "I would hope there's some gradual rectification of past errors. Particularly, between Carole and me, there's a strong sense of partnership, a strong mutual respect for each other's particular needs and directions, both spiritual and practical. I think of the marriage now with Carole as being a mature and adult relationship that recognizes our mutual needs to do certain things in our lives. Carole has been most understanding and positive with my work as a writer. And was a fantastic editorial reader on *The Practice of the Wild* as we were going on. She read it and we discussed it in detail. Section by section. She was a great help. And it was fun. We have a strong exchange of opinion and ideas that's very helpful."

That was lacking in other relationships? "Masa simply was not that good at English, even. She's a very bright woman but her intellectual tendencies were not in the direction that my mind would go. So we weren't able to have such probing conversations. There are not too many people you can have a probing conversation with anyway. And suppose I wrote stuff in English. It was never quite as accessible to her. She wasn't a verbal person. Her art form was dance. I don't think that even if we had removed the language barrier that there would necessarily have been such easy communication." Also, "She had such a burden of anger against her father, and against males, and against authority. Very unlike a Japanese person."

The new partnership with Koda paid off in tenderness—both toward his new family and to his readers. In "Off the Trail," dedicated to Koda, he writes, "*We have / Been here before. / It's more intimate somehow...*"

Koda notes in *Dimensions* that "the irritable, solipsistic, high-strung artist has emerged only occasionally [in our relationship]...a quick little snap and it's over.... Something [for Gary] is coming together—a confidence and joy with prose, a multilayered balance of going out and staying in, a feel for when to leap and when to nap. So now he thinks he'll be a writer, thinks he's getting the hang of it...."

"Carole's the easiest woman to live with I've ever been with," Snyder says. "Also in her own way the most independent. She has more confidence than any of the women I've been with. Her confidence means she's not paranoid. We can work things out by an intelligent conversation.

And she's able to be very clear about what she needs. Rather than moping around and then blowing up."

He studies the men at the bar. "Carole has her own background in being a feminist, but she in no way presents herself as a *victim*." He swirls the last of his draft. "Buddhism says, in its own way, 'The world is an illusion. The world is a made-up narrative. *But you are not a victim of that narrative.* You always have the option of stepping out of it.' The practice of meditation and its affiliated disciplines is a way to step out of the narrative of your society and your culture, and see the world for what it really is."

Koda told me, "Zazen teaches you to be aware of what your own mind and body state is, as much as possible, all the time. You can hear yourself say the habitual things you would say. So you can know when you're irritable, and cop to it. Know when you're stressed or very tired. Or when you're about to say the same tape you've said about thirty thousand times. The pop therapy is to express anger and to express all those emotions. The Zen teaching is that you don't need to express them, but you do need to know they're there."

Snyder says, "My mother, if she feels angry, will just let all of her anger out. And doesn't care about the consequences. That gave me a healthy respect for rationality and judgment and distance. Perhaps it made me excessively suspicious of too much trusting of your own feelings. My mother trusts *all* of her own feelings, indiscriminately. And indulges them. Yet I am very much at peace with my mother; the old rages I had against her—which made no difference to her—have evaporated, as I see her in her eluctable uniqueness and frailty."

What a nutty country this is, I reflect, in which someone like Snyder—after sixty-two years of unorthodoxy—could publish fifteen books, be a full professor at a major university, and otherwise be so applauded. "It is nutty, isn't it," he laughs. "It's nutty enough that it makes you think that, in a certain sense, society as an organism, so to speak, recognizes in its own way that there should be some counter voices. And that other ideas can be heard from. And in a sense my opposition has been a 'loyal' opposition, in that I only wish well. As a Buddhist I wish all sentient beings well."

He tugs at his ear, below its gold stud. "If anything, the total direction, the final direction of all of my work comes to presenting, making visible, describing, defining the complete interrelatedness and interconnectedness of things. Both in consciousness and in the natural world." His voice sounds fragile. "But saying that everything is interconnected doesn't necessarily mean that everything is benign and tranquil. Pain is part of it."

He hesitates, as if spotting some demon—a ghost, or the gentle shade of Jack Kerouac in the hazy twilight of this afternoon bar, so reminiscent of those both writers haunted after summers on Desolation Peak. Ray told Japhy in *Bums*, "I wonder which one of us'll die first... whoever it is, come on back, ghost, and give 'em the key."

"You know," Snyder confides, sadly, "I went to Kyoto in the spring of 1956, and I never saw Jack again. We talked on the phone few times, had a correspondence for a while. But I never saw him, physically, again."

Outside
1993

Acknowledgments

Thanks to Ken McCullough and Sandy Rock for their friendship and proofreading skills; to Seabring Davis and the editors of *Big Sky Journal* where many of these stories appeared; to the editors of *Esquire, Outside, Vanity Fair, Western Art & Architecture*, and *The Washington Post* where other pieces were commissioned or published; to Ralph White, Pat Miller, and Dan and Kathleen Kaul, who cared for me at the Murray; to Lynn Donaldson, whose friendship and photographic skills are invaluable; to Teresa and Stocky White, for lodging and heady times; to Katharine Meyer, in Peck's Place; to Rick Winking, on the trail; to Belinda Winslow, riding shotgun, and to Margot Kidder for her intelligent good humor and support. Thanks especially to Allen Jones for his editorial guidance at Bangtail Press. Without his vision, this collection would not exist.

ABOUT *the* AUTHOR

Toby Thompson is the author of three previous books: *Positively Main Street: Bob Dylan's Minnesota, Saloon* and *The '60s Report*. He has written for publications as diverse as *Vanity Fair, Esquire, Rolling Stone, Esquire, Gray's Sporting Journal, GQ, Men's Journal, Sports Afield, Playboy, Outside, Big Sky Journal, Western Art & Architecture, The New York Times, The Washington Post* and many others. He teaches creative nonfiction in the MFA program at Penn State. He lives in Livingston, Montana and Cabin John, Maryland.

CPSIA information can be obtained at www.ICGtesting.com
Printed in the USA
LVOW041601241012

304285LV00009B/60/P